4/6

E.J.C. Wolfe

April 1949.

WINDSOR CASTLE

WILLIAM HARRISON
AINSWORTH

was born in Manchester on February 4th, 1805, and was educated at the grammar school there. He studied law but left that profession on deciding to become a novelist. ROOKWOOD *was published from London in 1834, the first of many successes. He edited* BENTLEY'S MISCELLANY, *and for eleven years owned and edited his own journal,* AINSWORTH'S MAGAZINE. *He died on January 3rd, 1882. This book was first published in 1843.*

Printed in Great Britain

CONTENTS

Book One
ANNE BOLEYN
9

Book Two
HERNE THE HUNTER
99

Book Three
THE HISTORY OF THE CASTLE
165

Book Four
CARDINAL WOLSEY
205

Book Five
MABEL LYNDWOOD
293

Book Six
JANE SEYMOUR
341

CONTENTS

Part One
LOOSE SOILS

Part Two
DENSE FORMATIONS

Part Three
FROM MUD TO SOLID

"About, about!
Search Windsor Castle, elves, within and out"
Shakespeare.—*Merry Wives of Windsor.*

"There is an old tale goes that Herne the Hunter,
Sometime a keeper here in Windsor Forest,
Doth all the winter time, at still midnight,
Walk round about an oak, with great ragg'd horns,
And there he blasts the tree.—

"You have heard of such a spirit; and well you know
The superstitious idle-headed eld
Received, and did deliver to our age,
This tale of Herne the Hunter for a truth."—Ibid.

Book the First

ANNE BOLEYN

I

*Of the Earl of Surrey's solitary ramble in the Home
Park ; of the vision beheld by him in the haunted dell ;
and of his meeting with Morgan Fenwolf, the keeper,
beneath Herne's Oak*

IN the twentieth year of the reign of the right high
and puissant king Henry the Eighth, namely, in 1529,
on the 21st of April, and on one of the loveliest evenings
that ever fell on the loveliest district in England, a fair
youth, having somewhat the appearance of a page, was
leaning over the terrace-wall on the north side of
Windsor Castle, and gazing at the magnificent scene
before him. On his right stretched the broad green
expanse, forming the Home Park, studded with noble
trees, chiefly consisting of ancient oaks, of which
England had already learnt to be proud, thorns as old,
or older than the oaks, wide-spreading beeches, tall
elms, and hollies. The disposition of these trees was
picturesque and beautiful in the extreme. Here, at the
end of a sweeping vista, and in the midst of an open
space, covered with the greenest sward, stood a mighty,
broad-armed oak, beneath whose ample boughs, though
as yet almost destitute of foliage, while the sod beneath
them could scarcely boast a head of fern, couched a
herd of deer ; there lay a thicket of thorns skirting a
sand-bank, burrowed by rabbits; on this hand, grew a
dense and Druid-like grove, into whose intricacies the
slanting sunbeams pierced; on that, extended a long
glade, formed by a natural avenue of oaks, across which,
at intervals, deer were passing. Nor were human figures
wanting to give life and interest to the scene. Adown
the glade came two keepers of the forest, having each
a couple of buckhounds with them in leash, whose

11

baying sounded cheerily amid the woods. Nearer the castle, and bending their way towards it, marched a party of falconers, with their well-trained birds, whose skill they had been approving, upon their fists, their jesses ringing as they moved along; while nearer still and almost at the foot of the terrace wall, was a minstrel, playing on a rebec, to which a keeper, in a dress of Lincoln green, with a bow over his shoulder, a quiver of arrows at his back, and a comely damsel under his arm, was listening.

On the left, a view altogether different in character, though scarcely less beautiful, was offered to the gaze. It was formed by the town of Windsor, then not a third of its present size, but incomparably more picturesque in appearance, consisting almost entirely of a long straggling row of houses, chequered black and white, with tall gables and projecting stories, skirting the west and south sides of the castle; by the silver windings of the river, traceable for miles, and reflecting the glowing hues of the sky; by the venerable college of Eton, embowered in a grove of trees; and by a vast tract of well-wooded and well-cultivated country beyond it, interspersed with villages, churches, old halls, monasteries, and abbeys.

Taking out his tablets, the youth, after some reflection, traced a few lines upon them, and then, quitting the parapet, proceeded slowly, and with a musing air, towards the north-west angle of the terrace. He could not be more than fifteen, perhaps not so much; but he was tall and well-grown, with slight, though remarkably well-proportioned limbs; and it might have been safely predicted, that, when arrived at years of maturity, he would possess great personal vigour. His countenance was full of thought and intelligence; and he had a broad, lofty brow, shaded by a profusion of light brown ringlets, a long, straight, and finely-formed nose, a full, sensitive, and well-chiselled mouth, and a pointed chin. His eyes were large, dark, and somewhat melancholy in expression, and his complexion possessed that rich, clear, brown tint, constantly met with in Italy or Spain, though but seldom seen in a native of our own colder clime. His dress was rich, but sombre; consisting of a doublet of black satin, worked with threads of Venetian gold; hose of the same material, and similarly embroidered; a shirt curiously wrought with black silk, and fastened at the collar with black enamelled clasps; a cloak of black velvet, passmented with gold, and lined with crimson satin; a flat black velvet cap, set with pearls and goldsmith's work, and adorned with a short white plume; and black velvet buskins. His arms were rapier and dagger, both having gilt and graven handles, and sheaths of black velvet.

As he moved along, the sound of voices chanting vespers arose from St. George's Chapel; and while he paused to listen to the solemn strains, a door in that part of the castle used as the king's privy-lodgings, opened, and a person advanced towards him. The newcomer had broad, brown, martial-looking features, darkened still more by a thick, coal-black beard, clipped short in the fashion of the time, and a pair of enormous moustachios. He was accoutred in a habergeon, which gleamed from beneath the folds of a russet-coloured mantle, and wore a steel cap, in lieu of a bonnet, on his head, while a long sword dangled from beneath his cloak. When within a few paces of the youth, whose back was towards him, and who did not hear his approach, he announced himself by a loud cough, that proved the excellence of his lungs, and made the old walls ring again, startling the jackdaws roosting in the battlements.

" What ! composing a vesper hymn, my Lord of Surrey ? " he cried, with a laugh, as the other hastily thrust the tablets, which he had hitherto held in his hand, into his bosom. " You will rival Master Skelton, the poet-laureate, and your friend, Sir Thomas Wyat, too, ere long. But will it please your lordship to quit for a moment the society of the celestial Nine, and descend to earth, while I inform you that, acting as your representative, I have given all needful directions for his majesty's reception to-morrow."

"You have not failed, I trust, to give orders to the groom of the chambers for the lodging of my fair cousin, Mistress Anne Boleyn, Captain Bouchier?" inquired the Earl of Surrey, with a significant smile.

"Assuredly not, my lord!" replied the other, smiling in his turn. "She will be lodged as royally as if she were Queen of England. Indeed, the queen's own apartments are assigned her."

"It is well," rejoined Surrey. "And you have also provided for the reception of the Pope's legate, Cardinal Campeggio?"

Bouchier bowed.

"And for Cardinal Wolsey?" pursued the other.

The captain bowed again.

"To save your lordship the necessity of asking any further questions," he said, "I may state briefly, that I have done all as if you had done it yourself."

"Be a little more particular, captain, I pray you," said Surrey.

"Willingly, my lord," replied Bouchier. "In your lordship's name, then, as vice-chamberlain, in which character I presented myself, I summoned together the dean and canons of the College of St. George, the usher of the black-rod, the governor of the alms-knights, and the whole of the officers of the household, and acquainted them, in a set speech, which, I flatter myself, was quite equal to any that your lordship, with all your poetical talents, could have delivered, that the king's highness being at Hampton Court, with the two cardinals, Wolsey and Campeggio, debating the matter of divorce from his queen, Catharine of Arragon, proposes to hold the grand feast of the most noble Order of the Garter, at this his castle of Windsor, on St. George's Day—that is to say, the day after to-morrow—and that it is therefore his majesty's sovereign pleasure that the Chapel of St. George, in the said castle, be set forth, and adorned with its richest furniture; that the

14

high altar with arras representing the patron saint of the order on horseback, and garnished with the costliest images and ornaments in gold and silver; that the pulpit be covered with crimson damask, inwrought with flowers-de-luces of gold, portcullises, and roses; that the royal stall be canopied with a rich cloth of state, with a hautpas beneath it of a foot high; that the stalls of the knights-companions be decked with cloth of tissue, with their scutcheons set at the back; and that all be ready at the hour of tierce—*horâ tertiâ vespertinâ,* as appointed by his majesty's own statute—at which time the eve of the feast shall be held to commence."

" Take breath, captain," laughed the earl.

" I have no need," replied Bouchier. " Furthermore, I delivered your lordship's warrant from the lord chamberlain to the usher of the black-rod, to make ready and furnish St. George's Hall, both for the supper to-morrow and the grand feast on the following day; and I enjoined the dean and canons of the college, the alms-knights, and all the other officers of the order, to be in readiness for the occasion. And now having fulfilled my devoir, or rather your lordship's, I am content to resign my post as vice-chamberlain, to resume my ordinary one, that of your simple gentleman, and to attend you back to Hampton Court, whenever it shall please you to set forth."

" And that will not be for an hour at the least," replied the earl; " for I intend to take a solitary ramble in the Home Park."

" What ! to seek inspiration for a song—or to meditate upon the charms of the fair Geraldine, eh ! my lord ? " rejoined Bouchier. " But I will not question you too shrewdly. Only let me caution you against going near Herne's Oak. It is said that the demon hunter walks at nightfall, and scares, if he does not injure, all those who cross his path. At curfew toll I must quit the castle, and will then, with your attendants, proceed to the Garter, in Thames Street, where I will await your arrival. If we reach Hampton Court by

15

midnight, it will be time enough, and as the moon will rise in an hour, we shall have a pleasant ride."

"Commend me to Bryan Bowntance, the worthy host of the Garter," said the earl; "and bid him provide you with a bottle of his best sack in which to drink my health."

"Fear me not," replied the other. "And I pray your lordship not to neglect my caution respecting Herne the Hunter. In sober sooth, I have heard strange stories of his appearance of late, and should not care to go near the tree after dark."

The earl laughed somewhat sceptically, and the captain reiterating his caution, they separated— Bouchier returning the way he came, and Surrey proceeding towards a small drawbridge crossing the ditch on the eastern side of the castle, and forming a means of communication with the Little Park. He was challenged by a sentinel at the drawbridge, but on giving the password, he was allowed to cross it, and to pass through a gate on the further side opening upon the park.

Brushing the soft and dewy turf, with a footstep almost as light and bounding as that of a fawn, he speeded on for more than a quarter of a mile, when he reached a noble beech-tree, standing at the end of a clump of timber. A number of rabbits were feeding beneath it, but at his approach they instantly plunged into their burrows.

Here he halted to look at the castle. The sun had sunk behind it, dilating its massive keep to almost its present height, and tinging the summits of the whole line of ramparts and towers, since rebuilt and known as the Brunswick Tower, the Chester Tower, the Clarence Tower, and the Victoria Tower, with rosy lustre.

Flinging himself at the foot of the beech-tree, the youthful earl indulged his poetical reveries for a short time, and then rising, retraced his steps, and in a few minutes the whole of the south side of the castle lay before him. The view comprehended the two fortifications recently removed to make way for the York and Lancaster Towers, between which stood a gate approached by a drawbridge; the Earl Marshal's Tower, now styled from the monarch in whose reign it was erected, Edward the Third's Tower; the Black-rod's lodgings; the Lieutenant's—now Henry the Third's Tower; the line of embattled walls, constituting the lodgings of the Alms-Knights; the tower tenanted by the governor of that body, and still allotted to the same officer; Henry the Eighth's Gateway; and the Chancellor of the Garter's Tower—the latter terminating the line of building. A few rosy beams tipped the pinnacles of St. George's Chapel, seen behind the towers above mentioned, with fire; but with this exception, the whole of the mighty fabric looked cold and gray.

At this juncture, the upper gate was opened, and Captain Bouchier and his attendants issued from it, and passed over the drawbridge. The curfew bell then tolled; the drawbridge was raised; the horsemen disappeared; and no sound reached the listener's ear, except the measured tread of the sentinels on the ramparts, audible in the profound stillness.

The youthful earl made no attempt to join his followers, but having gazed on the ancient pile before him, till its battlements and towers grew dim in the twilight, he struck into a footpath leading across the park, towards Datchet, and pursued it until it brought him near a dell filled with thorns, hollies, and underwood, and overhung by mighty oaks, into which he unhesitatingly plunged, and soon gained the deepest part of it. Here, owing to the thickness of the hollies, and the projecting arms of other large overhanging timber, added to the uncertain light above, the gloom was almost impervious, and he could scarcely see a yard before him. Still, he pressed on unhesitatingly, and with a sort of pleasurable sensation at the difficulties he was encountering. Suddenly, however, he was startled by a blue phosphoric light streaming through the bushes on the left, and, looking up, he beheld at the foot of an

17

enormous oak, whose giant roots protruded like twisted snakes from the bank, a wild, spectral-looking object, possessing some slight resemblance to humanity, and habited, so far as it could be determined, in the skins of deer, strangely disposed about its gaunt and tawny-coloured limbs. On its head was seen a sort of helmet, formed of the skull of a stag, from which branched a large pair of antlers; from its left arm hung a heavy and rusty-looking chain, in the links of which burned the phosphoric fire before mentioned; while on its right wrist was perched a large horned owl, with feathers erected, and red, staring eyes.

Impressed with the superstitious feelings common to the age, the young earl, fully believing he was in the presence of a supernatural being, could scarcely, despite his courageous nature, which no ordinary matter would have shaken, repress a cry. Crossing himself, he repeated, with great fervency, a prayer against evil spirits, and as he uttered it, the light was extinguished, and the spectral figure vanished. The clanking of the chain was heard, succeeded by the hooting of the owl; then came a horrible burst of laughter; then a fearful wail; and all was silent.

Up to this moment, the young earl had stood still as if spell-bound; but being now convinced that the spirit had fled, he pressed forward, and, ere many seconds, emerged from the brake. The full moon was rising, as he issued forth, and illuminating the glades and vistas, and the calmness and beauty of all around seemed at total variance with the fearful vision he had just witnessed. Throwing a shuddering glance at the haunted dell, he was about to hurry towards the castle, when a large, lightning-scathed and solitary oak, standing a little distance from him, attracted his attention.

This was the very tree connected with the wild legend of Herne the Hunter, which Captain Bouchier had warned him not to approach, and he now forcibly recalled the caution. Beneath it he perceived a figure,

18

which he at first took for that of the spectral hunter; but his fears were relieved by a shout from the person, who, at the same moment, appeared to catch sight of him.

Satisfied that, in the present instance, he had to do with a being of this world, Surrey ran towards the tree, and on approaching it perceived that the object of his alarm was a young man, of very athletic proportions, and evidently, from his garb, a keeper of the forest.

He was habited in a jerkin of Lincoln-green cloth, with the royal badge woven in silver on the breast, and his head was protected by a flat green cloth cap, ornamented with a pheasant's tail. Under his right arm he carried a cross-bow; a long, silver-tipped horn was slung in his baldric; and he was armed with a short hanger, or wood-knife. His features were harsh and prominent; and he had black, beetling brows, a large, coarse mouth, and dark eyes, lighted up with a very sinister and malignant expression.

He was attended by a large, savage-looking stag-hound, whom he addressed as Bawsey, and whose fierceness had to be restrained as Surrey approached.

" Have you seen anything ? " he demanded of the earl.

" I have seen Herne the hunter himself, or the fiend in his likeness," replied Surrey.

And he briefly related the vision he had beheld.

" Ay, ay, you have seen the demon hunter, no doubt," replied the keeper, at the close of the recital. " I neither saw the light, nor heard the laughter nor the wailing cry you speak of; but Bawsey crouched at my feet, and whined, and I knew some evil thing was at hand. Heaven shield us ! " he exclaimed, as the hound crouched at his feet, and directed her gaze towards the oak, utter-ing a low, ominous whine. " She is at the same trick again."

The earl glanced in the same direction, and half expected to see the knotted trunk of the tree burst open and disclose the figure of the spectral hunter. But nothing was visible—at least to him; though it would seem, from the shaking limbs, fixed eyes, and ghastly

19

visage of the keeper, that some appalling object was presented to his gaze.

"Do you not see him?" cried the latter at length, in thrilling accents. "He is circling the tree, and blasting it. There! he passes us now—do you not see him?"

"No," replied Surrey; "but do not let us tarry here longer."

So saying, he laid his hand upon the keeper's arm. The touch seemed to rouse him to exertion. He uttered a fearful cry, and set off at a quick pace along the park, followed by Bawsey, with her tail between her legs. The earl kept up with him, and neither halted till they had left the wizard oak at a considerable distance behind them.

"And so you did not see him?" said the keeper, in a tone of exhaustion, as he wiped the thick drops from his brow.

"I did not," replied Surrey.

"That is passing strange," rejoined the other. "I myself have seen him before, but never as he appeared to-night."

"You are a keeper of the forest, I presume, friend?" said Surrey. "How are you named?"

"I am called Morgan Fenwolf," replied the keeper; "and you?"

"I am the Earl of Surrey," returned the young noble.

"What!" exclaimed Fenwolf, making a reverence; "the son to his grace of Norfolk?"

The earl replied in the affirmative.

"Why, then, you must be the young nobleman whom I used to see so often with the king's son, the Duke of Richmond, three or four years ago, at the castle?" rejoined Fenwolf. "You are altogether grown out of my recollection."

"Not unlikely," returned the earl. "I have been at Oxford, and have only just completed my studies. This is the first time I have been at Windsor since the period you mention."

"I have heard that the Duke of Richmond was at Oxford, likewise," observed Fenwolf.

"We were at Cardinal College together," replied Surrey. "But the duke's term was completed before mine. He is my senior by three years."

"I suppose your lordship is returning to the castle?" said Fenwolf.

"No," replied Surrey. "My attendants are waiting for me at the Garter, and if you will accompany me thither, I will bestow a cup of good ale upon you to recruit you after the fright you have undergone."

Fenwolf signified his grateful acquiescence, and they walked on in silence, for the earl could not help dwelling upon the vision he had witnessed, and his companion appeared equally abstracted.

In this sort, they descended the hill near Henry the Eighth's Gate, and entered Thames Street.

II

Of Bryan Bowntance, the host of the Garter; of the Duke of Shoreditch; of the bold words uttered by Mark Fytton, the butcher, and how he was cast into the vault of the Curfew Tower

TURNING off on the right, the earl and his companion continued to descend the hill, until they came in sight of the Garter—a snug little hostel, situated immediately beneath the Curfew Tower.

Before the porch were grouped the earl's attendants, most of whom had dismounted, and were holding their steeds by the bridles. At this juncture, the door of the hostel opened, and a fat, jolly-looking personage, with a bald head, and bushy gray beard, and clad in a brown serge doublet, and hose to match, issued forth, bearing a foaming jug of ale, and a horn cup. His appearance was welcomed by a joyful shout from the attendants.

"Come, my masters!" he cried, filling the horn— "here is a cup of stout Windsor ale, in which to drink

21

the health of our jolly monarch, bluff King Hal ; and there's no harm, I trust, in calling him so."

" Marry, is there not, mine host," cried the foremost attendant. " I spoke of him as such in his own hearing not long ago, and he laughed at me in right merry sort. I love the royal bully, and will drink his health gladly, and Mistress Anne Boelyn's to boot."

And he emptied the horn.

" They tell me Mistress Anne Boleyn is coming to Windsor with the king and the knights-companions to-morrow—is it so ? " asked the host, again filling the horn, and handing it to another attendant.

The person addressed nodded, but he was too much engrossed by the horn to speak.

" Then there will be rare doings in the castle," chuckled the host; " and many a lusty pot will be drained at the Garter. Alack a day ! how times are changed since I, Bryan Bowntance, first stepped into my father's shoes, and became host of the Garter. It was in 1501—twenty-eight years ago—when King Henry the Seventh, of blessed memory, ruled the land, and when his elder son, Prince Arthur, was alive likewise. In that year, the young prince espoused Catharine of Arragon, our present queen, and soon afterwards died; whereupon the old king, not liking—for he loved his treasure better than his own flesh —to part with her dowry, gave her to his second son, Henry, our gracious sovereign, whom God preserve ! Folks said then the match wouldn't come to good; and now we find they spoke the truth, for it is likely to end in a divorce."

" Not so loud, mine host ! " cried the foremost attendant; " here comes our young master, the Earl of Surrey."

" Well, I care not," replied the host bluffly. " I've spoken no treason. I love my kind; and if he wishes to have a divorce, I hope his holiness the Pope will grant him one, that's all."

As he said this, a loud noise was heard within the hostel, and a man was so suddenly and so forcibly driven forth, that he almost knocked down Bryan Bowntance, who was rushing in to see what was the matter. The person thus ejected, who was a powerfully built young man, in a leathern doublet, with his muscular arms bared to the shoulder, turned his rage upon the host, and seized him by the throat with a gripe that threatened him with strangulation. Indeed, but for the intervention of the earl's attendants, who rushed to his assistance, such might have been his fate. As soon as he was liberated, Bryan cried, in a voice of mingled rage and surprise, to his assailant—" Why, what's the matter, Mark Fytton ?— are you gone mad, or do you mistake me for a sheep or a bullock, that you attack me in this fashion? My strong ale must have got into your adle pate with a vengeance."

" The knave has been speaking treason of the king's highness," said a tall man, whose doublet and hose of the finest green cloth, as well as the bow and quiverful of arrows at his back, proclaimed him an archer—" and therefore we turned him out ! "

" And you did well, Captain Barlow," cried the host.

" Call me rather, the Duke of Shoreditch," rejoined the tall archer; " for since his majesty conferred the title upon me, though it were but in jest, when I won this silver bugle, I shall ever claim it. I am always designated by my neighbours in Shoreditch as his grace ; and I require the same attention at your hands. To-morrow I shall have my comrades, the Marquesses of Clerkenwell, Islington, Hogsden, Pancras, and Paddington, with me, and then you will see the gallant figure we shall cut."

" I crave your grace's pardon for my want of respect," replied the host. " I am not ignorant of the distinction conferred upon you at the last match at the castle-butts by the king. But to the matter in hand. What treason hath Mark Fytton, the butcher, been talking? "

" I care not to repeat his words, mine host," replied the duke; " but he hath spoken in unbecoming terms of his highness and Mistress Anne Boleyn."

" He means not what he says," rejoined the host. " He is a loyal subject of the king; but he is apt to get quarrelsome over his cups."

23

"Well said, honest Bryan," cried the duke; "you have one quality of a good landlord—that of a peacemaker. Give the knave a cup of ale, and let him wash down his foul words in a health to the king, wishing him a speedy divorce and a new queen, and he shall then sit among us again."

"I do not desire to sit with you, you self-dubbed duke," rejoined Mark; "but if you will doff your fine jerkin, and stand up with me on the green, I will give you cause to remember laying hands on me."

"Well challenged, bold butcher!" cried one of Surrey's attendants. "You shall be made a duke yourself."

"Or a cardinal," cried Mark. "I should not be the first of my brethren who has met with such preferment."

"He derides the Church in the person of Cardinal Wolsey!" cried the duke. "He is a blasphemer as well as traitor."

"Drink the king's health in a full cup, Mark," interposed the host, anxious to set matters right, "and keep your mischievous tongue between your teeth."

"Beshrew me if I drink the king's health, or that of his minion, Anne Boleyn!" cried Mark boldly. "But I will tell you what I *will* drink. I will drink the health of King Henry's lawful consort, Catharine of Arragon; and I will add to it a wish, that the Pope may forge her marriage chains to her royal husband faster than ever."

"A foolish wish," cried Bryan. "Why, Mark, you are clean crazed!"

"It is the king who is crazed, not me!" cried Mark. "He would sacrifice his rightful consort to his unlawful passion; and you, base hirelings, support the tyrant in his wrongful conduct!"

"Saints protect us!" exclaimed Bryan. "Why, this is flat treason. Mark, I can no longer uphold you."

"Not if you do not desire to share his prison, mine host," cried the Duke of Shoreditch. "You have all heard him call the king a tyrant. Seize him, my masters!"

"Let them lay hands upon me, if they dare!" cried

24

the butcher resolutely. " I have felled an ox with a blow of my fist before this, and I promise you I will show them no better treatment."

Awed by Mark's determined manner, the bystanders kept aloof.

" I command you, in the king's name, to seize him ! " roared Shoreditch. " If he offers resistance, he will assuredly be hanged."

" No one shall touch me ! " cried Mark firecely.

" That remains to be seen," said the foremost of the Earl of Surrey's attendants. " Yield, fellow ! "

" Never ! " replied Mark; " and I warn you to keep off."

The attendant, however, advanced; but before he could lay hands on the butcher, he received a blow from his ox-like fist that sent him reeling backwards for several paces, and finally stretched him at full length upon the ground. His companions drew their swords, and would have instantly fallen upon the sturdy offender, if Morgan Fenwolf, who, with the Earl of Surrey, was standing among the spectators, had not rushed forward, and, closing with Mark before the latter could strike a blow, grappled with him, and held him fast till he was secured, and his arms tied behind him.

" And so it is you, Morgan Fenwolf, who have served me this ill turn, eh ? " cried the butcher, regarding him fiercely. " I now believe all I have heard of you."

" What have you heard of him ? " asked Surrey, advancing.

" That he has dealings with the fiend—with Herne the hunter," replied Mark. " If I am hanged for a traitor, he ought to be burned for a wizard."

" Heed not what the villain says, my good fellow," said the Duke of Shoreditch; " you have captured him bravely, and I will take care your conduct is duly reported to his majesty. To the castle with him ! To the castle ! He will lodge to-night in the deepest dungeon of yon fortification," pointing to the Curfew Tower above them, " there to await the king's judgment; and to-morrow

25

night it will be well for him if he is not swinging from the gibbet near the bridge. Bring him along ! "

And followed by Morgan Fenwolf and the others, with the prisoner, he strode up the hill.

Long before this, Captain Bouchier had issued from the hostel, and joined the earl, and they walked together after the crowd. In a few minutes, the Duke of Shoreditch reached Henry the Eighth's gate, where he shouted to a sentinel, and told him what had occurred. After some delay, a wicket in the gate was opened, and the chief persons of the party were allowed to pass through it, with the prisoner, who was assigned to the custody of a couple of arquebusiers.

By this time an officer had arrived, and it was agreed, at the suggestion of the Duke of Shoreditch, to take the offender to the Curfew Tower. Accordingly, they crossed the lower ward, and passing beneath an archway near the semicircular range of habitations allotted to the petty canons, traversed the space before the west end of St. George's Chapel, and descending a short flight of stone steps at the left, and threading a narrow passage, presently arrived at the arched entrance in the Curfew Tower, whose hoary walls shone brightly in the moonlight.

They had to knock for some time against the stout oak door, before any notice was taken of the summons. At length an old man, who acted as bellringer, thrust his head out of one of the narrow pointed windows above, and demanded their business. Satisfied with the reply, he descended, and opening the door, admitted them into a lofty chamber, the roof of which was composed of stout planks, crossed by heavy oaken rafters, and supported by beams of the same material. On the left, a steep, ladder-like flight of wooden steps led to an upper room; and from a hole in the roof, descended a bell-rope, which was fastened to one of the beams, showing the use to which the chamber was put.

Some further consultation was now held among the party as to the propriety of leaving the prisoner in this chamber, under the guard of the arquebusiers; but it was at last decided against doing so, and the old bell-ringer being called upon for the keys of the dungeon beneath, he speedily produced them. They then went forth; and descending a flight of stone steps on the left, came to a low, strong door, which they unlocked, and obtained admission to a large octangular chamber with a vaulted roof, and deep embrasures terminated by narrow loopholes. The light of a lamp carried by the bellringer showed the dreary extent of the vault, and the enormous thickness of its walls.

"A night's solitary confinement in this place will be of infinite service to our prisoner," said the Duke of Shoreditch, gazing around. "I'll be sworn he is now ready to bite off the foolish tongue that has brought him to such a pass."

The butcher made no reply; but being released by the arquebusiers, sat down upon a bench that constituted the sole furniture of the vault.

"Shall I leave him the lamp?" asked the bellringer. "He may beguile the time by reading the names of former prisoners scratched on the walls and in the embrasures."

"No; he shall not even have that miserable satisfaction," returned the Duke of Shoreditch. "He shall be left in the darkness to his own bad and bitter thoughts."

With this the party withdrew, and the door was fastened upon the prisoner. An arquebusier was stationed at the foot of the steps; and the Earl of Surrey and Captain Bouchier having fully satisfied their curiosity, shaped their course towards the castle gate. On their way thither, the earl looked about for Morgan Fenwolf, but could nowhere discern him. He then passed through the wicket with Bouchier, and proceeding to the Garter, they mounted their steeds, and galloped off towards Datchet, and thence to Staines and Hampton Court.

III

Of the Grand Procession to Windsor Castle ; of the Meeting of King Henry the Eighth and Anne Boleyn at the Lower Gate ; of their Entrance into the Castle ; and how the Butcher was Hanged from the Curfew Tower.

A JOYOUS day was it for Windsor, and great were the preparations made by its loyal inhabitants for a suitable reception to their sovereign. At an early hour, the town was thronged with strangers from the neighbouring villages, and later on, crowds began to arrive from London ; some having come along the highway on horseback, and others having rowed in various craft up the river. All were clad in holiday attire, and the streets presented an appearance of unwonted bustle and gaiety. The may-pole in Bachelors' Acre was hung with flowers. Several booths, with flags floating above them, and erected in the same place, where ale, mead, and hippocras, together with cold pasties, hams, capons, and large joints of beef and mutton, might be obtained. Mummers and minstrels were in attendance, and every kind of diversion was going forward. Here was one party wrestling ; there, another casting the bar ; on this side a set of rustics were dancing a merry round with a bevy of buxom Berkshire lasses ; on that, stood a fourth group listening to a youth playing on the recorders. At one end of the Acre large fires were lighted, before which two whole oxen were roasting, provided in honour of the occasion, by the mayor and burgesses of the town ; at the other, butts were set, against which the Duke of Shoreditch and his companions, the five marquesses, were practising. The duke himself shot admirably, and never failed to hit the bull's eye ; but the great feat of the day was performed by Morgan Fenwolf, who thrice split the duke's shafts as they stuck in the mark.

" Well done ! " cried the duke, as he witnessed the

28

achievement; " why, you shoot as bravely as Herne the hunter. Old wives tell us he used to split the arrows of comrades in that fashion."

" He must have learned the trick from Herne himself in the forest," cried one of the bystanders.

Morgan Fenwolf looked fiercely round in search of the speaker, but could not discern him. He, however, shot no more, and refusing a cup of hippocras offered him by Shoreditch, disappeared among the crowd.

Soon after this, the booths were emptied, the bar thrown down, the may-pole and the butts deserted, and the whole of Bachelors' Acre cleared of its occupants— except those who were compelled to attend to the mighty spits turning before the fires—by the loud discharge of ordnance from the castle gates, accompanied by the ringing of bells, announcing that the mayor and burgesses of Windsor, together with the officers of the Order of the Garter, were setting forth to Datchet Bridge, to meet the royal procession.

Those who most promptly obeyed the summons beheld the lower castle gate, built by the then reigning monarch, open, while from it issued four trumpeters clad in emblazoned coats, with silken bandrols depending from their horns, blowing loud fanfares. They were followed by twelve henchmen, walking four abreast, arrayed in scarlet tunics, with the royal cipher, *H.R.*, worked in gold on the breast, and carrying gilt pole-axes over their shoulders. Next came a company of archers, equipped in helm and brigandine, and armed with long pikes, glittering, as did their steel accoutrements, in the bright sunshine. They were succeeded by the bailiffs and burgesses of the town, riding three abreast, and enveloped in gowns of scarlet cloth; after whom rode the mayor of Windsor, in a gown of crimson velvet, and attended by two footmen, in white and red damask, carrying white wands. The mayor was followed by a company of the town guard, with partisans over the shoulders. Then came the sheriff of the county and his attendants. Next followed the twenty-six alms-knights (for such was then their number) walking two and two, and wearing red mantles, with a scutcheon of St. George on the shoulder, but without the garter surrounding it. Then came the thirteen petty canons, in murrey-coloured gowns, with the arms of St. George wrought in a roundel on the shoulder; then the twelve canons, similarly attired, and lastly, the dean of the college in his cope.

A slight pause ensued, and the chief officers of the Garter made their appearance. First walked the Black-rod, clothed in a russet-coloured mantle, faced with alternate panes of blue and red, emblazoned with flower-de-luces of gold, and crowned lions. He carried a small black rod, the ensign of his office, surmounted with the lion of England in silver. After the Black-rod came the Garter, habited in a gown of crimson satin, paned and emblazoned like that of the officer who preceded him, bearing a white crown, with a sceptre upon it, and having a gilt crown, in lieu of a cap upon his head. The Garter was followed by the Register, a grave personage, in a black gown, with a surplice over it, covered by a mantelet of furs. Then came the Chancellor of the Order, in his robe of murrey-coloured velvet lined with sarcenet, with a badge on the shoulder consisting of a gold rose, en-closed in a garter wrought with pearls of damask gold. Lastly, came the Bishop of Winchester, the prelate of the Order, wearing his mitre, and habited in a robe of crimson velvet lined with white taffeta, faced with blue, and embroidered on the right shoulder with a scutcheon of St. George, encompassed with the garter, and adorned with cordons of blue silk mingled with gold.

Brought up by a rear-guard of halberdiers, the proces-sion moved slowly along Thames Street, the houses of which, as well as those in Peascod Street, were all more or less decorated—the humbler sort being covered with branches of trees, intermingled with garlands of flowers, while the better description was hung with pieces of tapestry, carpets, and rich stuffs. Nor should it pass un-noticed that the loyalty of Bryan Bowntance, the host of the Garter, had exhibited itself in an arch thrown across

mented at the corners with silver bells, ringing forth sweet music as it moved along. Each staff was borne by a knight, of whom sixteen were in attendance to relieve one another when fatigued.

In this litter sat Anne Boleyn. She wore a surcoat of white tissue, and a mantle of the same material lined with ermine. Her gown, which, however, was now concealed by the surcoat, was of cloth-of-gold tissue, raised with pearls of silver damask, with a stomacher of purple gold similarly raised, and large open sleeves lined with chequered tissue. Around her neck she wore a chain of orient pearls, from which depended a diamond cross. A black velvet cap, richly embroidered with pearls and other precious stones, and ornamented with a small white plume, covered her head; and her small feet were hidden in blue velvet brodequins, decorated with diamond stars.

Anne Boleyn's features were exquisitely formed, and though not regular, far more charming than if they had been so. Her nose was slightly aquiline, but not enough so to detract from its beauty, and had a little *retrousse* point that completed its attraction. The rest of her features were delicately chiselled; the chin being beautifully rounded, the brows smooth and white as snow, while the rose could not vie with the bloom of her cheek. Her neck—alas! that the fell hand of the executioner should ever touch it—was long and slender, her eyes large and blue, and of irresistible witchery—sometimes scorching the beholder like a sunbeam, anon melting him with soul-subduing softness.

Of her accomplishments other opportunities will be found to speak; but it may be mentioned that she was skilled on many instruments, danced and sung divinely, and had rare powers of conversation and wit. If to these she had not added the dangerous desire to please, and the wish to hold other hearts than the royal one she had enslaved, in thraldom, all might, perhaps, have been well. But, alas! like many other beautiful women, she had a strong tendency to coquetry. How severely she suffered for it, it is the purpose of this history to relate. An

excellent description of her has been given by a contemporary writer, the Comte de Chateaubriand, who, while somewhat disparaging her personal attractions, speaks in rapturous terms of her accomplishments:—
"Anne," write the Comte, "avait un esprit si deslié quie c'estoit a qui l'ouïroit desgoiser; et ci venoit-elle a poetiser, telle qu'Orpheus, elle eust faict les ours et rochers attenifs: puis saltoit, balloit, et dançoit toutes dances Anglaises ou Estranges, et en imagina nombre qui ont gardé son nom ou celluy du galant pour qui les feit: puis sçavoit tous les jeux, qu'elle jouoit avec non plus d'heur que d'habilité; puis chantoit comme syrene, s'accompagnant de luth; harpoit mieuelx que le roy David, et manioit fort gentilment fleuste et rebec; puis s'accoustroit de tant et si merveilleuses façons, que ses inventions, faisoient d'elle le parangon de toutes les dames les plus sucrées de la court; mais nulle n'avoit sa grace, laquelle, au dire d'un ancien, passe venusté." Such was the opinion of one who knew her well during her residence at the French court, when in attendance on Mary of England, consort of Louis the Twelfth, and afterwards Duchess of Suffolk.

At this moment Anne's eyes were fixed with some tenderness upon one of the supporters of her canopy on the right—a very handsome young man, attired in a doublet and hose of black tylsent, paned and cut, and whose tall, well-proportioned figure was seen to the greatest advantage, inasmuch as he had divested himself of his mantle, for his better convenience in walking.

"I fear me you will fatigue yourself, Sir Thomas Wyat," said Anne Boleyn, in tones of musical sweetness, which made the heart beat, and the colour mount to the cheeks of him she addressed. "You had better allow Sir Thomas Arundel or Sir John Hulstone to relieve you."

"I can feel no fatigue when near you, madam," replied Wyat, in a low tone.

A slight blush overspread Anne's features, and she raised her embroidered kerchief to her lips.

"If I had that kerchief I would wear it at the next lists, and defy all comers," said Wyat.

"You shall have it, then," rejoined Anne. "I love all chivalrous exploits, and will do my best to encourage them."

"Take heed, Sir Thomas," said Sir Francis Weston, the knight who held the staff on the other side, "or we shall have the canopy down. Let Sir Thomas Arundel relieve you."

"No," rejoined Wyat, recovering himself; "I will not rest till we come to the bridge."

"You are in no haste to possess the kerchief," said Anne petulantly.

"There you wrong me, madam!" cried Sir Thomas eagerly. "What ho, good fellows!" he shouted to the attendants at the palfreys' heads; "your lady desires you to stop."

"And I desire them to go on,—I, Will Sommers, jester to the high and mighty King Harry the Eighth!" cried a voice of mock authority behind the knight; "what if Sir Thomas Wyat has undertaken to carry the canopy farther than any of his companions, is that a reason he should be relieved? Of a surety not—go on, I say!"

The person who thus spoke then stepped forward, and threw a glance so full of significance at Anne Boleyn that she did not care to dispute the order, but on the contrary, laughingly acquiesced in it.

Will Sommers, the king's jester, as he described himself, was a small, middle-aged personage, with a physiognomy in which good-nature and malice, folly and shrewdness, were so oddly blended, that it was difficult to say which predominated. His look was cunning and sarcastic, but it was tempered by great drollery and oddity of manner, and he laughed so heartily at his own jests and jibes, that it was scarcely possible to help joining him. His attire consisted of a long, loose gown, of spotted crimson silk, with the royal cipher woven in front in gold; hose of blue cloth, guarded with red and black cloth; and red cordovan buskins. A sash tied round his waist served him instead of a girdle, and he wore a trencher-shaped velvet cap on his head, with a white tufted feather in it. In his hand he carried a small horn. He was generally attended by a monkey, habited in a crimson doublet and hood, which sat upon his shoulder, and played very diverting tricks, but the animal was not with him on the present occasion.

Will Sommers was a great favourite with the king, and ventured upon familiarities which no one else dared to use with him. The favour in which he stood with his royal master procured him admittance to his presence at all hours, and at all seasons, and his influence, though seldom exerted, was very great. He was especially serviceable in turning aside the edge of the king's displeasure, and more frequently exerted himself to allay the storm, than to raise it. His principal hostility was directed against Wolsey, whose arrogance and grasping practices were the constant subjects of his railing. It was seldom, such was his privileged character, and the protection he enjoyed from the sovereign, that any of the courtiers resented his remarks; but Sir Thomas Wyat's feelings being now deeply interested, he turned sharply round, and said—

" How now, thou meddling varlet, what business hast thou to interfere ? "

" I interfere to prove my authority, gossip Wyat," replied Sommers, " and to show that, varlet as I am, I am as powerful as Mistress Anne Boleyn; nay, that I am yet more powerful, because I am obeyed, while she is not."

" Were I at liberty," said Sir Thomas angrily, " I would make thee repent thine insolence."

" But thou art not at liberty, good gossip," replied the jester, screaming with laughter; " thou are tied like a slave to the oar, and cannot free thyself from it—ha ! ha ! " Having enjoyed the knight's discomposure for a few seconds, he advanced towards him, and whispered in his ear—" Don't mistake me, gossip. I have done thee good service in preventing thee from taking that kerchief. Hadst thou received it in the presence of these witnesses, thou wouldst have been lodged in the Round Tower of

Windsor Castle to-morrow, instead of feasting with the knights-companions in St. George's Hall."

" I believe thou art right, gossip," said Wyat, in the same tone.

" Rest assured I am," replied Sommers; " and I furthermore counsel thee to decline this dangerous gift altogether, and to think no more of the fair profferer, or if thou *must* think of her, let it be as of one beyond thy reach. Cross not the lion's path. Take a friendly hint from the jackal."

And without waiting for a reply, he darted away, and mingled with the cavalcade in the rear.

Immediately after Anne Boleyn's litter rode a company of henchmen of the royal household, armed with gilt partisans. Next succeeded a chariot covered with red cloth-of-gold, and drawn by four horses richly caparisoned, containing the old Duchess of Norfolk and the old Marchioness of Dorset. Then came the king's natural son, the Duke of Richmond—a young man formed on the same large scale, and distinguished by the same haughty port and the same bluff manner, as his royal sire. The duke's mother was the Lady Talboys, esteemed one of the most beautiful women of the age, and who had, for a long time, held the capricious monarch captive. Henry was warmly attached to his son, showered favours without number upon him; and might have done yet more, if fate had not snatched him away at an early age.

Though scarcely eighteen, the Duke of Richmond looked more than twenty, and his lips and chin were clothed with a well-grown, though closely-cropped beard. He was magnificently habited in a doublet of cloth-of-gold of bawdekin, the placard and sleeves of which were wrought with flat gold, and fastened with aiglets. A girdle of crimson velvet, enriched with precious stones, encircled his waist, and sustained a poniard, and a Toledo sword, damascened with gold. Over all he wore a loose robe, or *housse*, of scarlet mohair, trimmed with miniver; and was further decorated with the collar of the

Order of the Garter. His cap was of white velvet, ornamented with emeralds, and from the side depended a small azure plume. He rode a magnificent black charger trapped in housings of cloth-of-gold, powdered with ermine.

By the duke's side rode the Earl of Surrey, attired as upon the previous day, and mounted on a fiery Arabian, trapped in crimson velvet, fringed with Venetian gold. Both nobles were attended by their esquires in their liveries.

Behind them came a chariot covered with cloth-of-silver, and drawn, like the first, by four horses in rich housings, containing two very beautiful damsels, one of whom attracted so much of the attention of the youthful nobles, that it was with difficulty they could preserve due order of march. The young dame in question was about seventeen; her face was oval in form, with features of the utmost delicacy and regularity. Her complexion was fair and pale, and contrasted strikingly with her jetty brows and magnificent black eyes, of Oriental size, tenderness, and lustre. Her dark and luxuriant tresses were confined by a cap of black velvet faced with white satin, and ornamented with pearls. Her gown was of white satin worked with gold, and had long, open, pendent sleeves; while from her slender and marble neck hung a cordeliere—a species of necklace imitated from the cord worn by Franciscan friars, and formed of crimson silk twisted with threads of Venetian gold.

This fair creature was the Lady Elizabeth Fitzgerald, daughter of Gerald Fitzgerald, ninth Earl of Kildare, who claimed descent from the Geraldi family of Florence; but she was generally known by the appellation of the Fair Geraldine—a title bestowed upon her, on account of her beauty, by the king, and by which she still lives, and will continue to live, as long as poetry endures, in the deathless and enchanting strains of her lover, the Earl of Surrey. At the instance of her mother, Lady Kildare, the fair Geraldine was brought up with the Princess Mary, afterwards Queen of England; but she had been lately

assigned by the royal order as one of the attendants
—a post equivalent to that of maid of honour—to
Anne Boleyn.

Her companion was the Lady Mary Howard, the sister
of the Earl of Surrey, a nymph about her own age, and
possessed of great personal attractions, having nobly-
formed features, radiant blue eyes, light tresses, and a
complexion of dazzling clearness. Lady Mary Howard
nourished a passion for the Duke of Richmond, whom
she saw with secret chagrin captivated by the superior
charms of the fair Geraldine. Her uneasiness, however,
was in some degree abated by the knowledge, which, as
confidante of the latter she had obtained, that her brother
was master of her heart. Lady Mary was dressed in blue
velvet, cut and lined with cloth-of-gold, and wore a head-
gear of white velvet, ornamented with pearls.

Just as the cavalcade came in sight of Datchet Bridge,
the Duke of Richmond turned his horse's head, and rode
up to the side of the chariot on which the fair Geraldine
was sitting.

" I am come to tell you of a marvellous adventure that
befell Surrey in the Home Park at Windsor, last night,"
he said. " He declares he has seen the demon-hunter,
Herne."

" Then pray let the Earl of Surrey relate the adventure
to us himself," replied the fair Geraldine. " No one can
tell a story so well as the hero of it."

The duke signed to the youthful earl, who was glancing
rather wistfully at them, and he immediately joined them,
while Richmond passed over to the Lady Mary Howard.
Surrey then proceeded to relate what had happened to
him in the park, and the fair Geraldine listened to his
recital with breathless interest.

" Heaven shield us from evil spirits ! " she exclaimed,
crossing herself. " But what is the history of this wicked
hunter, my lord ?—and why did he incur such a dreadful
doom ? "

" I know nothing more than that he was a keeper in
the forest, who, having committed some heinous crime,

hanged himself from a branch of the oak beneath which I found the keeper, Morgan Fenwolf—and which still bears his name," replied the earl. " For this unrighteous act, he cannot obtain rest, but is condemned to wander through the forest at midnight, where he wreaks his vengeance in blasting the trees."

" The legend I have heard differs from yours," observed the Duke of Richmond. " It runs that the spirit by which the forest is haunted is a wood-demon, who assumes the shape of the ghostly hunter, and seeks to tempt or terrify the keepers to sell their souls to him."

" Your grace's legend is the better of the two," said Lady Mary Howard, " or rather, I should say, the more probable. I trust the evil spirit did not make you any such offer, brother of Surrey ? "

The earl gravely shook his head.

" If I were to meet him, and he offered me my heart's dearest wish, I fear he would prevail with me," observed the duke, glancing tenderly at the fair Geraldine.

" Tush !—the subject is too serious for jesting, Richmond," said Surrey, almost sternly.

" His grace, as is usual in compacts with the fiend, might have reason to rue his bargain," observed Lady Mary Howard peevishly.

" If the Earl of Surrey were my brother," remarked the fair Geraldine to the Lady Mary, " I would interdict him from roaming in the park after nightfall."

" He is very wilful," said Lady Mary, smiling, " and holds my commands but lightly."

" Let the fair Geraldine lay hers upon me, and she shall not have to reproach me with disobedience," rejoined the earl.

" I must interpose to prevent their utterance," cried Richmond, with a somewhat jealous look at his friend —" for I have determined to know more of this mystery, and shall require the earl's assistance to unravel it. I think I remember Morgan Fenwolf, the keeper, and will send for him to the castle and question him. But in any case, I and Surrey will visit Herne's Oak to-night."

The remonstrances of both ladies were interrupted by the sudden appearance of Will Sommers.

" What ho ! my lords—to your places ! to your places ! " cried the jester, in a shrill, angry voice. " See ye not we are close upon Datchet Bridge ? Ye can converse with these fair dames at a more fitting season; but it is the king's pleasure that the cavalcade should make a goodly show. To your places, I say ! "

Laughing at the jester's peremptory injunction, the two young nobles nevertheless obeyed it, and, bending almost to the saddle-bow to the ladies, resumed their posts.

The concourse assembled on Datchet Bridge welcomed Anne Boleyn's arrival with loud acclamations, while joyous strains proceeded from sackbut and psaltery, and echoing blasts from the trumpets. Caps were flung into the air, and a piece of ordnance was fired from the barge, which was presently afterwards answered by the castle guns. Having paid his homage to Anne Boleyn, the mayor rejoined the company of bailiffs and burgesses, and the whole cavalcade crossed the bridge, winding their way slowly along the banks of the river, the barge, with the minstrels playing in it, accompanying them the while. In this way they reached Windsor, and as Anne Boleyn gazed up at the lordly castle, above which the royal standard now floated, proud and aspiring thoughts swelled her heart, and she longed for the hour when she should approach it as its mistress. Just then, her eye chanced on Sir Thomas Wyat, who was riding behind her amongst the knights, and she felt, though it might cost her a struggle, that love would yield to ambition.

Leaving the barge and its occupants to await the king's arrival, the cavalcade ascended Thames Street, and were welcomed everywhere with acclamations and rejoicing. Bryan Bowntance, who had stationed himself on the right of the arch in front of his house, attempted to address Anne Boleyn, but could not bring forth a word. His failure, however, was more successful than his speech

41

might have been, inasmuch as it excited abundance of merriment.

Arrived at the area in front of the lower gateway, Anne Boleyn's litter was drawn up in the midst of it, and the whole of the cavalcade grouping around her, presented a magnificent sight to the archers and arquebusiers stationed on the towers and walls.

Just at this moment, a signal gun was heard from Datchet Bridge, announcing that the king had reached it, and the Dukes of Suffolk, Norfolk, and Richmond, together with the Earl of Surrey, Sir Thomas Wyat, and a few of their gentlemen, rode back to meet him. They had scarcely, however, reached the foot of the hill when the royal party appeared in view, for the king with his characteristic impatience, on drawing near the castle, had urged his attendants quickly forward.

First came half a dozen trumpeters, with silken bandrols fluttering in the breeze, blowing loud flourishes. Then a party of halberdiers, whose leaders had pennons streaming from the tops of their tall pikes. Next came two gentlemen-ushers bareheaded, but mounted and richly habited, belonging to the Cardinal of York, who cried out as they pressed forward—" On before, my masters, on before !—make way for my lord's grace."

Then came a sergeant of arms bearing a great mace of silver, and two gentlemen carrying each a pillar of silver. Next rode a gentleman carrying the cardinal's hat, and after him came Wolsey himself, mounted on a mule trapped in crimson velvet, with a saddle covered with the same stuff, and gilt stirrups. His large person was arrayed in robes of the finest crimson satin engrained, and a silky cap of the same colour contrasted by its brightness with the pale, purple tint of his sullen, morose, and bloated features. The cardinal took no notice of the clamour around him, but now and then, when an expression of dislike was uttered against him, for he had already begun to be unpopular with the people, he would raise his eyes and direct a withering glance at the hardy speaker. But these expressions were few, for, though tottering, Wolsey was yet too formidable to be insulted with impunity. On either side of him were two mounted attendants each carrying a gilt pole-axe, who, if he had given the word, would have instantly chastised the insolence of the by-standers; while behind him rode his two cross-bearers, upon horses trapped in scarlet.

Wolsey's princely retinue was followed by a litter of crimson velvet, in which lay the pope's legate, Cardinal Campeggio, whose infirmities were so great that he could not move without assistance. Campeggio was likewise attended by a numerous train.

After a long line of lords, knights, and esquires, came Henry the Eighth. He was apparelled in a robe of crimson velvet furred with ermines, and wore a doublet of raised gold, the placard of which was embroidered with diamonds, rubies, emeralds, large pearls, and other precious stones. About his neck was a baldric of balas rubies, and over his robe he wore the collar of the Order of the Garter. His horse, a charger of the largest size, and well able to sustain his vast weight, was trapped in crimson velvet, purfled with ermines. His knights and esquires were clothed in purple velvet, and his henchmen in scarlet tunics of the same make as those worn by the warders of the Tower at the present day.

Henry was in his thirty-eighth year, and though some-what overgrown and heavy, had lost none of his activity, and but little of the grace of his noble proportions. His size and breadth of limb were well displayed in his magnificent habiliments. His countenance was handsome and manly, with a certain broad, burly look thoroughly English in its character, which won him much admiration from his subjects; and though it might be objected that the eyes were too small, and the mouth somewhat too diminutive, it could not be denied that the general expression of the face was kindly in the extreme. A prince of a more " royal presence " than Henry the Eighth was never seen, and though he had many and grave faults, want of dignity was not amongst the number.

Henry entered Windsor amid the acclamations of the

spectators, the fanfares of trumpeters, and the roar of ordnance from the castle walls.

Meanwhile, Anne Boleyn, having descended from her litter, which passed through the gate into the lower ward, stood with her ladies beneath the canopy awaiting his arrival.

A wide, clear space was preserved before her, into which, however, Wolsey penetrated, and, dismounting, placed himself so that he could witness the meeting between her and the king. Behind him stood the jester, Will Sommers, who was equally curious with himself. The litter of Cardinal Campeggio passed through the gateway and proceeded to the lodgings reserved for his eminence.

Scarcely had Wolsey taken up his station than Henry rode up, and, alighting, consigned his horse to a page, and, followed by the Duke of Richmond and the Earl of Surrey, advanced towards Anne Boleyn, who immediately stepped forward to meet him.

" Fair mistress," he said, taking her hand, and regarding her with a look of passionate devotion, " I welcome you to this my castle of Windsor, and trust soon to make you as absolute mistress of it, as I am lord and master."

Anne Boleyn blushed and cast down her eyes, and Sir Thomas Wyat, who stood at some little distance with his hand upon his saddle, regarding her, felt that any hopes he might have entertained were utterly annihilated.

" Heard you that, my lord cardinal ? " said Will Sommers to Wolsey. " She will soon be mistress here. As she comes in, you go out—mind that ! "

The cardinal made no answer further than was conveyed by the deepened colour of his cheeks.

Amid continued fanfares and acclamations, Harry then led Anne Boleyn through the gateway, followed by the ladies in waiting, who were joined by Richmond and Surrey. The prelate, chancellor, register, black-rod, and other officers of the Garter, together with the whole of the royal retinue who had dismounted, came after them. A vast concourse of spectators, extending almost as far as the Lieutenant's Tower, was collected in front of the Alms-Knights' Houses; but a wide space had been kept clear of the henchmen for the passage of the sovereign and his train, and along this, Henry proceeded with Anne Boleyn, in the direction of the upper ward. Just as he reached the Norman Tower, and passed the entrance to the keep, the Duke of Shoreditch, who was standing beneath the gateway, advanced towards him, and prostrated himself on one knee.

" May it please your majesty," said Shoreditch, " I last night arrested a butcher of Windsor, for uttering words highly disrespectful of your highness, and of the fair and virtuous lady by your side."

" Ah ! God's death ! " exclaimed the king. " Where is the traitor ? Bring him before us."

" He is here," replied Shoreditch.

And immediately Mark Fytton was brought forward by a couple of halberdiers. He still preserved his undaunted demeanour, and gazed sternly at the king.

" So, fellow, thou hast dared to speak disrespectfully of us—ha ! " cried Henry.

" I have spoken the truth," replied the butcher, fearlessly. " I have said you were about to divorce your lawful consort, Catharine of Arragon, and to take the minion, Anne Boleyn, who stands beside you, to your bed. And I added, it was a wrongful act."

" Foul befall thy lying tongue for saying so ! " replied Henry furiously. " I have a mind to pluck it from thy throat, and cast it to the dogs. What ho ! guards, take this caitiff to the summit of the highest tower of the castle—the Curfew Tower—and hang him from it, so that all my loyal subjects in Windsor may see how traitors are served."

" Your highness has judged him justly," said Anne Boleyn.

" You say so now, Mistress Anne Boleyn," rejoined the butcher, " but you shall yourself one day stand in as much peril of your life as I do, and shall plead as vainly as I should, were I to plead at all, which I will never do, to this inexorable tyrant. You will then remember my end."

"Away with him!" cried Henry. "I myself will go to the Garter Tower to see it done. Farewell for a short while, sweetheart. I will read these partisans of Catharine a terrible lesson."

As the butcher was hurried off to the Curfew Tower, the king proceeded with his attendants to the Garter Tower, and ascended to its summit.

In less than ten minutes, a stout pole, like the mast of a ship, was thrust through the battlements of the Curfew Tower, on the side looking towards the town. To this pole a rope, of some dozen feet in length, and having a noose at one end, was firmly secured. The butcher was then brought forth, bound hand and foot, and the noose was thrown over his neck.

While this was passing, the wretched man descried a person looking at him from a window in a wooden structure projecting from the side of the tower.

"What, are you there, Morgan Fenwolf?" he cried. "Remember what passed between us in the dungeon last night, and be warned! You will not meet your end as firmly as I meet mine."

"Make thy shrift quickly, fellow, if thou hast aught to say," interposed one of the halberdiers.

"I have no shrift to make," rejoined the butcher, "I have already settled my account with Heaven. God preserve Queen Catharine!"

As he uttered these words, he was thrust off from the battlements by the halberdiers, and his body swung into the abyss amid the hootings and execrations of the spectators below.

Having glutted his eyes with the horrible sight, Henry descended from the tower, and returned to Anne Boleyn.

I V

How King Henry the Eighth held a Chapter of the Garter ; how he attended Vespers and Matins in Saint George's Chapel ; and how he feasted with the Knights-Companions in Saint George's Hall.

FROM a balcony overlooking the upper ward, Anne Boleyn beheld the king's approach on his return from the Garter Tower, and, waving her hand smilingly to him, she withdrew into the presence-chamber. Hastening to her, Henry found her surrounded by her ladies of honour, by the chief of the nobles and knights who had composed her train from Hampton Court, and by the Cardinals Wolsey and Campeggio; and having exchanged a few words with her, he took her hand, and led her to the upper part of the chamber, where two chairs of state were set beneath a canopy of crimson velvet embroidered with the royal arms, and placed her in the seat hitherto allotted to Catharine of Arragon. A smile of triumph irradiated Anne's lovely countenance at this mark of distinction; nor was her satisfaction diminished, as Henry turned to address the assemblage.

" My lords," he said, " ye are right well aware of the scruples of conscience I entertain in regard to my marriage with my brother's widow, Catharine of Arragon. The more I weight the matter, the more convinced am I of its unlawfulness; and were it possible to blind myself to my sinful condition, the preachers, who openly rebuke me from the pulpit, would take care to remind me of it. Misunderstand me not, my lords, I have no ground of complaint against the queen. Far otherwise. She is a lady of most excellent character—full of devotion, loyalty, nobility, and gentleness. And if I could divest myself of my misgivings, so far from seeking to put her from me, I should cherish her with the greatest tenderness. Ye may marvel that I have delayed the divorce thus long. But

47

it is only of late that my eyes have been opened; and the step was hard to take. Old affections clung to me—old chains restrained me—nor could I, without compunction, separate myself from one who has ever been to me a virtuous and devoted consort."

" Thou hast undergone a martyrdom, gossip," observed Will Sommers, who had posted himself at the foot of the canopy, near the king, " and shall henceforth be denominated Saint Henry."

The gravity of the hearers might have been discomposed by this remark, but for the stern looks of the king.

" Ye may make a jest of my scruples, my lords," he continued, " and think I hold them lightly; but my treatise on the subject, which has cost me much labour and meditation, will avouch to the contrary. What would befall this realm if my marriage were called in question after my decease ? The same trouble and confusion would ensue that followed on the death of my noble grandfather, King Edward the Fourth. To prevent such mischance I have resolved, most reluctantly, to put away my present queen, and to take another consort, by whom I trust to raise up a worthy successor, and inheritor of my kingdom."

A murmur of applause followed this speech, and the two cardinals exchanged significant glances, which were not unobserved by the king.

" I doubt not ye will all approve the choice I shall make," he pursued, looking fiercely at Wolsey, and taking Anne Boleyn's hand, who arose as he turned to her. " And now, fair mistress," he added to her, " as an earnest of the regard I have for you, and of the honours I intend you, I hereby create you Marchioness of Pembroke, and bestow upon you a thousand marks a year in land, and another thousand to be paid out of my treasury to support your dignity."

" Your majesty is too generous," replied Anne, bending the knee, and kissing his hand.

" Not a whit, sweetheart—not a whit," replied Henry, tenderly raising her; " this is but a slight mark of my goodwill. Sir Thomas Boleyn," he added to her father, " henceforth your style and title will be that of Viscount Rochford, and your patent will be made out at the same time as that of your daughter, the Marchioness of Pembroke. I also elect you a knight-companion of the most honourable Order of the Garter, and your investiture and installation will take place to-day."

Having received the thanks and homage of the newly-created noble, Henry descended from the canopy, and passed into an inner room with the Lady Anne, where a collation was prepared for them. Their slight meal over, Anne took up her lute, and playing a lively prelude, sang two or three French songs with so much skill and grace, that Henry, who was passionately fond of music, was quite enraptured. Two delightful hours having passed by, almost imperceptibly, an usher approached the king, and whispering a few words to him, he reluctantly withdrew, and Anne retired with her ladies to an inner apartment.

On reaching his closet, the king's attendants proceeded to array him in a surcoat of crimson velvet, powdered with garters embroidered in silk and gold, with the motto—*Honi soit qui mal y pense*—wrought within them. Over the surcoat was thrown a mantle of blue velvet with a magnificent train, lined with white damask, and having on the left shoulder a large garter, wrought in pearls and Venice twists, containing the motto, and encircling the arms of Saint George—argent, a cross, gules. The royal habiliments were completed by a hood of the same stuff as the surcoat, decorated like it with small embroidered garters, and lined with white satin. From the king's neck was suspended the collar of the Great George, composed of pieces of gold, fashioned like garters, the ground of which was enamelled, and the letters gold.

While Henry was thus arrayed, the knights-companions, robed in their mantles, hoods, and collars, entered the closet, and waiting till he was ready, marched before him into the presence-chamber, where were assembled the two provincial kings-at-arms, Clarenceux and Norroy, the heralds, and pursuivants, wearing their coats-of-arms, together with the band of pensioners, carrying gilt pole-axes, and drawn up in two lines. At the king's approach, one of the gentlemen-ushers who carried the sword of state, with the point resting upon the ground, delivered it to the Duke of Richmond—the latter having been appointed to bear it before the king during all the proceedings of the feast. Meanwhile, the knights-companions having drawn up on either side of the canopy, Henry advanced with a slow and stately step towards it, his train borne by the Earl of Surrey, Sir Thomas Wyat, and other nobles and knights. As he ascended the canopy, and faced the assemblage, the Duke of Richmond and the chief officers of the order drew up a little on his right. The knights-companions then made their salutation to him, which he returned by removing his jewelled cap with infinite grace and dignity; and as soon as he was again covered, they put on their caps, and ranging themselves in order, set forward to Saint George's Chapel.

Quitting the royal lodgings, and passing through the gateway of the Norman Tower, the procession wound its way along the base of the Round Tower, the battlements of which bristled with spearmen, as did the walls on the right, and the summit of the Winchester Tower, and crossing the middle ward, skirted the tomb-house, then newly erected by Wolsey, and threading a narrow passage, between it and Saint George's Chapel, entered the north-east door of the latter structure.

Dividing, on their entrance into the chapel, into two lines, the attendants of the knights-companions flanked either side of the north aisle; while between them walked the alms-knights, the verger, the prebends of the college, and the officers-of-arms, who proceeded as far as the west door of the choir, where they stopped. A slight pause then ensued, after which, the king, the knights-companions, and the chief officers of the order, entered the chapter-house—a chamber situated at the north-east corner of the chapel—leaving the Duke of Richmond, the sword-bearer, Lord Rochford, the knight-elect, the train-bearers, and pensioners, outside. The door of the chapter-house being closed by the black-rod, the king proceeded to the upper end of the vestments'-board—as the table was designated—where a chair, cushions and cloth of state, were provided for him; the knights-companions, whose stalls in the choir were on the same side as his own, seating themselves on his right, and those whose posts were on the prince's side taking their places on the left. The prelate and the chancellor stood at the upper end of the table; the garter and register at the foot; while the door was kept by the black-rod.

As soon as the king and the knights were seated, intimation was given by an usher to the black-rod, that the newly-elected knight, Lord Rochford, was without. This intelligence being communicated to the king, he ordered the Dukes of Suffolk and Norfolk to bring him into his presence. The injunction was obeyed, and the knight-elect presently made his appearance, the garter marching before him to the king. Bowing reverently to the sovereign, Rochford, in a brief speech, expressed his gratitude for the signal honour conferred upon him, and at its close, set his left foot upon a gilt stool, placed for him by the garter, who pronounced the following admonition:—" My good lord, the loving company of the Order of the Garter have received you as their brother and fellow. In token whereof, they give you this garter which God grant you may receive and wear from henceforth, to His praise and glory, and to the exultation and honour of the noble order and yourself."

Meanwhile, the garter was girded on the leg of the newly-elected knight, and buckled by the Duke of Suffolk. This done, he knelt before the king, who hung a gold chain, with the image of Saint George attached to about his neck, while another admonition was pronounced by the chancellor. Rochford then arose, bowed to the monarch, and to the knights-companions, who returned his salutations, and the investiture was complete.

Other affairs of the chapter were next discussed. Certain officers, nominated since the last meeting, were sworn; letters from absent knights-companions, praying to be excused from attendance, were read—and their pleas, except in the instance of Sir Thomas Cheney, allowed. After reading the excuse of the latter, Henry uttered an angry oath, declaring he would deprive him of his vote in the chapter-house, banish him from his stall, and mulct him a hundred marks, to be paid at Saint George's altar, when Will Sommers, who was permitted to be present, whispered in his ear that the offender was kept away by the devices of Wolsey, because he was known to be friendly to the divorce, and to the interests of the Lady Anne.

" Aha ! by Saint Mary, is it so ? " exclaimed Henry, knitting his brows. " This shall be looked into. I have hanged a butcher just now. Let the butcher's son take warning by his fate. He has bearded me long enough. See that Sir Thomas Cheney be sent for with all despatch. I will hear the truth from his own lips."

He then arose, and quitting the chapter-house, proceeded with the knights-companions to the choir—the roof and the walls of the sacred structure resounding with the solemn notes of the organ as they traversed the aisle. The first to enter the choir were the alms-knights, who passed through the door in a body, and making low obeisances toward the altar and the royal stall, divided into two lines. They were succeeded by the prebends of the college, who, making similar obeisances, stationed themselves in front of the benches before the stalls of the knights-companions. Next followed the pursuivants, heralds, and provincial kings-of-arms, making like reverences, and ranging themselves with the alms-knights. Then came the knights-companions, who performed double reverences like the others, and took their stations under their stalls; then came the black-rod, garter, and register, who having gone through the same ceremony as the others, proceeded to their form, which was placed on the south side of the choir before the sovereign's stall; then came the chancellor and prelate, whose form was likewise placed before the royal stall, but nearer to it than that allotted to the other officers; and, lastly, Henry himself, with the sword borne before him by the Duke of Richmond, who, as he approached the steps of his stall, bowed reverently towards the altar, and made another obeisance before seating himself.

Meanwhile, the Duke of Richmond posted himself in front of the royal stall, the Earl of Oxford, as lord-chamberlain, taking his station on the knight's right, and the Earl of Surrey, as vice-chamberlain, on the left. As these arrangements were made, the two cardinals arrived, and proceeded to the altar.

Mass was then said, and nothing could be more striking than the appearance of the chapel during its performance. The glorious choir, with its groined and pendent roof, its walls adorned with the richest stuffs, its exquisitely carved stalls, above which hung the banners of the knights-companions, together with their helmets, crests, and swords, its sumptuously-decorated altar, glittering with costly vessels, its pulpit hung with crimson damask inter-woven with gold, the magnificent and varied dresses of the assemblage—all these constituted a picture of surpassing splendour.

Vespers over, the king and his train departed with the same ceremonies, and in the same order as had been observed on their entrance of the choir.

On returning to the royal lodgings, Henry proceeded to his closet, where, having divested himself of his mantle, he went in search of the Lady Anne. He found her walking with her dames on the stately terrace at the north of the castle, and the attendants retiring as he joined her, he was left at full liberty for amorous converse. After pacing the terrace for some time, he adjourned with Anne to her own apartments, where he remained till summoned to supper with the knight-companions in Saint George's Hall.

The next morning betimes, it being the day of the patron saint of the Order of the Garter, a numerous cavalcade assembled in the upper ward of the castle, to conduct the king to hear matins in Saint George's Chapel. In order to render the sight as imposing as possible, Henry had arranged that the procession should take place on horseback, and the whole of the retinue were accordingly mounted. The large quadrangle was filled with steeds and their attendants, and the castle walls resounded with the fanfares of trumpets, and the beating of kettle-drums. The most attractive feature of the procession in the eyes of the beholders was the Lady Anne, who, mounted on a snow-white palfrey richly trapped, rode on the right of the king. She was dressed in a rich gown of raised cloth-of-gold; and had a coronet of black velvet, decorated with orient pearls, on her head. Never had she looked so lovely as on this occasion, and the king's passion increased as he gazed upon her. Henry himself was more sumptuously attired than on the preceding day. He wore a robe of purple velvet made somewhat like a frock, embroidered with flat damask gold, and small lace intermixed. His doublet was very curiously embroidered, the sleeves and breast being lined with cloth-of-gold, and fastened with great buttons of diamonds and rubies. His sword and girdle were adorned with magnificent emeralds, and his bonnet glistened with precious stones. His charger was trapped in cloth-of-gold, traversed lattice-wise, square, embroidered with gold damask, pearled on every side, and having buckles and pendants of fine gold. By his side ran ten footmen, richly attired in velvet and goldsmith's work. They were followed by the pages of honour, mounted on great horses, trapped in crimson velvet embroidered with new devices and knots of gold.

In this state Henry and his favourite proceeded to the great western door of Saint George's Chapel. Here twelve gentlemen of the privy-chamber attended with a canopy of cloth-of-gold, which they bore over the king's head, and that of the Lady Anne, as she walked beside him to the entrance of the choir, where they separated— he proceeding to his stall, and she to a closet at the north-east corner of the choir over the altar, while her ladies repaired to one adjoining it.

Matins then commenced, and at the appointed part of the service, the dean of the college took a silver box, containing the heart of Saint George, bestowed upon King Henry the Fifth by the Emperor Sigismund, and after incense had been shed upon it by one of the canons, presented it to the king and the knights-companions to kiss.

After the offertory, a carpet was spread on the steps before the altar, the alms-knights, pursuivants, and heralds stationing themselves on either side of it. The garter then descended from his seat, and waving his rod, the knights-companions descended likewise, but remained before their stalls. The black-rod next descended, and proceeding towards the altar, a groom of the wardrobe brought him a small carpet of cloth-of-gold, and a cushion of the same stuff, which were placed on the larger carpet, the cushion being set on the head of the steps. Taking a large gilt basin to receive the offerings, the prelate stationed himself with one of the prebends in the midst of the altar. The king then rose from his stall, and making a reverence as before, proceeded to the altar, attended by the garter, register, and chancellor, together with the Duke of Richmond bearing the sword, and having reached the upper step, prostrated himself on the cushion, while the black-rod bending the knee delivered a chain of gold, intended afterwards to be redeemed, to the Duke of Suffolk, who was appointed to make the royal offering, and who placed it in the basin held by the prelate. This ceremony over, the king got up, and with similar reverences returned to his stall. Then the two provincial kings, Clarenceux and Norroy, proceeded along the choir, and making due reverences to the altar and the sovereign, bowed to the two senior knights, who thereupon advanced towards the altar, and kneeling down, made their offering. The others imitated their example, coming forward according to their seniority.

The service ended, the officers and knights-companions

quitted the chapel in the same order they had entered it, the king being received under the canopy at the door of the choir, and passing through the west entrance of the chapel, where he waited for the Lady Anne. On her arrival, they both mounted their steeds, and rode up to the royal lodgings amid flourishes of trumpets and acclamations. Dismounting at the great gate, Henry proceeded to the presence-chamber, where the knights-companions had assembled, and having received their salutations, retired to his closet. Here he remained in deep consultation with the Duke of Suffolk for some hours, when, it having been announced to him that the first course of the banquet was served, he came forth, and proceeded to the presence-chamber, where he greeted the knights-companions, who were there assembled, and who immediately put themselves in order of procession. After this, the alms-knights, prebends, and officers-of-arms, passed on through the guard-chamber into Saint George's Hall. They were followed by the knights-companions, who drew up in double file, the seniors taking the upper-most place ; and through these lines the king passed, his train borne up as before, until reaching the table set apart for him, beneath a canopy, he turned round, and received the knights' reverences. The Earl of Oxford, as vice-chamberlain, then brought him a ewer containing water, the Earl of Surrey a basin, and Lord Rochford a napkin. Henry having performed his ablutions, grace was said by the prelate, after which the king seated him-self beneath the canopy in an ancient chair with a curiously-carved back representing the exploit of Saint George, which had once belonged to the founder, King Edward the Third, and called up the two cardinals, who by this time had entered the hall, and who remained standing beside him, on either hand, during the repast.

As soon as the king was seated, the knights-com-panions put on their caps, and retired to the table prepared for them, on the right side of the hall, where they seated themselves, according to their degree; the Duke of Richmond occupying the first place, the Duke of Suffolk the second, the Duke of Norfolk the third. On the opposite side of the hall was a long beaufet covered with flasks of wine, meat, and dishes, for the service of the knights' table. Before this stood the attendants, near whom were drawn up two lines of pensioners bearing the second course on great gilt dishes, and headed by the sewer. In front of the sewer were the treasurer, and comptroller of the household, each bearing a white wand. Next them stood the officers-at-arms, in two lines, headed by the garter. The bottom of the hall was thronged with yeomen of the guard, halberdiers, and henchmen. In a gallery at the lower end were stationed a band of minstrels; and near them sat the Lady Anne and her dames to view the proceedings.

The appearance of the hall during the banquet was magnificent; the upper part being hung with arras representing the legend of Saint George, placed there by Henry the Sixth; and the walls behind the knights-companions adorned with other tapestries and rich stuffs. The tables groaned with the weight of dishes, some of which may be enumerated for the benefit of modern gastronomers. There were Georges on horseback, chickens in brewis, cygnets, capons of high grease, carpes of venison, herons, calvered salmon, custards planted with garters, tarts closed with arms, godwits, peafowl, halibut engrailed, porpoise in armour, pickled mullets, perch in foyle, venison pasties, hippocras jelly, and mainemy royal.

Before the second course was served, the garter, followed by Clarenceux and Norroy, together with the heralds and pursuivants, advanced towards the sovereign's canopy, and cried thrice, in a loud voice, " Largesse ! "

Upon this all the knights-companions arose and took off their caps. The garter then proceeded to proclaim the king's titles in Latin and French, and lastly in English, as follows :—" Of the most high, most excellent, and most mighty monarch, Henry the Eighth, by the grace of God, King of England, France, and Ireland, Defender of the Faith, and sovereign of the most noble Order of the Garter."

This proclamation made, the treasurer of the household put ten golden marks into the garter's cap, who making a reverence to the sovereign, retired from the hall with his followers.

" Come, my lord legate," said Henry, when this ceremony was at an end; " we will drink to my future queen. What ho ! wine ! " he added, to the Earl of Surrey, who officiated as cup-bearer.

" Your highness is not yet divorced from your present consort," replied Campeggio. " If it please you, I should prefer drinking the health of Catharine of Arragon."

" Well, as your eminence pleases," replied the king, taking the goblet from the hand of Surrey; " I shall not constrain you."

And looking towards the gallery, he fixed his eyes on the Lady Anne, and drained the cup to the last drop.

" Would it were poison," muttered Sir Thomas Wyat, who stood behind the Earl of Surrey, and witnessed what was passing.

" Give not thy treasonable thoughts vent, gossip," said Will Sommers, who formed one of the group near the royal table, " or it may chance that some one less friendly-disposed towards thee than myself may overhear them. I tell thee, the Lady Anne is lost to thee for ever. Think'st thou aught of womankind would hesitate between a simple knight and a king ? My lord duke," he added, sharply, to Richmond, who was looking round at him, " you would rather be in yonder gallery than here."

" Why so, knave ? " asked the duke.

" Because the fair Geraldine is there," replied the jester. " And yet your grace is not the person she would most desire to have with her."

" Whom would she prefer ? " inquired the duke angrily.

The jester nodded at Surrey, and laughed maliciously.

" You heard the health given by the king just now, my lord," observed the Duke of Suffolk to his neighbour the Duke of Norfolk : " it was a shrewd hint to the lord legate which way his judgment should incline. Your niece will assuredly be Queen of England."

"I did not note what was said, my lord," replied Norfolk; "I pray you repeat it to me."

Suffolk complied, and they continued in close debate until the termination of the banquet, when the king, having saluted the company, returned to the presence-chamber.

V

Of the Ghostly Chase beheld by the Earl of Surrey and the Duke of Richmond, in Windsor Forest

ON that same night, and just as the castle clock was on the stroke of twelve, the Earl of Surrey and the Duke of Richmond issued from the upper gate, and took their way towards Herne's Oak. The moon was shining brightly, and its beams silvered the foliage of the noble trees with which the park was studded. The youthful friends soon reached the blasted tree; but nothing was to be seen near it, and all looked so tranquil, so free from malignant influence, that the Duke of Richmond could not help laughing at his companion, telling him that the supposed vision must have been the offspring of his over-excited fancy. Angry at being thus doubted, the earl walked off, and plunged into the haunted dell. The duke followed, but though they paused for some time beneath the gnarled oak-tree, the spirit did not appear.

"And thus ends the adventure of Herne the hunter!" laughed the duke, as they emerged from the brake. "By my halidom, Surrey, I am grievously disappointed. You must have mistaken some large stag, caught by its antlers in the branches of the oak-tree, for the demon."

"I have told you precisely what occurred," replied Surrey angrily. "Ha! there he is—look! look!"

And he pointed to a weird figure, mounted on a steed

as weird-looking as itself, galloping through the trees
with extraordinary swiftness, at a little distance from
them. This ghostly rider wore the antlered helmet
described by Surrey, and seemed to be habited in a garb
of deer skins. Before him flew a large owl, and a couple
of great black dogs ran beside him. Staring in speechless
wonder at the sight, the two youths watched the mysterious being scour a glade brightly illumined by the
moon, until reaching the pales marking the confines of
the Home Park, he leaped them, and disappeared.

"What think you of that?" cried Surrey, as soon as
he had recovered from his surprise, glancing triumphantly
at the duke. "Was that the offspring of my fancy?"

"It was a marvellous sight, truly!" exclaimed Richmond. "Would we had our steeds to follow him!"

"We can follow him on foot," replied the earl—"he
is evidently gone into the forest."

And they set off at a quick pace in the direction taken
by the ghostly rider. Clambering the park pales, they
crossed the road leading to Old Windsor, and entered that
part of the forest which, in more recent times, has been
enclosed and allotted to the grounds of Frogmore.
Tracking a long vista, they came to a thick dell, overgrown with large oaks, at the bottom of which lay a
small pool. Fleeter than his companion, and therefore
somewhat in advance of him, the Earl of Surrey, as he
approached this dell, perceived the spectral huntsman
and his dogs standing at the edge of the water. The earl
instantly shouted to him, and the horseman, turning his
head, shook his hand menacingly, while the hounds
glared fiercely at the intruder, and displayed their fangs,
but did not bark. As Surrey, however, despite this
caution, continued to advance, the huntsman took a
strangely-shaped horn that hung by his side, and placing
it to his lips, flames and thick smoke presently issued
from it, and before the vapour had cleared off, he and
his dogs had disappeared. The witnesses of this
marvellous spectacle crossed themselves reverently, and
descended to the brink of the pool; but the numerous

footprints of deer, that came there to drink, prevented them from distinguishing any marks of the steed of the ghostly hunter.

" Shall we return, Surrey ? " asked the duke.

" No," replied the earl; " I am persuaded we shall see the mysterious huntsman again. You can return, if you think proper. I will go on."

" Nay, I will not leave you," rejoined Richmond.

And they set off again at the same quick pace as before. Mounting a hill covered with noble beeches and elms, a magnificent view of the castle burst upon them, towering over the groves they had tracked, and looking almost like the work of enchantment. Charmed with the view, the young men continued to contemplate it for some time. They then struck off on the right, and ascended still higher, until they came to a beautiful grove of beeches cresting the hill where the equestrian statue of George the Third is now placed. Skirting this grove, they disturbed a herd of deer, which starting up, darted into the valley below.

At the foot of two fine beech-trees lay another small pool, and Surrey almost expected to see the spectral huntsman beside it.

From this spot they could discern the whole of the valley beyond, and they scanned it in the hope of perceiving the object of their search. Though not comparable to the view on the nearer side, the prospect was nevertheless exceedingly beautiful. Long vistas and glades stretched out before them, while in the far distance might be seen glittering in the moonbeams the lake or mere, which in later days has received the name of Virginia Water.

While they were gazing at this scene, a figure habited like a keeper of the forest suddenly emerged from the trees at the lower end of one of the glades. Persuaded that this person had some mysterious connection with the ghostly huntsman, the earl determined to follow him, and hastily mentioning his supicions and design to Richmond, he hurried down the hill. But before he

accomplished the descent, the keeper was gone. At
length, however, on looking about, they perceived him
mounting the rising ground on the left, and immediately
started after him, taking care to keep out of sight. The
policy of this course was soon apparent. Supposing himself no longer pursued, the keeper relaxed his pace, and
the others got nearer to him.

In this way both parties went on, the keeper still
hurrying forward, every now and then turning his head
to see whether any one was on his track, until he came
to a road cut through the trees, that brought him to the
edge of a descent leading to the lake. Just at this moment,
a cloud passed over the moon, burying all in com-
parative obscurity. The watchers, however, could
perceive the keeper approach an ancient beech-tree of
enormous growth, and strike it thrice with the short
hunting-spear which he held in his grasp.

The signal remaining unanswered, he quitted the tree,
and shaped his course along the side of a hill on the right.
Keeping under the shelter of the thicket on the top of the
same hill, Surrey and Richmond followed, and saw him
direct his steps towards another beech-tree of almost
double the girth of that he had just visited. Arrived at
this mighty tree, he struck it with his spear, while a large
owl, seated on a leafless branch, began to hoot; a bat
circled the tree; and two large snakes, glistening in the
moonlight, glided from its roots. As the tree was stricken
for the third time, the same weird figure that the watchers
had seen ride along the Home Park burst from its rifted
truck, and addressed its summoner in tones apparently
menacing and imperious, but whose import was lost upon
the listeners. The curiosity of the beholders was roused
to the highest pitch; but an undefinable awe prevented
them from rushing forward.

Suddenly, the demon-hunter waved a pike with which
he was armed, and uttered a peculiar cry, resembling the
hooting of an owl. At this sound, and as if by magic, a
couple of steeds, accompanied by the two hounds, started
from the brake. In an instant, the demon huntsman

vaulted upon the back of the horse nearest to him, and the keeper almost as quickly mounted the other. The pair then galloped off through the glen, the owl flying before them, and the hounds coursing by their side.

The two friends gazed at each other, for some time, in speechless wonder. Taking heart, they then descended to the haunted tree, but could perceive no traces of the strange being by whom it had been recently tenanted. After awhile, they retraced their course towards the castle, hoping they might once more encounter the wild huntsmen. Nor were they disappointed. As they crossed a glen, a noble stag darted by. Close at its heels came the two black hounds, and after them the riders hurrying forward at a furious pace, their steeds appearing to breathe forth flame and smoke.

In an instant the huntsmen and hounds were gone, and the trampling of the horses died away in the distance. Soon afterwards, a low sound, like the winding of a horn, broke upon the ear, and the listeners had no doubt that the buck was brought down. They hurried in the direction of the sound, but though the view was wholly unobstructed for a considerable distance, they could see nothing either of horsemen, hounds, or deer.

VI

*How the Fair Geraldine bestowed a Relic upon her Lover;
how Surrey and Richmond rode in the Forest at Midnight;
and where they found the Body of Mark Fytton, the
Butcher*

SURREY and Richmond agreed to say nothing for the
present of their mysterious adventure in the forest; but
their haggard looks, as they presented themselves to the
Lady Anne Boleyn in the reception-chamber, on the
following morning, proclaimed that something had
happened, and they had to undergo much questioning
from the fair Geraldine and the Lady Mary Howard.

" I never saw you so out of spirits, my lord," remarked
the fair Geraldine to Surrey; " you must have spent the
whole night in study—or what is more probable, you
have again seen Herne the hunter. Confess now, you
have been in the forest."

" I will confess anything you please," replied Surrey
evasively.

" And what have you seen ?—a stranger vision than
the first ? " rejoined the fair Geraldine.

" Since your ladyship answers for me, there is no need
for explanation on my part," rejoined Surrey, with a faint
laugh. " And know you not, that those who encounter
supernatural beings are generally bound to profound
secrecy ? "

" Such, I hope, is not your case, Henry ? " cried the
Lady Mary Howard, in alarm;—" nor yours, my lord ? "
she added, to the Duke of Richmond.

" I am bound equally with Surrey," returned the duke
mysteriously.

" You pique my curiosity, my lords," said the fair
Geraldine; " and since there is no other way of gratifying
it, if the Lady Mary Howard will accompany me, we will
ourselves venture into the forest, and try whether we

cannot have a meeting with this wild huntsman. Shall we go to-night ? "

" Not for worlds," replied the Lady Mary, shuddering; " were I to see Herne, I should die of fright."

" Your alarm is groundless," observed Richmond gallantly. " The presence of two beings, fair and pure as yourself and the Lady Elizabeth Fitzgerald, would scare away aught of evil."

The Lady Mary thanked him with a beaming smile, but the fair Geraldine could not suppress a slight laugh.

" Your grace is highly flattering," she said. " But with all faith in beauty and purity, I should place most reliance in a relic I possess—the virtue of which has often been approved against evil spirits. It was given by a monk—who had been sorely tempted by a demon, and who owed his deliverance to it—to my ancestor, Luigi Geraldi of Florence; and from him it descended to me."

" Would I had an opportunity of proving its efficacy ! " exclaimed the Earl of Surrey.

" You shall prove it, if you choose," rejoined the fair Geraldine. " I will give you the relic, on the condition that you never part with it to friend or foe."

And detaching a small cross of gold, suspended by a chain from her neck, she presented it to the Earl of Surrey.

" This cross encloses the relic," she continued; " wear it, and may it protect you from all ill ! "

Surrey's pale cheek glowed as he took the gift.

" I will never part with it but with life ! " he cried, pressing the cross to his lips, and afterwards placing it next his heart.

" I would have given half my dukedom to be so favoured," said Richmond moodily.

And quitting the little group, he walked towards the Lady Anne.

" Henry," said the Lady Mary, taking her brother aside; " you will lose your friend."

" I care not," replied Surrey.

" But you may incur his enmity," pursued the Lady

Mary. " I saw the glance he threw at you just now, and it was exactly like the king's terrible look, when offended."

" Again I say I care not," replied Surrey. " Armed with this relic, I defy all hostility."

" It will avail little against Richmond's rivalry and opposition," rejoined his sister.

" We shall see," retorted Surrey. " Were the king himself my rival, I would not resign my pretensions to the fair Geraldine ! "

" Bravely resolved, my lord," said Sir Thomas Wyat, who, having overheard the exclamation, advanced towards him. " Heaven grant you may never be placed in such jeopardy ! "

" I say amen to that prayer, Sir Thomas," rejoined Surrey. " I would not prove disloyal, and yet under such circumstances——"

" What would you do ? " interrupted Wyat.

" My brother is but a hasty boy, and has not learned discretion, Sir Thomas," interposed the Lady Mary, trying by a significant glance to impose silence on the earl.

" Young as he is, he loves well, and truly," remarked Wyat, in a sombre tone.

" What is all this ? " inquired the fair Geraldine, who had been gazing through the casement into the court below.

" I was merely expressing a wish that Surrey may never have a monarch for a rival, fair lady," replied Wyat.

" It matters little who may be his rival," rejoined Geraldine, " provided she he loves be constant."

" Right, lady, right," said Wyat, with great bitterness.

At this moment, Will Sommers approached them.

" I come to bid you to the Lady Anne's presence, Sir Thomas, and you to the king's, my Lord of Surrey," said the jester. " I noticed what has just taken place," he remarked to the latter, as they proceeded towards the royal canopy, beneath which Henry and the Lady Anne Boleyn were seated ; but Richmond will not relinquish her tamely for all that."

Anne Boleyn had summoned Sir Thomas Wyat, in order to gratify her vanity, by showing him the unbounded influence she possessed over his royal rival; and the half-suppressed agony displayed by the unfortunate lover at the exhibition afforded her a pleasure such as only the most refined coquette can feel.

Surrey was sent for by the king to receive instructions, in his quality of vice-chamberlain, respecting a tilting-match and hunting-party to be held on successive days—the one in the upper quadrangle of the castle, the other in the forest.

Anxious, now that he was somewhat calmer, to avoid a rupture with Richmond, Surrey, as soon as he had received the king's instructions, drew near the duke; and the latter, who had likewise reasoned himself out of his resentment, was speedily appeased, and they became, to all appearance, as good friends as ever.

Soon afterwards, the Lady Anne and her dames retired, and the court breaking up, the two young nobles trolled forth to the stately terrace at the north of the castle, where, while gazing at the glorious view it commanded, they talked over the mysterious event of the previous night.

" I cannot help suspecting that the keeper we beheld with the demon-hunter was Morgan Fenwolf," remarked the earl. " Suppose we make inquiry whether he was at home last night. We can readily find out his dwelling from Bryan Bowntance, the host of the Garter."

Richmond acquiesced in the proposal, and they accordingly proceeded to the cloisters of Saint George's Chapel, and threading some tortuous passages contrived among the canons' houses, passed through a small porch, guarded by a sentinel, and opening upon a precipitous and somewhat dangerous flight of steps, hewn out of the rock, and leading to the town.

None except the more important members of the royal household were allowed to use this means of exit from the castle; but of course the privilege extended to Richmond and Surrey. Here in later times, and when the castle was not so strictly guarded, a more convenient approach was built, and designated, from the number of its stairs, " The hundred steps."

Having accomplished the descent in safety, and given the pass-word to the sentinel at the foot of the steps, the two young nobles emerged into the street, and the first object they beheld was the body of the miserable butcher swinging from the summit of the Curfew Tower, where it was left by order of the king.

Averting their gaze from this ghastly spectacle, they took their way up Thames Street, and soon reached the Garter. Honest Bryan was seated on a bench before the dwelling, with a flagon of his own ale beside him, and rising as he saw the others approach, he made them a profound salutation.

On learning what they sought, he told them that Morgan Fenwolf dwelt in a small cottage by the river side, not far from the bridge, and if it pleased them he would guide them to it himself,—an offer which they gladly accepted.

" Do you know anything of this Fenwolf ? " asked Surrey, as they proceeded on their way.

" Nothing particular," replied Bryan, with some hesitation ; " there are some strange reports about him, but I don't believe 'em."

" What reports are they, friend ? " asked the Duke of Richmond.

" Why, your grace, one ought to be cautious what one says, for fear of bringing an innocent man into trouble," returned the host. " But if the truth must be spoken, people *do* say that Morgan Fenwolf is in league with the devil—or with Herne the hunter, which is the same thing."

Richmond exchanged a look with his friend.

" Folks say strange sights have been seen in the forest, of late," pursued Bryan—" and it may be so. But I myself have seen nothing,—but then, to be sure, I never go there. The keepers used to talk of Herne the hunter when I was a lad, but I believe it was only a tale to frighten deer-stealers; and I fancy it's much the same thing now."

Neither Surrey nor Richmond made any remark, and they presently reached the keeper's dwelling.

It was a small wooden tenement standing, as the host had stated, on the bank of the river, about a bow-shot from the bridge. The door was opened by Bryan, and the party entered without further ceremony. They found no one within except an old woman, with harsh, wrinkled features, and a glance as ill-omened as that of a witch, whom Bryan Bowntance told them was Fenwolf's mother. The old crone regarded the intruders uneasily.

" Where is your son, dame ? " demanded the duke.

" On his walk in the forest," replied the old crone bluntly.

" What time did he go forth ? " inquired Surrey.

" An hour before daybreak, as is his custom," returned the woman, in the same short tone as before.

" You are sure he slept at home last night, dame ? " said Surrey.

" As sure as I am that the question is asked me," she replied. " I can show you the very bed on which he slept, if you desire to see it. He retired soon after sunset—slept soundly, as he always sleeps—and arose as I have told you. I lighted a fire, and made him some hot pottage myself."

" If she speaks the truth, you must be mistaken," observed Richmond, in a whisper to his friend.

" I do believe her not," replied Surrey, in the same tone. " Show us his chamber, dame."

The old crone sullenly complied, and throwing open a side door, disclosed an inner apartment, in which there was a small bed. There was nothing noticeable in the room, except a couple of fishing-nets, a hunting-spear, and an old cross-bow. A small open casement looked upon the river, whose clear, sparkling waters flowed immediately beneath it.

Surrey approached the window, and obtained a fine view of the Brocas meads on the one hand, and the embowered college of Eton on the other. His attention, however, was diverted by a fierce barking without; and the next moment, in spite of the vociferations of the old woman, a large, black staghound, which Surrey recognised as Fenwolf's dog, Bawsey, burst through the door, and rushed furiously towards him. Surrey drew his dagger to defend himself from the hound's attack, but the precaution was needless. Bawsey's fierceness changed suddenly to the most abject submission, and with a terrified howl, she retreated from the room with her tail between her legs. Even the old woman uttered a cry of surprise.

" Lord help us ! " exclaimed Bryan—" was ever the like o' that seen ? Your lordship must have a strange mastery over dogs. That hound," he added, in a whisper, " is said to be a familiar spirit."

" The virtue of the relic is approved," observed Surrey to Richmond, in an undertone.

" It would seem so," replied the duke.

The old woman now thought proper to assume a more respectful demeanour towards her visitors, and inquired whether her son should attend upon them on his return from the forest; but they said it was unnecessary.

" The king is about to have a grand hunting-party the day after to-morrow," observed Surrey, " and we wished to give your son some instructions respecting it. They can, however, be delivered to another keeper."

And they departed with Bryan and returned to the castle.

At midnight they again issued forth. Their steeds awaited them near the upper gate, and mounting, they galloped across the greensward in the direction of Herne's Oak. Discerning no trace of the ghostly huntsman, they shaped their course towards the forest.

Urging their steeds to their utmost speed, and skirting the long avenue, they did not draw the rein till they reached the eminence beyond it; having climbed which, they dashed down the further side, at the same swift pace as before. The ride greatly excited them; but they saw nothing of the wild huntsman; nor did any sound salute their ears, except the tramp of their own horses, or the occasional darting forth of a startled deer.

Less than a quarter of an hour brought them to the haunted beech-tree. But all was as silent and solitary here at the blasted oak. In vain Surrey smote the tree. No answer was returned to the summons, and finding all efforts to evoke the demon fruitless, they quitted the spot, and, turning their horses' heads to the right, slowly ascended the hill-side.

Before they had gained the brow of the hill, the faint blast of a horn saluted their ears, apparently proceeding from the vallley, near the lake. They instantly stopped, and looked in that direction, but could see nothing. Presently, however, the blast was repeated more loudly than before, and, guided by the sound, they discerned the spectral huntsman riding beneath the trees at some quarter of a mile's distance.

Striking spurs into their steeds, they instantly gave him chase; but though he lured them on through thicket and over glade—now climbing a hill, now plunging into a valley, until their steeds began to show symptoms of exhaustion—they got no nearer to him; and at length, as they drew near the Home Park, to which he had gradually led them, he disappeared from view.

" I will take my station near the blasted oak," said Surrey, galloping towards it; " the demon is sure to revisit his favourite tree before cock-crowing."

" What is that ? " cried the Earl of Surrey, pointing to a strange and ghastly-looking object depending from the tree. " Some one has hanged himself ! It may be the caitiff, Morgan Fenwolf."

With one accord they dashed forward; and as they drew nearer the tree, they perceived that the object that had attracted their attention was the body of Mark Fytton, the butcher, which they had so recently seen swinging from the summit of the Curfew Tower. It was now suspended from an arm of the wizard oak.

A small scroll was stuck upon the breast of the corpse, and, taking it off, Surrey read these words, traced in uncouth characters: "*Mark Fytton is now one of the band of Herne the Hunter.*"

"By my fay, this passes all comprehension," said Richmond, after a few moments' silence. "This castle and forest seem under the sway of the powers of darkness. Let us return. I have had enough of adventure for to-night."

And he rode towards the castle, followed more slowly by the earl.

VII

How the Earl of Surrey and the Fair Geraldine Plighted their Troth in the Cloisters of Saint George's Chapel

BARRIERS were erected on the following day in the upper ward of the castle, and the Lady Anne and her dames assembled in the balcony in front of the royal lodgings, which was decorated with arras, costly carpets, and rich stuffs, to view the spectacle.

Perfect in all manly accomplishments, Henry splintered several lances, with his brother-in-law, the Duke of Suffolk, who formed an admirable match for him in point of weight and strength; and at last, though he did not succeed in unhorsing the duke, he struck off his helmet, the clasp of which, it was whispered, was left designedly unfastened; and being thereupon declared the victor, he received the prize—a scarf embroidered by her own hands—from the fair Anne herself.

He then retired from the lists, leaving them free for the younger knights to run a course at the ring. The first to enter the arena was Sir Thomas Wyat; and as he was known to be a skilful jouster, it was expected he would come off triumphantly. But a glance from the royal balcony rendered his arm unsteady, and he missed the mark.

Next came the Duke of Richmond, superbly accoutred.

Laughing at Wyat's ill success, he bowed to the fair Geraldine, and taking a lance from his esquire, placed it in the rest, and rode gallantly forward. But he was equally unsuccessful, and retired, looking deeply chagrined.

The third knight who presented himself was Surrey. Mounted on his favourite black Arabian—a steed which, though of fiery temper, obeyed his slightest movement—his light symmetrical figure was seen to the greatest advantage in his close-fitting habiliments of silk and velvet. Without venturing a look at the royal balcony, the earl couched his lance, and bounding forward, bore away the ring on its point.

Amid the plaudits of the spectators, he then careered round the arena, and approaching the royal balcony, raised his lance, and proffered the ring to the fair Geraldine, who blushingly received it. Henry, though by no means pleased with Surrey's success, earned as it was at the expense of his son, complimented him upon his skill, and Anne Boleyn joined warmly in his praises.

The lists were then closed, and the royal party retired to partake of refreshments, after which they proceeded to the butts erected in the broad mead at the north of the castle, where the Duke of Shoreditch and his companions shot a well-contested match with the long bow.

During these sports, Surrey placed himself as near as he could to the fair Geraldine, and though but few opportunities occurred of exchanging a syllable with her, his looks spoke a sufficiently intelligible language. At last, just as they were about to return to the palace, he breathed in an imploring tone in her ear—

" You will attend vespers at Saint George's Chapel this evening. Return through the cloisters. Grant me a moment's interview alone there."

" I cannot promise," replied the fair Geraldine.

And she followed in the train of the Lady Anne.

The earl's request had not been unheard. As the royal

train proceeded towards the castle. Will Sommers contrived to approach the Duke of Richmond, and said to him, in a jeering tone—

" You ran but indifferently at the ring to-day, gossip. The galliard Surrey rode better, and carried off the prize."

" Pest on thee, scurril knave, be silent ! " cried Richmond angrily. " Failure is bad enough without thy taunts ! "

" If you had only missed the ring, gossip, I should have thought nothing of it," pursued Will Sommers; " but you lost a golden opportunity of ingratiating yourself with your lady-love. All your hopes are now at an end. A word in your ear. The fair Geraldine will meet Surrey alone, this evening."

" Thou liest, knave ! " cried the duke fiercely.

" Your grace will find the contrary, if you will be at Wolsey's tomb-house at vesper-time," replied the jester.

" I will be there," replied the duke: " but if I am brought on a bootless errand, not even my royal father shall save thee from chastisement."

" I will bear any chastisement your grace may choose to inflict upon me, if I prove not the truth of my assertion," replied Sommers. And he dropped into the rear of the train.

The two friends, as if by mutual consent, avoided each other during the rest of the day—Surrey feeling he could not unburthen his heart to Richmond, and Richmond brooding jealously over the intelligence he had received from the jester.

At the appointed hour, the duke proceeded to the lower ward, and stationed himself near Wolsey's tomb-house. Just as he arrived there, the vesper hymn arose from the adjoining fane, and its solemn strains somewhat soothed his troubled spirit. But they died away; and as the jester came not, Richmond grew impatient, and began to fear he had been duped by his informant. At length, the service concluded, and, losing all patience, he was about to depart, when the jester peered round the lower angle of the tomb-house, and beckoned to him. Obeying the summons, the duke followed his conductor down the arched passage leading to the cloisters.

"Tread softly, gossip, or you will alarm them," said Sommers, in a low tone.

They turned the corner of the cloisters; and there, near the entrance of the chapel, stood the youthful pair —the fair Geraldine, half reclining upon the earl's breast, while his arm encircled her slender waist.

"There!" whispered the jester, chuckling maliciously —"there! did I speak falsely—eh! gossip?"

Richmond laid his hand upon his sword.

"Hist!" said the jester—"hear what the fair Geraldine has to say."

"We must meet no more thus, Surrey," she murmured; "I feel I was wrong in granting the interview, but I could not help it. If, when a few more years have flown over your head, your heart remains unchanged——"

"It will never change!" interrupted Surrey. "I here solemnly pledge my troth to you."

"And I return the pledge," replied the fair Geraldine earnestly. "I vow to be yours, and yours only."

"Would that Richmond could hear your vow!" said Surrey—"it would extinguish his hopes."

"He *has* heard it!" cried the duke, advancing. "But his hopes are not yet extinguished."

The fair Geraldine uttered a slight scream, and disengaged herself from the earl.

"Richmond, you have acted unworthily in thus playing the spy," said Surrey angrily.

"None but a spy can surprise interviews like these," rejoined Richmond bitterly. "The Lady Elizabeth Fitzgerald had better have kept her chamber, than come here to plight her troth with a boy, who will change his mind before his beard is grown."

"Your grace shall find the boy man enough to avenge an insult," rejoined Surrey sternly.

"I am glad to hear it!" returned the duke. "Lady Elizabeth Fitzgerald, I must pray you to return to your lodgings. The king's jester will attend you. This way, my lord!"

Too much exasperated to hesitate, Surrey followed the duke down the passage, and the next moment, the clashing of swords was heard. The fair Geraldine screamed loudly, and Will Sommers began to think the jest had been carried too far.

"What is to be done?" he cried. "If the king hears of this quarrel, he will assuredly place the Earl of Surrey in arrest. I now repent having brought the duke here."

"You acted most maliciously," cried the fair Geraldine; "but fly, and prevent further mischief."

Thus urged, the jester ran towards the lower ward, and finding an officer of the guard and a couple of halberdiers near the entrance of Saint George's Chapel, told them what was taking place, and they immediately hastened with him to the scene of the conflict.

"My lords!" cried the officer to the combatants, "I command you to lay down your weapons."

But finding no respect paid to his injunctions, he rushed between them, and with the aid of the halberdiers, forcibly separated them.

"My Lord of Surrey," said the officer, "you are my prisoner. I demand your sword."

"On what plea, sir?" rejoined the other.

"You have drawn it against the king's son—and the act is treason," replied the officer. "I shall take you to the guard-house until the king's pleasure is known."

"But I provoked the earl to the conflict," said Richmond: "I was the aggressor."

"Your grace will represent the matter as you see fit to your royal father," rejoined the officer: "I shall fulfil my duty. My lord, to the guard-house!"

"I will procure your instant liberation, Surrey," said Richmond.

The earl was then led away, and conveyed to a chamber in the lower part of Henry the Eighth's gate, now used as a place of military punishment, and denominated the "black hole."

VIII

*Of Tristram Lyndwood, the old forester, and his grand-
daughter Mabel; of the peril in which the Lady Anne
Boleyn was placed during the chase; and by whom she
was rescued*

IN consequence of the announcement that a grand
hunting-party would be held in the forest, all the
verderers, rangers, and keepers assembled at an early
hour on the fourth day after the king's arrival at Windsor,
in an open space on the west side of the great avenue,
where a wooden stand was erected, canopied over with
green boughs and festooned with garlands of flowers, for
the accommodation of the Lady Anne Boleyn and her
dames, who, it was understood, would be present at the
chase.

At a little distance from the stand, an extensive covert
was fenced round with stout poles, to which nets were
attached, so as to form a haye or preserve, where the
game intended for the royal sport was confined; and
though many of the animals thus brought together were
of hostile natures, they were all so terrified, and seemingly
so conscious of the danger impending over them, that
they did not molest each other. The foxes and martens,
of which there were abundance, slunk into the brushwood
with the hares and rabbits, but left their prey untouched.
The harts made violent efforts to break forth, and
entangling their horns in the nets, were with difficulty
extricated and driven back; while the timid does, not
daring to follow them, stood warily watching the result
of the struggle.

Amongst the antlered captives was a fine buck, which,
having been once before hunted by the king, was styled
a "hart royal," and this noble animal would certainly
have effected his escape, if he had not been attacked and
driven back by Morgan Fenwolf, who throughout the

morning's proceedings displayed great energy and skill. The compliments bestowed on Fenwolf for his address by the chief verderer excited the jealousy of some of his comrades; and more than one asserted that he had been assisted in his task by some evil being, and that Bawsey herself was no better than a familiar spirit in the form of a hound.

Morgan Fenwolf scouted these remarks; and he was supported by some others among the keepers, who declared that it required no supernatural aid to accomplish what he had done—that he was nothing more than a good huntsman, who could ride fast and boldly—that he was skilled in all the exercises of the chase—and possessed a staunch and well-trained hound.

The party then sat down to breakfast beneath the trees, and the talk fell upon Herne the hunter, and his frequent appearance of late in the forest (for most of the keepers had heard of, or encountered the spectral huntsman); and while they were discussing this topic, and a plentiful allowance of cold meat, bread, ale, and mead, at the same time, two persons were seen approaching along a vista on the right, who specially attracted their attention, and caused Morgan Fenwolf to drop the hunting-knife, with which he was carving his viands, and start to his feet.

" I am glad your grandfather has brought you out to see the chase to-day, Mabel," observed Morgan Fenwolf.

" I came not to see the chase, but the king," she replied, somewhat petulantly.

" It is not every fair maid who would confess so much," observed Fenwolf, frowning.

" Then I am franker than some of my sex," replied Mabel. " But who is the strange man looking at us from behind that tree, grandfather ? "

" I see no one," replied the old forester.

" Neither do I," added Morgan Fenwolf, with a shudder.

" You are wilfully blind," rejoined Mabel. " But see, the person I mentioned stalks forth. Now, perhaps, he is visible to you both."

78

And as she spoke, a tall, wild-looking figure armed with a hunting spear, emerged from the trees, and advanced towards them. The garb of the newcomer somewhat resembled that of a forester; but his arms and lower limbs were destitute of covering, and appeared singularly muscular, while his skin was swarthy as that of a gipsy. His jet black hair hung in elf-locks over his savage-looking features.

In another moment, he was beside them, and fixed his dark, piercing eyes on Mabel, in such a manner as to compel her to avert her gaze.

" What brings you here this morning, Tristram Lyndwood ? " he demanded, in a hoarse, imperious tone.

" The same motive that brought you, Valentine Hagthorne," replied the old forester—" to see the royal chase."

" This, I suppose, is your grand-daughter ? " pursued Hagthorne.

" Ay," replied Tristram bluntly.

" Strange I should never have seen her before," rejoined the other. " She is very fair. Be ruled by me, friend Tristram—take her home again. If she sees the king, ill will come of it. You know, or should know, his character."

" Hagthorne advises well," interposed Fenwolf. " Mabel will be better at home."

" But she has no intention of returning at present," replied Mabel. " You brought me for pastime, dear grandfather, and will not take me back at the recommendation of this strange man."

" Content you, child—content you," replied Tristram, kindly. " You shall remain where you are."

" You will repent it ! " cried Hagthorne.

And hastily darting among the trees, he disappeared from view.

Affecting to laugh at the occurrence, though evidently annoyed by it, the old forester led his grand-daughter towards the stand, where he was cordially greeted by the keepers, most of whom, while expressing their pleasure at seeing him, strove to render themselves agreeable in the eyes of Mabel.

From this scene Morgan Fenwolf kept aloof, and remained leaning against a tree, with his eyes riveted upon the damsel. He was roused from his reverie by a slight tap upon the shoulder; and turning at the touch, beheld Valentine Hagthorne. Obedient to a sign from the latter, he followed him amongst the trees, and they both plunged into a dell.

An hour or two after this, when the sun was higher in the heavens, and the dew dried upon the greensward, the king and a large company of lords and ladies rode forth from the upper gate of the castle, and taking their way along the great avenue, struck off on the right, when about half-way up it, and shaped their course towards the haye.

A goodly sight it was to see this gallant company riding beneath the trees; and pleasant was it, also, to listen to the blithe sound of their voices, amid which Anne Boleyn's musical laugh could be plainly distinguished. Henry was attended by his customary band of archers and yeomen of the guard; and by the Duke of Shoreditch and his followers. On reaching the haye, the king dismounted, and assisting the Lady Anne from her steed, ascended the stand with her.

He then took a small and beautifully-fashioned bow from an attendant, and stringing it, presented it to her.

"I trust this will not prove too strong for your fair hands," he said.

"I will make shift to draw it," replied Anne, raising the bow, and gracefully pulling the string. "Would I could wound your majesty as surely as I shall hit the first roe that passes."

"That were a needless labour," rejoined Henry, "seeing that you have already stricken me to the heart. You should cure the wound you have already made, sweetheart—not inflict a new one."

At this juncture, the chief verderer, mounted on a powerful steed, and followed by two keepers, each holding a couple of stag-hounds in leash, rode up to the royal stand, and placing his horn to his lips, blew three long notes from it. At the same moment, part of the network of the haye was lifted up, and a roebuck set free.

By the management of the keepers, the animal was driven past the royal stand; and Anne Boleyn, who had drawn an arrow nearly to the head, let it fly with such good aim that she pierced the buck to the heart. A loud shout from the spectators rewarded the prowess of the fair huntress; and Henry was so enchanted that he bent the knee to her and pressed her hand to his lips. Satisfied, however, with the achievement, Anne prudently declined another shot. Henry then took a bow from one of the archers, and other roes being turned out, he approved upon them his unerring skill as a marksman.

Meanwhile, the hounds, being held in leash, kept up a loud and incessant baying; and Henry, wearying of his slaughterous sport, turned to Anne, and asked her whether she was disposed for the chase. She answered in the affirmative, and the king motioned his henchmen to bring forward the steeds.

In doing this, he caught sight of Mabel, who was standing with her grandsire among the keepers, at a little distance from the stand, and, struck with her extraordinary beauty, he regarded her for a moment intently, and then called to Gabriel Lapp, who chanced to be near him, and demanded her name.

"It is Mabel Lyndwood, and please your majesty," replied Gabriel. "She is grand-daughter to old Tristram Lyndwood, who dwells at Black Nest, near the lake, at the further extremity of Windsor Forest, and who was forester to your royal father, King Henry the Seventh, of blessed memory."

"Ha ! is it so ? " cried Henry.

But he was prevented from further remark by Anne Boleyn, who, perceiving how his attention was attracted, suddenly interposed.

"Your majesty spoke of the chase," she said impatiently. " But perhaps you have found other pastime more diverting ? "

" Not so—not so, sweetheart," he replied hastily.

" There is a hart royal in the haye," said Gabriel Lapp. " Is it your majesty's pleasure that I set him free ? "

" It is, good fellow—it is," replied the king.

And as Gabriel hastened to the netted fencework, and prepared to drive forth the hart, Henry assisted Anne Boleyn, who could not help exhibiting some slight jealous pique, to mount her steed, and having sprung into his own saddle, they waited the liberation of the buck, which was accomplished in a somewhat unexpected manner.

Separated from the rest of the herd, the noble animal made a sudden dart towards Gabriel, and upsetting him in his wild career, darted past the king, and made towards the upper part of the forest. In another instant, the hounds were uncoupled, and at his heels, while Henry and Anne urged their steeds after him, the king shouting at the top of his lusty voice. The rest of the royal party followed as they might, and the woods resounded with their joyous cries.

The hart royal proved himself worthy of his designation. Dashing forward with extraordinary swiftness, he rapidly gained upon his pursuers—for though Henry, by putting his courser to his utmost speed, could have kept near him, he did not choose to quit his fair companion.

In this way they scoured the forest, until the king, seeing they should be speedily distanced, commanded Sir Thomas Wyat, who, with the Dukes of Suffolk and Norfolk, was riding close behind him, to cross by the lower ground on the left, and turn the stag. Wyat instantly obeyed, and plunging his spurs deeply into his horse's sides, started off at a furious pace, and was soon after seen shaping his rapid course through a devious glade.

Meanwhile, Henry and his fair companion rode on without relaxing their pace, until they reached the summit of a knoll, crowned by an old oak and beech-tree, and commanding a superb view of the castle, where they drew in the rein.

From this eminence they could witness the progress of the chase, as it continued in the valley beyond. An ardent lover of hunting, the king watched it with the deepest interest, rose in his saddle, and uttering various exclamations, showed, from his impatience, that he was only restrained by the stronger passion of love from joining it.

Ere long, stag, hounds, and huntsmen were lost amid a thicket, and nothing could be distinguished but a distant baying and shouts. At last, even these sounds died away.

Henry, who had ill brooked the previous restraint, now grew so impatient that Anne begged him to set off after them, when, suddenly, the cry of hounds burst upon their ear, and the hart was seen issuing from the dell, closely followed by his pursuers.

The affrighted animal, to the king's great satisfaction, made his way directly towards the spot where he was stationed; but on reaching the side of the knoll, and seeing his new foes, he darted off on the right, and tried to regain the thicket below. But he was turned by another band of keepers, and again driven towards the knoll.

Scarcely had Sir Thomas Wyat reined in his steed by the side of the king than the hart again appeared bounding up the hill. Anne Boleyn, who had turned her horse's head to obtain a better view of the hunt, alarmed by the animal's menacing appearance, tried to get out of his way. But it was too late. Hemmed in on all sides, and driven to desperation by the cries of hounds and huntsmen in front, the hart lowered his horns, and made a furious push at her.

Dreadfully alarmed, Anne drew in the rein so suddenly and sharply that she almost pulled her steed back upon his haunches; and in trying to avoid the stag's attack, caught hold of Sir Thomas Wyat, who was close beside her.

In all probability, she would have received some serious injury from the infuriated animal, who was just about to repeat his assault, and more successfully, when a bolt from a cross-bow, discharged by Morgan Fenwolf, who suddenly made his appearance from behind the beech-tree, brought him to the ground.

But Anne Boleyn escaped one danger only to encounter another equally serious. On seeing her fling herself into the arms of Sir Thomas Wyat, Henry regarded her in stern displeasure for a moment, and then calling angrily to his train, without so much as deigning to inquire whether she had sustained any damage from the accident, or making the slightest remark upon her conduct, rode sullenly towards the castle.

IX

By what means Sir Thomas Wyat obtained an interview with Anne Boleyn; and how the Earl of Surrey saved them from the King's anger

THE incident above related gave new life to the adherents of Catharine of Arragon, while it filled those devoted to Anne Boleyn with alarm. Immediately on Anne's return to the castle, Lord Rochford had a private interview with her, and bitterly reproached her for endangering her splendid prospects. Anne treated the matter very lightly; said it was only a temporary gust of jealousy; and added that the king would be at her feet again before the day was past.

" You are over-confident, mistress ! " cried Rochford, angrily. " Henry is not an ordinary gallant."

" It is you who are mistaken, father," replied Anne. " The king differs in no respect from any of his love-smitten subjects. I have him in my toils, and will not let him escape."

" You have a tiger in your toils, daughter, and take

heed he breaks not forcibly through them," rejoined Rochford. "Henry is more wayward than you suppose him. Once let him take up a notion, and nothing can shake him from it. He has resolved upon the divorce as much from self-will as from any other consideration. If you regain your position with him, of which you seem so confident, do not consider yourself secure—not even when you are crowned queen—but be warned by Catharine of Arragon."

"Catharine has not the art to retain him," said Anne. "Henry will never divorce *me*."

"Take care he does not rid himself of you in a more summary manner, daughter," rejoined Rochford. "If you would stand well with him, you must study his lightest word, look, and action—humour him in every whim—and yield to every caprice. Above all, you must exhibit no jealousy."

"You are wrong in all but the last, father," returned Anne. "Henry is not to be pleased by such nice attention to his humours. It is because I have shown myself careless of them that I have captivated him. But I will take care not to exhibit jealousy, and, sooth to say, I do not think I shall have cause."

"Be not too sure of that," replied Rochford. "And, at all events, let not the king have cause to be jealous of you. I trust Wyat will be banished from court. But if he is not, do not let him approach you more."

"Poor Sir Thomas!" sighed Anne. "He loved me very dearly."

"But what is his love compared to the king's?" cried Rochford. "Tut, tut, girl! think no more of him."

"I will not, my lord," she rejoined; "I see the prudence of your counsel, and will obey it. Leave me, I pray you. I will soon win back the affections of the king."

No sooner had Rochford quitted the chamber than the arras at the further end was raised, and Wyat stepped from behind it. His first proceeding was to bar the door.

"What means this, Sir Thomas?" cried Anne, in alarm. "How have you obtained admittance here?"

85

" Through the secret staircase," replied Wyat, bending the knee before her.

" Rise, sir ! " cried Anne, in great alarm. " Return, I beseech you, as you came. You have greatly endangered me by coming here. If you are seen to leave this chamber, it will be in vain to assert my innocence to Henry. Oh, Sir Thomas, you cannot love me, or you would not have done this ! "

" Not love you, Anne ! " he repeated bitterly; " not love you ! Words cannot speak my devotion. I would lay down my head on the scaffold to prove it. But for my love for you, I would throw open that door, and walk forth so that all might see me—so that Henry might experience some part of the anguish I now feel."

" But you will not do so, good Sir Thomas—dear Sir Thomas," cried Anne Boleyn, in alarm.

" Have no fear," rejoined Wyat, with some contempt— " I will sacrifice even vengeance to love."

" Sir Thomas, I have tolerated this too long," said Anne; " begone—you terrify me."

" It is my last interview with you, Anne," said Wyat imploringly,—" do not abridge it. Oh, bethink you of the happy hours we have passed together—of the vows we have interchanged—of the protestations you have listened to, and returned—ay, returned, Anne. Are all these forgotten ? "

" Not forgotten, Sir Thomas," replied Anne mournfully; " but they must not be recalled. I cannot listen to you longer. You must go. Heaven grant you may get hence in safety ! "

" Anne," replied Wyat, in a sombre tone, " the thought of Henry's happiness drives me mad. I feel that I am grown a traitor,—that I could slay him."

" Sir Thomas ! " she exclaimed, in mingled fear and anger.

" I will *not* go," he continued, flinging himself into a seat. " Let them put what construction they will upon my presence. I shall at least wring Henry's heart. I shall see him suffer as I have suffered; and I shall be content."

"This is not like you, Wyat," cried Anne, in great alarm. "You were wont to be noble, generous, kind. You will not act thus disloyally?"

"Who has acted disloyally, Anne," cried Wyat, springing to his feet, and fixing his dark eyes, blazing with jealous fury upon her—"you or I? Have you not sacrificed your old affections at the shrine of ambition? Are you not about to give yourself to one to whom—unless you are forsworn—you cannot give your heart? Better had you been the mistress of Allington Castle—better the wife of a humble knight like myself, than the queen of the ruthless Henry."

"No more of this, Wyat," said Anne.

"Better far you should perish by his tyranny for a supposed fault now than hereafter," pursued Wyat fiercely. "Think not Henry will respect you more than her who has been eight and twenty years his wife. No, when he is tired of your charms—when some other dame, fair as yourself, shall enslave his fancy, he will cast you off, or, as your father truly intimated, will seek a readier means of ridding himself of you. Then you will think of the different fate that might have been yours if you had adhered to your early love."

"Wyat! Wyat! I cannot bear this,—in mercy spare me!" cried Anne.

"I am glad to see you weep," said Wyat; "your tears make you look more like your former self."

"Oh, Wyat, do not view my conduct too harshly!" she said. "Few of my sex would have acted other than I have done."

"I do not think so," replied Wyat sternly; "nor will I forego my vengeance. Anne, you shall die. You know Henry too well to doubt your fate if he finds me here."

"You cannot mean this," she rejoined, with difficulty repressing a scream; "but if I perish, you will perish with me."

"I wish to do so," he rejoined, with a bitter laugh.

"Wyat," cried Anne, throwing herself on her knees

before him, " by your former love for me, I implore you to spare me ! Do not disgrace me thus."

But Wyat continued inexorable. " Oh, God ! " exclaimed Anne, wringing her hands in agony.

A terrible silence ensued, during which Anne regarded Wyat, but she could discern no change in his countenance.

At this juncture, the tapestry was again raised, and the Earl of Surrey issued from it.

" You here, my lord ?" said Anne, rushing towards him.

" I am come to save you, madam," said the earl; " I have just been liberated from arrest, and was about to implore your intercession with the king, when I learned he had been informed by one of his pages that a man was in your chamber. Luckily, he knows now who it is, and while he was summoning his attendants to accompany him, I hurried thither by the secret staircase. I have arrived in time. Fly—fly ! Sir Thomas Wyat ! "

But Wyat moved not.

At this moment, footsteps were heard approaching the door—the handle was tried—and the stern voice of the king was heard commanding that it might be opened.

" Will you destroy me, Wyat ? " cried Anne.

" You have destroyed yourself," he rejoined.

" Why stay you here, Sir Thomas ? " said Surrey, seizing his arm. " You may yet escape. By heaven ! if you move not, I will stab you to the heart ! "

" You would do me a favour, young man," said Wyat coldly; " but I will go. I yield to love, and not to you, tyrant ! " he added, shaking his hand at the door. " May the worst pangs of jealousy rend your heart ! " And he disappeared behind the arras.

" I hear voices," cried Henry from without. " God's death ! madam, open the door—or I will burst it open ! "

" Oh heaven ! what is to be done ? " cried Anne Boleyn, in despair.

" Open the door, and leave all to me, madam," said Surrey; " I will save you, though it cost me my life ! "

Anne pressed his hand, with a look of ineffable gratitude, and Surrey concealed himself behind the arras.

The door was opened, and Henry rushed in, followed by Richmond, Norfolk, Suffolk, and a host of attendants.

" Ah ! God's death ! where is the traitor ? " roared the king, gazing round.

" Why is my privacy thus broken upon ? " said Anne, assuming a look of indignation.

" Your privacy ! " echoed Henry, in a tone of deep derision—" your privacy !—ha ! ha ! You bear yourself bravely, it must be confessed. My lords, you heard the voices as well as myself. Where is Sir Thomas Wyat?"

" He is not here," replied Anne firmly.

" Aha ! we shall see that, mistress," rejoined Henry fiercely. " But if Sir Thomas Wyat is not here—who is ? for I am well assured that some one is hidden in your chamber."

" What if there be ? " rejoined Anne, coldly.

" Ah ! by Saint Mary, you confess it ! " cried the king. " Let the traitor come forth."

" Your majesty shall not need to bid twice," said Surrey, issuing from his concealment.

" The Earl of Surrey ! " exclaimed Henry, in surprise. " How came you here, my lord ? Methought you were under arrest at the guard-house."

" He was set free by my orders," said the Duke of Richmond.

" First of all, I must entreat your majesty to turn your resentment against me," said the earl. " I am solely to blame, and I would not have the Lady Anne suffer for my fault. I forced myself into her presence. She knew not of my coming."

" And wherefore did you so, my lord ? " demanded Henry, sternly.

" Liberated from the guard-house, at the Duke of Richmond's instance, my liege, I came to entreat the Lady Anne to mediate between me and your majesty, and to use her influence with your majesty to have me betrothed to the Lady Elizabeth Fitzgerald."

" Is this so, madam ? " asked the king.

Anne bowed her head.

"But why was the door barred?" demanded Henry.

"I barred it myself," said Surrey, "and vowed that the Lady Anne should not go forth till she had granted my request."

"By our Lady! you have placed yourself in peril, my lord," said Henry sternly.

"Your majesty will bear in mind his youth," said the Duke of Norfolk anxiously.

"For my sake overlook the indiscretion," cried the Duke of Richmond.

"It will not, perhaps, avail him to hope that it may be overlooked for mine," added Anne Boleyn.

"The offence must not pass unpunished," said Henry musingly. "My Lord of Surrey, you must be content to remain for two months a prisoner in the Round Tower of this castle."

"Your majesty!" cried Richmond, bending the knee in supplication.

"The sentence is passed," replied Henry coldly; "and the earl may thank you it is not heavier. Richmond, you will think no more of the fair Geraldine; and it is my pleasure, Lady Anne, that the young dame withdraw from the court for a short while."

"Your majesty shall be obeyed," said Anne; "but——"

"But me no buts, sweetheart," said the king peremptorily. "Surrey's explanation is satisfactory so far as it goes, but I was told Sir Thomas Wyat was here."

"Sir Thomas Wyat *is* here," said Will Sommers, pointing out the knight, who had just joined the throng of courtiers at the door.

"I have hurried hither from my chamber, my liege," said Wyat, stepping forward, "hearing there was some inquiry concerning me."

"Is your majesty now satisfied?" asked Anne Boleyn.

"Why, ay, sweetheart, well enough," rejoined Henry. "Sir Thomas Wyat, we have a special mission for you to the court of our brother of France. You will set out to-morrow."

Wyat bowed.

"You have saved your head, gossip," whispered Will Sommers in the knight's ear. "A visit to Francis the First is better than a visit to the Tower."

"Retire, my lords," said Henry, to the assemblage; "we owe some apology to the Lady Anne for our intrusion, and desire an opportunity to make it."

Upon this the chamber was instantly cleared of its occupants, and the Earl of Surrey was conducted under a guard to the Round Tower.

Henry, however, did not find it an easy matter to make peace with the Lady Anne. Conscious of the advantage she had gained, she determined not to relinquish it, and after half an hour's vain suing her royal lover proposed a turn in the long gallery, upon which her apartments opened. Here they continued conversing—Henry pleading in the most passionate manner, and Anne maintaining a show of offended pride.

At last she exhibited some signs of relenting, and Henry led her into a recess in the gallery, lighted by a window filled with magnificent stained glass. In this recess was a seat and a small table, on which stood a vase filled with flowers, arranged by Anne's own hand; and here the monarch hoped to adjust his differences with her.

Meanwhile, word having reached Wolsey and Campeggio of the new cause of jealousy which the king had received, it was instantly resolved that the former should present to him, while in his present favourable mood, a despatch received that morning from Catharine of Arragon.

Armed with the letter, Wolsey repaired to the king's closet. Not finding him there, and being given to understand by an usher that he was in the great gallery, he proceeded thither. As he walked softly along the polished oak floor, he heard voices in one of the recesses and, distinguished the tones of Henry and Anne Boleyn.

Henry was clasping the snowy fingers of his favourite, and gazing passionately at her, as the cardinal approached.

"Your majesty shall not detain my hand," said Anne, "unless you swear to me, by your crown, that you will not again be jealous without cause."

"I swear it!" replied Henry.

"Were your majesty as devoted to me as you would have me believe, you would soon bring this matter of the divorce to an issue," said Anne.

"I would fain do so, sweetheart," rejoined Henry, "but these cardinals perplex me sorely."

"I am told by one who overheard him, that Wolsey has declared the divorce shall not be settled these two years," said Anne; "in which case it had better not be settled at all; for I care not to avow I cannot brook so much delay. The warmth of my affection will grow icy cold by that time."

"It were enough to try the patience of the most forbearing," rejoined the king, smiling—"but it shall not be so—by this lily hand it shall not! And now, sweetheart, are we entirely reconciled?"

"Not yet," replied Anne. "I shall claim a boon from your majesty, before I accord my entire forgiveness."

"Name it," said the king, still clasping her hand tenderly, and intoxicated by the witchery of her glance.

"I ask an important favour," said Anne—"but as it is one which will benefit your majesty as much as myself, I have the less scruple in requesting it. I ask the dismissal of one who has abused your favour—who, by his extortion and rapacity, has in some degree alienated the affections of your subjects from you—and who solely opposes your divorce from Catharine of Arragon because he fears my influence may be prejudicial to him."

"You cannot mean Wolsey?" said Henry uneasily.

"Your majesty has guessed aright," replied Anne.

"Wolsey has incurred my displeasure oft of late," said Henry; "and yet his fidelity——"

"Be not deceived, my liege," said Anne, "he is faithful to you only so far as serves his turn. He thinks he rules you."

Before Henry could reply the cardinal stepped forward.

"I bring your majesty a despatch, just received from the queen," he said.

"And you have been listening to our discourse?" rejoined Henry sternly. "You have overheard——"

"Enough to convince me, if I had previously doubted it, that the Lady Anne Boleyn is my mortal foe," replied Wolsey.

"Foe though I am, I will make terms with your eminence," said Anne. "Expedite the divorce—you can do so if you will—and I am your fast friend."

"I know too well the value of your friendship, noble lady, not to do all in my power to gain it," replied Wolsey. "I will further the matter, if possible. But it rests chiefly in the hands of his holiness, Pope Clement the Seventh."

"If his majesty will listen to my counsel, he will throw off the pope's yoke altogether," rejoined Anne.

"Nay, your eminence may frown at me if you will. Such, I repeat, shall be my counsel. If the divorce is speedily obtained, I am your friend: if not—look to yourself."

"Do not appeal to me, Wolsey," said Henry, smiling approval at Anne—"I shall uphold her."

"Will it please your majesty to peruse this despatch?" said Wolsey, again offering Catharine's letter.

"Take it to my closet," replied the king; "I will join you there. And now at last we are good friends, sweetheart."

"Excellent friends, my dear liege," replied Anne; "but I shall never be your queen while Wolsey holds his place!"

"Then, indeed, he shall lose it," replied Henry.

"She is a bitter enemy, certes," muttered Wolsey, as he walked away. "I must overthrow her quickly, or she will overthrow me. A rival must be found—ay, a rival —but where? I was told that Henry cast eyes on a comely forester's daughter at the chase this morning. She may do for the nonce."

X

Of the Mysterious Disappearance of Herne the Hunter in the Lake

UNABLE to procure any mitigation of Surrey's sentence, the Duke of Richmond proceeded to the Round Tower, where he found his friend in a small chamber, endeavouring to beguile his captivity by study.

Richmond endeavoured to console him, and was glad to find him in better spirits than he expected. Early youth is seldom long dejected; and misfortunes, at that buoyant season, seem lighter than they appear later on in life. The cause for which he suffered, moreover, sustained Surrey, and confident of the fair Geraldine's attachment, he cared little for the restraint imposed upon him. On one point he expressed some regret—namely, his inability to prosecute the adventure of Herne the hunter with the duke.

" I grieve that I cannot accompany you, Richmond," he said, " but since that is impossible, let me recommend you to take the stout archer who goes by the name of the Duke of Shoreditch with you. He is the very man you require."

After some consideration the duke assented, and, promising to return on the following day and report what had occurred, he took his leave, and went in search of the archer in question. Finding he had taken up his quarters at the Garter, he sent for him and proposed the matter.

Shoreditch heard the duke's relation with astonishment, but expressed the greatest willingness to accompany him, pledging himself, as Richmond demanded, to profound secrecy on the subject.

At the appointed hour—namely, midnight—the duke quitted the castle, and found Shoreditch waiting for him near the upper gate. The latter was armed with a stout staff, and a bow and arrows.

" If we gain sight of the mysterious horseman to-night," he said, " a cloth-yard shaft shall try whether he is of mortal mould or not. If he be not a demon, I will warrant he rides no more."

Quitting the Home Park, they shaped their course at once towards the forest. It was a stormy night, and the moon was obscured by thick clouds. Before they reached the hill, at the head of the long avenue, a heavy thunder-storm came on, and the lightning, playing among the trees, seemed to reveal a thousand fantastic forms to their half-blinded gaze. Presently the rain began to descend in torrents, and compelled them to take refuge beneath a large beech-tree.

It was evident, notwithstanding his boasting, that the courage of Shoreditch was waning fast, and he at last proposed to his leader that they should return as soon as the rain abated. But the duke indignantly rejected the proposal.

While they were thus sheltering themselves, the low winding of a horn was heard. The sound was succeeded by the trampling of horses' hoofs, and the next moment, a vivid flash of lightning showed a hart darting past, followed by a troop of some twenty ghostly horsemen, headed by the demon-hunter.

The Duke of Richmond bade his companion send a shaft after them; but the latter was so overcome by terror that he could scarcely fix an arrow on the string, and when he bent the bow the shaft glanced from the branches of an adjoining tree.

The storm continued with unabated fury for nearly an hour, at the expiration of which time it partially cleared off, and, though it was still profoundly dark, the duke insisted upon going on. So they pressed forward beneath the dripping trees, and through the wet grass. Ever and anon, the moon broke through the rifted clouds, and shed a wild glimmer upon the scene.

As they were tracking a glade on the further side of the hill, the spectral huntsmen again swept past them, and so closely that they could almost touch their horses.

To the duke's horror, he perceived among them the body of the butcher, Mark Fytton, sitting erect upon a powerful black steed.

By this time, Shoreditch, having somewhat regained his courage, discharged another shaft at the troop. The arrow struck the body of the butcher, and completely transfixed it, but did not check his career; while wild and derisive laughter broke from the rest of the cavalcade.

The Duke of Richmond hurried after the band, trying to keep them in sight; and Shoreditch, flinging down his bow, which he found useless, and grasping his staff, endeavoured to keep up with him. But though they ran swiftly down the glade, and tried to peer through the darkness, they could see nothing more of the ghostly company.

After a while, they arrived at a hill-side, at the foot of which lay the lake, whose darkling waters were just distinguishable through an opening in the trees. As the duke was debating with himself whether to go on or retrace his course, the trampling of a horse was heard behind them, and looking in the direction of the sound they beheld Herne the hunter, mounted on his swarthy steed, and accompanied only by his two black hounds, galloping furiously down the declivity. Before him flew the owl, whooping as it sailed along the air.

The demon-hunter was so close to them that they could perfectly discern his horrible lineaments, the chain depending from his neck, and his antlered helm. Richmond shouted to him, but the rider continued his headlong course towards the lake, heedless of the call.

The two beholders rushed forward, but by this time the huntsman had gained the edge of the lake. One of his sable hounds plunged into it, and the owl skimmed over its surface. Even in the hasty view which the duke caught of the flying figure, he fancied he perceived that it was attended by a fantastic shadow, whether cast by its ray or arising from some supernatural cause he could not determine.

But what followed was equally marvellous and incomprehensible. As the wild huntsman reached the brink of the lake, he placed a horn to his mouth, and blew from it a bright blue flame, which illumined his own dusky and hideous features, and shed a wild and unearthly glimmer over the surrounding objects.

While enveloped in this flame, the demon plunged into the lake, and apparently descended to its abysses, for as soon as the duke could muster courage to approach its brink, nothing could be seen of him, his steed, or his hounds.

Book the Second

HERNE THE HUNTER

I

On the Compact between Sir Thomas Wyat and Herne the Hunter

ON the day after his secret interview with Anne Boleyn, Sir Thomas Wyat received despatches from the king for the court of France. "His majesty bade me tell you to make your preparations quickly, Sir Thomas," said the messenger who delivered the despatches. "He cares not how soon you set forth."

"The king's pleasure shall be obeyed," rejoined Wyat. And the messenger retired.

Left alone, Wyat remained for some time in profound and melancholy thought. Heaving a deep sigh, he then rose, and paced the chamber with rapid strides.

"Yes, it is better thus," he ejaculated; "if I remain near her, I shall do some desperate deed. Better—far better—I should go. And yet to leave her with Henry—to know that he is ever near her—that he drinks in the music of her voice, and basks in the sunshine of her smile—while I am driven forth to darkness and despair—the thought is madness! I will not obey the hateful mandate! I will stay and defy him!"

As he uttered aloud this wild and unguarded speech, the arras screening the door was drawn aside, and gave admittance to Wolsey.

Wyat's gaze sank before the penetrating glance fixed upon him by the cardinal.

"I did not come to play the eavesdropper, Sir Thomas," said Wolsey; "but I have heard enough to place your life in my power. So, you refuse to obey the king's injunctions. You refuse to proceed to Paris. You refuse to assist in bringing about the divorce, and prefer remaining here to brave your sovereign, and avenge yourself upon a fickle mistress. Ha?"

Wyat returned no answer.

" If such be your purpose," pursued Wolsey, after a pause, during which he intently scrutinised the knight's countenance, " I will assist you in it. Be ruled by me, and you shall have a deep and full revenge."

" Say on," rejoined Wyat, his eyes blazing with infernal fire, and his hand involuntarily clutching the handle of his dagger.

" If I read you aright," continued the cardinal, " you are arrived at that pitch of desperation, when life itself becomes indifferent, and when but one object remains to be gained——"

" And that is vengeance ! " interrupted Wyat fiercely.

" Right, cardinal—right. I will have vengeance—terrible vengeance ! "

" You shall. But I will not deceive you. You will purchase what you seek at the price of your own head."

" I care not," replied Wyat. " All sentiments of love and loyalty are swallowed up by jealousy and burning hate. Nothing but blood can allay the fever that consumes me. Show me how to slay him ! "

" Him ! " echoed the cardinal, in alarm and horror. " Wretch ! would you kill your king ? God forbid that I should counsel the injury of a hair of his head ! I do not want to play the assassin, Wyat," he added, more calmly, " but the just avenger. Liberate the king from the thraldom of the capricious siren who enslaves him, and you will do a service to the whole country. A word from you—a letter—a token—will cast her from the king, and place her on the block. And what matter ? The gory scaffold were better than Henry's bed."

" I cannot harm her," cried Wyat, distractedly. " I love her still, devotedly as ever. She was in my power yesterday, and without your aid, cardinal, I could have wreaked my vengeance upon her if I had been so minded."

" You were then in her chamber, as the king suspected ? " cried Wolsey, with a look of exultation.

" Trouble yourself no more, Sir Thomas. I will take the part of vengeance off your hands."

" My indiscretion will avail you little, cardinal," replied Wyat sternly. " A hasty word proves nothing. I will perish on the rack sooner than accuse Anne Boleyn. I am a desperate man, but not so desperate as you suppose me. A moment ago I might have been led on, by the murtherous and traitorous impulse that prompted me, to lift my hand against the king, but I never could have injured her."

" You are a madman ! " cried Wolsey impatiently; " and it is waste of time to argue with you. I wish you good speed on your journey. On your return you will find Anne Boleyn Queen of England."

" And you disgraced," rejoined Wyat, as, with a malignant and vindictive look the cardinal quitted the chamber.

Again left alone, Wyat fell into another fit of despondency, from which he roused himself with difficulty and went forth to visit the Earl of Surrey in the Round Tower.

Some delay occurred before he could obtain access to the earl. The halberdier stationed at the entrance to the keep near the Norman Tower refused to admit him without the order of the officer in command of the tower, and as the latter was not in the way at the moment, Wyat had to remain without till he made his appearance.

While thus detained, he beheld Anne Boleyn and her royal lover mount their steeds, in the upper ward, and ride forth, with their attendants, on a hawking expedition. Anne Boleyn bore a beautiful falcon on her wrist— Wyat's own gift to her in happier days—and looked full of coquetry, animation, and delight—without the vestige of a cloud upon her brow, or a care on her countenance. With increased bitterness of heart, he turned from the sight, and shrouded himself beneath the gateway of the Norman Tower.

Soon after this, the officer appeared, and at once according to Wyat permission to see the earl, preceded him up the long flight of stone steps communicating with the upper part of the keep, and screened by an embattled and turreted structure, constituting a covered way to the Round Tower.

Arrived at the landing, the officer unlocked a door on the left, and ushered his companion into the prisoner's chamber.

Influenced by the circular shape of the structure in which it was situated, and of which it formed a segment, the further part of this chamber was almost lost to view, and a number of cross-beams and wooden pillars added to its sombre and mysterious appearance. The walls were of enormous thickness, and a narrow loophole, terminating a deep embrasure, afforded but scanty light. Opposite the embrasure sat Surrey, at a small table covered with books and writing materials. A lute lay beside him on the floor, and there were several astrological and alchemical implements within reach.

So immersed was the youthful prisoner in study, that he was not aware, until a slight exclamation was uttered by Wyat, of the entrance of the latter. He then arose, and gave him welcome.

Nothing material passed between them as long as the officer remained in the chamber, but on his departure Surrey observed, laughingly, to his friend, " And how doth my fair cousin, the Lady Anne Boleyn ? "

" She has just ridden forth with the king, to hawk in the park," replied Wyat moodily. " For myself, I am ordered on a mission to France, but I could not depart without entreating your forgiveness for the jeopardy in which I have placed you. Would I could take your place."

" Do not heed me," replied Surrey; " I am well content with what has happened. Virgil and Homer, Dante and Petrarch, are the companions of my confinement; and, in good sooth, I am glad to be alone. Amid the distractions of the court, I could find little leisure for the Muse."

" Your situation is, in many respects, enviable,

Surrey," replied Wyat. "Disturbed by no jealous doubts and fears, you can beguile the tedious hours in the cultivation of your poetical tastes, or in study. Still, I must needs reproach myself with being the cause of your imprisonment."

"I repeat, you have done me a service," rejoined the earl. "I would lay down my life for my fair cousin, Anne Boleyn, and I am glad to be able to prove the sincerity of my regard for you, Wyat. I applaud the king's judment in sending you to France, and if you will be counselled by me, you will stay there long enough to forget her who now occasions you so much uneasiness."

"Will the fair Geraldine be forgotten when the term of your imprisonment shall expire, my lord?" asked Wyat.

"Of a surety, not," replied the earl.

"And yet, in less than two months, I shall return from France," rejoined Wyat.

"Our cases are not alike," said Surrey. "The Lady Elizabeth Fitzgerald has plighted her troth to me."

"Anne Boleyn vowed eternal constancy to me," cried Wyat bitterly; "and you see how she kept her oath! The absent are always in danger; and few women are proof against ambition. Vanity—vanity is the rock they split upon. May you never experience from Richmond the wrong I have experienced from his father."

"I have no fear," replied Surrey.

As he spoke, there was a slight noise in that part of the chamber which was buried in darkness.

"Have we a listener here?" cried Wyat, grasping his sword.

"Not unless it be a four-legged one from the dungeons beneath," replied Surrey. "But you were speaking of Richmond. He visited me this morning, and came to relate the particulars of a mysterious adventure that occurred to him last night."

And the earl proceeded to detail what had befallen the duke in the forest.

"A marvellous story, truly!" said Wyat, pondering

upon the relation. " I will seek out the demon huntsman myself."

Again, a noise similar to that heard a moment before, resounded from the lower part of the room. Wyat immediately flew thither, and drawing his sword, searched about with its point, but ineffectually.

" It could not be fancy," he said, " and yet nothing is to be found."

" I do not like jesting about Herne the hunter," remarked Surrey, " after what I have myself seen. In your present frame of mind, I advise you not to hazard an interview with the fiend. He has power over the desperate."

Wyat returned no answer. He seemed lost in gloomy thought, and soon afterwards took his leave.

On returning to his lodgings, he summoned his attendants, and ordered them to proceed to Kingston; adding that he would join them there early the next morning. One of them, an old serving-man, noticing the exceeding haggardness of his looks, endeavoured to persuade him to go with them; but Wyat, with a harshness totally unlike his customary manner, which was gracious and kindly in the extreme, peremptorily refused.

" You look very ill, Sir Thomas," said the old servant; " worse than I ever remember seeing you. Listen to my counsel, I beseech you. Plead ill health with the king in excuse of your mission to France, and retire, for some months, to recruit your strength and spirits at Allington."

" Tush! Adam Twisden—I am well enough," exclaimed Wyat impatiently. " Go and prepare my mails."

" My dear, dear master," cried old Adam, bending the knee before him, and pressing his hand to his lips; " something tells me that if I leave you now, I shall never see you again. There is a paleness in your cheek, and a fire in your eye, such as I have never before observed in you, or in mortal man. I tremble to say it, but you look like one possessed by the fiend. Forgive my boldness, sir. I speak from affection and duty. I was serving-man to your father, good Sir Henry Wyat, before you, and I love you as a son, while I honour you as a master. I have heard that there are evil beings in the forest—nay, even within the castle—who lure men to perdition by promising to accomplish their wicked desires. I trust no such being has crossed your path."

"Make yourself easy, good Adam," replied Wyat; "no fiend has tempted me."

"Swear it, sir," cried the old man eagerly—"swear it by the Holy Trinity !"

"By the Holy Trinity, I swear it !" replied Wyat.

As the words were uttered, the door behind the arras was suddenly shut with violence.

"Curses on you, villain ! you have left the door open!" cried Wyat fiercely. "Our conversation has been over-heard."

"I will soon see by whom," cried Adam, springing to his feet, and rushing towards the door, which opened upon a long corridor.

"Well !" cried Wyat, as Adam returned the next moment, with cheeks almost as white as his own—"was it the cardinal ?"

"It was the devil, I believe !" replied the old man. "I could see no one."

"It would not require supernatural power to retreat into an adjoining chamber, fool !" replied Wyat, affecting an incredulity he was far from feeling.

"Your worship's adjuration was strangely inter-rupted," cried the old man, crossing himself devoutly. "Saint Dunstan and Saint Christopher shield us from evil spirits !"

"A truce to your idle terrors, Adam," said Wyat. "Take these packets," he added, giving him Henry's despatches, "and guard them as you would your life. I am going on an expedition of some peril to-night, and do not choose to keep them about me. Bid the grooms have my steed in readiness an hour before midnight."

"I hope your worship is not about to ride into the forest at that hour ?" said Adam, trembling. "I was told by the stout archer, whom the king dubbed Duke of

Shoreditch, that he and the Duke of Richmond ventured thither last night ; and that they saw a legion of demons mounted on coal-black horses, and amongst them Mark Fytton, the butcher who was hanged a few days ago from the Curfew Tower by the king's orders, and whose body so strangely disappeared. Do not go into the forest, dear Sir Thomas ! "

" No more of this ! " cried Wyat fiercely. " Do as I bid you, and if I join you not before noon to-morrow, proceed to Rochester, and there await my coming."

" I never expect to see you again, sir ! " groaned the old man, as he took his leave.

The anxious concern evinced in his behalf by his old and trusty servant, was not without effect on Sir Thomas Wyat, and made him hesitate in his design; but, by and by, another access of jealous rage come on, and overwhelmed all his better resolutions. He remained within his chamber to a late hour, and then issuing forth, proceeded to the terrace at the north of the castle, where he was challenged by a sentinel, but was suffered to pass on, on giving the watch-word.

The night was profoundly dark, and the whole of the glorious prospect commanded by the terrace shrouded from view. But Wyat's object in coming thither was to gaze, for the last time, at that part of the castle which enclosed Anne Boleyn; and knowing well the situation of her apartments, he fixed his eyes upon the windows; but though numerous lights streamed from the adjoining corridor, all here was buried in obscurity.

Suddenly, however, the chamber was illumined, and he beheld Henry and Anne Boleyn enter it, preceded by a band of attendants bearing tapers. It needed not Wyat's jealousy-sharpened gaze to read, even at that distance, the king's enamoured looks, or Anne Boleyn's responsive glances. He saw that one of Henry's arms encircled her waist, while the other caressed her yielding hand. They paused. Henry bent forward, and Anne half averted her head, but not so much so as to prevent the king from imprinting a long and fervid kiss upon her lips.

Terrible was its effect upon Wyat. An adder's bite would have been less painful. His hands convulsively clutched together; his hair stood erect upon his head; a shiver ran through his frame; and he tottered back several paces. When he recovered, Henry had bidden good-night to the object of his love, and having nearly gained the door, turned and waved a tender valediction to her. As soon as he was gone, Anne looked round with a smile of ineffable pride and pleasure at her attendants, but a cloud of curtains dropping over the window, shrouded her from the sight of her wretched lover.

In a state of agitation wholly indescribable, Wyat staggered towards the edge of the terrace—it might be with the design of flinging himself from it—but when within a few yards of the low parapet wall, defending its precipitous side, he perceived a tall, dark figure standing directly in his path, and halted. Whether the object he beheld was human or not, he could not determine, but it seemed of more than mortal stature. It was wrapped in a long black cloak, and wore a high conical cap on its head. Before Wyat could speak, the figure addressed him.

"You desire to see Herne the hunter," said the figure, in a deep, sepulchral tone. "Ride hence to the haunted beech-tree near the marsh, at the further side of the forest, and you will find him."

"You are Herne—I feel it," cried Wyat. "Why go into the forest? Speak now."

And he stepped forward, with the intention of grasping the figure. But it eluded him, and, with a mocking laugh, melted into the darkness.

Wyat avanced to the edge of the terrace and looked over the parapet, but he could see nothing except the tops of the tall trees springing from the side of the moat. Flying to the sentinel, he inquired whether any one had passed him, but the man returned an angry denial.

Awe-stricken and agitated. Wyat quitted the terrace, and, seeking his steed, mounted him, and galloped into the forest.

" If he I have seen be not indeed the fiend, he will scarcely outstrip me in the race," he cried, as his steed bore him at a furious pace up the long avenue.

The gloom was here profound, being increased by the dense masses of foliage beneath which he was riding. By the time, however, that he reached the summit of Snow Hill, the moon struggled through the clouds, and threw a wan glimmer over the leafy wilderness around. The deep slumber of the woods was unbroken by any sound save that of the frenzied rider bursting through them.

Well acquainted with the forest, Wyat held on a direct course. His brain was on fire, and the fury of his career increased his fearful excitement. Heedless of all impediments, he pressed forward—now dashing beneath overhanging boughs at the risk of his neck—now skirting the edge of a glen where a false step might have proved fatal. On—on he went, his frenzy increasing each moment.

At length, he reached the woody height overlooking the marshy tract that formed the limit of his ride. Once more the moon had withdrawn her lustre, and a huge, indistinct, black mass alone pointed out the position of the haunted tree. Around it wheeled a large, white owl, distinguishable by its ghostly plumage through the gloom, like a sea-bird in a storm; and hooting bodingly as it winged its mystic flight. No other sound was heard, nor living object seen.

While gazing into the dreary expanse beneath him, Wyat, for the first time since starting, experienced a sensation of doubt and dread; and the warning of his old and faithful attendant rushed upon his mind. He tried to recite a prayer, but the words died away on his lips—neither would his fingers fashion the symbol of the cross.

But even these admonitions did not restrain him. Springing from his foaming and panting steed, and taking the bridle in his hand, he descended the side of the acclivity. Ever and anon, a rustling among the grass told him that a snake, with which description of reptile the spot abounded, was gliding away from him. His horse, which had hitherto been all fire and impetuosity, now began to manifest symptoms of alarm, quivered in every limb, snorted, and required to be dragged along forcibly.

When within a few paces of the tree, its enormous rifted trunk became fully revealed to him. But no one was beside him. Wyat then stood still, and cried, in a loud, commanding tone—" Spirit, I summon thee !— appear ! "

At these words, a sound like a peal of thunder rolled overhead, accompanied by screeches of discordant laughter. Other strange and unearthly noises were heard, and amidst the din, a blue, phosphoric light issued from the yawning crevice in the tree, while a tall, gaunt figure, crested with an antlered helm, sprang from it. At the same moment, a swarm of horribly-grotesque, swart objects, looking like imps, appeared amid the branches of the tree, and grinned, and gesticulated at Wyat, whose courage remained unshaken during the fearful ordeal. Not so his steed. After rearing and plunging violently, the affrighted animal broke its hold, and darted off into the swamp, where it floundered, and was lost.

" You have called me, Sir Thomas Wyat," said the demon, in a sepulchral tone ; " I am here. What would you ? "

" My name being known to you, spirit of darkness, my errand should be also," replied Wyat boldly.

" Your errand *is* known to me," replied the demon. " You have lost a mistress, and would regain her ? "

" I would give my soul to win her back from my kingly rival," cried Wyat.

" I accept your offer," rejoined the spirit. " Anne Boleyn shall be yours. Your hand upon the compact."

Wyat stretched forth his hand, and grasped that of the demon. His fingers were compressed, as if by a vice, and he felt himself dragged towards the tree, while a stifling and sulphureous vapour rose around him. A black veil fell over his head, and was rapidly twined around his brow in thick folds.

111

Amid yells of fiendish laughter, he was then lifted from the ground, thrust into the hollow of the tree, and thence, as it seemed to him, conveyed into a deep subterranean cave.

II

In what manner Wolsey puts his scheme into operation

FOILED in his scheme of making Wyat the instrument of Anne Boleyn's overthrow, Wolsey determined to put into immediate operation the plan he had conceived of bringing forward a rival to her with the king. If a choice had been allowed him, he would have selected some high-born dame for the purpose; but as this was out of the question—and as, indeed, Henry had of late proved insensible to the attractions of all the beauties that crowded his court except Anne Boleyn—he trusted to the forester's fair grand-daughter to accomplish his object.

The source whence he had received intelligence of the king's admiration of Mabel Lyndwood, was his jester, Patch—a shrewd varlet who, under the mask of folly, picked up many an important secret for his master, and was proportionately rewarded.

Before excuting the scheme, it was necessary to ascertain whether the damsel's beauty was as extraordinary as it had been represented; and with this view, Wolsey mounted his mule one morning, and, accompanied by Patch and another attendant, rode towards the forest.

It was a bright and beautiful morning, and pre-occupied as he was, the plotting cardinal could not be wholly insensible to the loveliness of the scene around him. Crossing Spring Hill, he paused at the head of a long glade, skirted on the right by noble beech-trees, whose silver stems sparkled in the sunshine, and extending down to the thicket, now called Cooke's Hill Wood. From this point, as from every other eminence on the northern side of the forest, a magnificent view of the castle was obtained.

The sight of the kingly pile, towering above its vassal woods, kindled high and ambitious thoughts in his breast.

" The lord of that proud structure has been for years swayed by me," he mused, " and shall the royal puppet be at last wrested from me by a woman's hand ? Not if I can hold my own."

Roused by the reflection, he quickened his pace, and shaping his course towards Black Nest, reached, in a short time, the borders of a wide swamp lying between the great lake and another pool of water of less extent, situated in the heart of the forest. This wild and dreary marsh, the haunt of the bittern and the plover, contrasted forcibly and disagreeably with the rich sylvan district he had just quitted.

" I should not like to cross this swamp at night," he observed to Patch, who rode close behind him.

" Nor I, your grace," replied the buffoon. " We might chance to be led by a will-o'-the-wisp to a watery grave."

" Such treacherous fires are not confined to these regions, knave," rejoined Wolsey. " Mankind are often lured, by delusive gleams of glory and power, into quagmires and deep pitfalls. Holy Virgin ! what have we here ? "

The exclamation was occasioned by a figure that suddenly emerged from the ground, at a little distance on the right. Wolsey's mule swerved so much as almost to endanger his seat, and he called out, in a loud, angry tone, to the author of the annoyance, " Who are you, knave ?—and what do you here ? "

" I am a keeper of the forest, an please your grace," replied the other, doffing his cap, and disclosing harsh features, which by no means recommended him to the cardinal, " and am named Morgan Fenwolf. I was crouching among the weeds to get a shot at a fat buck, when your approach called me to my feet."

" By St. Jude, this is the very fellow your grace, who shot the hart-royal, the other day," cried Patch.

"And so preserved the Lady Anne Boleyn," rejoined the cardinal. "Art sure of it, knave?"

"As sure as your grace is of canonisation," replied Patch.

"That shot should have brought you a rich reward, friend—either from the king's highness, or the Lady Anne?" remarked Wolsey to the keeper.

"It has brought me nothing," rejoined Fenwolf sullenly.

"Hum!" exclaimed the cardinal. "Give the fellow a piece of gold, Patch."

"Methinks, I should have better earned your grace's bounty if I had let the hart work his will," said Fenwolf, reluctantly receiving the coin.

"How, fellow!" cried the cardinal, knitting his brows.

"Nay, I mean no offence," replied Fenwolf; "but the rumour goes that your grace and the Lady Anne are not well affected towards each other."

"The rumour is false," rejoined the cardinal; "and you can now contradict it on your own experience. Harkee, sirrah—where lies Tristram Lyndwood's hut?"

Fenwolf looked somewhat surprised and confused by the question.

"It lies on the other side of yonder rising ground, about half a mile hence," he said. "But if your grace is seeking old Tristram, you will not find him. I parted with him half an hour ago, on Hawk's Hill, and he was then on his way to the deer-pen at Bray Wood."

"If I see his grand-daughter, Mabel, it will suffice," rejoined the cardinal. "I am told she is a comely damsel. Is it so?"

"I am but an indifferent judge of beauty," replied Fenwolf moodily.

"Lead my mule across this swamp, thou senseless loon," said the cardinal, "and I will give thee my blessing."

With a very ill grace, Fenwolf complied, and conducted Wolsey to the further side of the marsh.

"If your grace pursues the path over the hill," he said, "and then strikes into the first opening on the right, it will bring you to the place you seek."

And, without waiting for the promised blessing, he disappeared among the trees.

On reaching the top of the hill, Wolsey descried the hut through an opening in the trees, at a few hundred yards distance. It was pleasantly situated on the brink of the lake, at the point where its width was greatest, and where it was fed by a brook that flowed into it from a large pool of water near Sunninghill.

From the high ground where Wolsey now stood, the view of the lake was beautiful. For nearly a mile its shining expanse was seen stretching out between banks of varied form—sometimes embayed, sometimes running out into little headlands, but everywhere clothed with timber almost to the water's edge. Wild fowl skimmed over its glassy surface, or dipped in search of its finny prey; and here and there a heron might be detected standing in some shallow nook, and feasting on the smaller fry. A flight of cawing rooks were settling upon the tall trees on the right bank, and the voices of the thrush, the blackbird, and other feathered songsters, burst in redundant melody from the nearer groves.

A verdant path, partly beneath the trees, and partly on the side of the lake, led Wolsey to the forester's hut. Constructed of wood and clay, with a thatched roof, green with moss, and half overgrown with ivy, the little building was in admirable keeping with the surrounding scenery. Opposite the door, and opening upon the lake, stood a little boat-house, and beside it, a few wooden steps, defended by a hand-rail, ran into the water. A few yards beyond the boat-house the brook before mentioned emptied its waters into the lake.

Gazing with much internal satisfaction at the hut, Wolsey bade Patch dismount, and ascertain whether Mabel was within. The buffoon obeyed, tried the door, and, finding it fastened, knocked, but to no purpose.

After a pause of a few minutes, the cardinal was turning

away in extreme disappointment, when a small skiff, rowed by a female hand, shot round an angle of the lake, and swiftly approached them. A glance from Patch would have told Wolsey, if he had required any such information, that this was the forester's grand-daughter. Her beauty quite ravished him, and drew from him an exclamation of wonder and delight. Features regular, exquisitely moulded, and of a joyous expression; a skin dyed like a peach by the sun, but so as to improve rather than impair its hue; eyes bright, laughing, and blue as a summer sky; ripe, ruddy lips, and pearly teeth; and hair of a light and glossy brown, constituted the sum of her attractions. Her sylph-like figure was charmingly displayed by the graceful exercise on which she was engaged, and her small hands, seemingly scarcely able to grasp an oar, impelled the skiff forwards with marvellous velocity, and apparently without much exertion on her part.

Unabashed by the presence of the strangers, though Wolsey's attire could leave her in no doubt as to his high ecclesiastical dignity, she sprang ashore at the landing-place, and fastened her bark to the side of a boat-house.

" You are Mabel Lyndwood, I presume, fair maiden ? " inquired the cardinal, in his blandest tones.

" Such is my name, your grace," she replied; " for your garb tells me I am addressing Cardinal Wolsey."

The cardinal graciously inclined his head.

" Chancing to ride in this part of the forest," he said, " and having heard of your beauty, I came to see whether the reality equalled the description, and I find it far transcends it."

Mabel blushed deeply and cast down her eyes.

" Would that Henry could see her now ! " thought the cardinal, " Anne Boleyn's reign were nigh at an end. How long have you dwelt in this cottage, fair maid ? " he added, aloud.

" My grandsire, Tristram Lyndwood, has lived here

fifty years and more," replied Mabel; " but I have only been its inmate within these few weeks. Before that time, I lived at Chertsey, under the care of one of the lay sisters of the monastery there—Sister Anastasia."

" And your parents—where are they ? " asked the cardinal curiously.

" Alas ! your grace, I have none," replied Mabel, with a sigh. " Tristram Lyndwood is my only living relative. He used to come over once a month to see me at Chertsey —and latterly, finding his dwelling lonely, for he lost the old dame who tended it for him, he brought me to dwell with him. Sister Anastasia was loth to part with me— and I was grieved to leave her—but I could not refuse my grandsire."

" Of a surety not," replied the cardinal musingly, and gazing hard at her. " And you know nothing of your parents ? "

" Little, beyond this," replied Mabel:—" My father was a keeper of the forest, and being unhappily gored by a stag, perished of the wound—for a hurt from a hart's horn, as your grace knows, is certain death—and my mother pined after him, and speedily followed him to the grave. I was then placed by my grandsire with Sister Anastasia, as I have just related—and this is all my history."

" A simple, yet a curious one," said Wolsey, still musing. " You are the fairest maid of low degree I ever beheld. You saw the king at the chase the other day, Mabel ? "

" Truly did I, your grace," she replied, her eyes brightening, and her colour rising—" and a right noble king he is."

" And as gentle and winning as he is goodly to look upon," said Wolsey, smiling.

" Report says otherwise," rejoined Mabel.

" Report speaks falsely," cried Wolsey; " I know him well—and he is what I describe him."

" I am glad to hear it," replied Mabel; " and I must own I formed the same opinion myself—for the smile he threw upon me was one of the sweetest and kindliest I ever beheld."

" Since you confess so much, fair maiden," rejoined Wolsey, " I will be equally frank, and tell you it was from the king's own lips I heard of your beauty."

" Your grace ! " she exclaimed.

" Well, well," said Wolsey, smiling; " if the king is bewitched, I cannot marvel at it. And now, good-day, fair maiden. You will hear more of me."

" Your grace will not refuse me your blessing ? " said Mabel.

" Assuredly not, my child," replied Wolsey, stretching his hands over her. " All good angels and saints bless you, and hold you in their keeping. Mark my words— a great destiny awaits you. But in all changes, rest assured you will find a friend in Cardinal Wolsey."

" Your grace overwhelms me with kindness," cried Mabel; " nor can I conceive how I have found an interest in your eyes—unless Sister Anastasia, or Father Anselm, of Chertsey Abbey, may have mentioned me to you."

" You have found a more potent advocate with me than either Sister Anastasia or Father Anselm," replied Wolsey, " and now, farewell."

And turning the head of his mule, he rode slowly away.

On the same day, there was a great banquet in the castle, and, as usual, Wolsey took his station on the right of the sovereign, while the papal legate occupied a place on the left. Watching a favourable opportunity, Wolsey observed to Henry, that he had been riding that morning in the forest, and had seen the loveliest damsel that eyes ever fell upon.

" Ah ! by our Lady ! and who may she be ? " asked the king curiously.

" She can boast little in regard to birth, being grand-child to an old forester," replied Wolsey. " But your majesty saw her at the hunting-party the other day."

" Ah, now I bethink me of her," said Henry. " A comely damsel, in good sooth."

"I know not where her match is to be found," cried
the cardinal. "Would your majesty had seen her skim
over the lake in a fairy boat managed by herself, as I
beheld her this morning. You would have taken her for
a water-sprite, except that no water-sprite was half so
beautiful."

"You must speak in raptures, cardinal," cried Henry
"I must see this damsel again. Where does she dwell?
I have heard—but it has slipped my memory."

"In a hut near the great lake," replied Wolsey.
"There is some mystery attached to her birth, which
I have not yet fathomed."

"Leave me to unriddle it," replied the king laughingly.

And he turned to talk on other subjects to Campeggio,
but Wolsey felt satisfied that the device was successful.

Nor was he mistaken. As Henry retired from the
banquet, he motioned the Duke of Suffolk towards him,
and said, in an under tone—

"I shall go forth at dusk to-morrow even, in disguise,
and shall require your attendance."

"On a love affair?" asked the duke, in the same tone.

"Perchance," replied Henry; "but I will explain
myself more fully anon."

This muttered colloquy was overheard by Patch, and
faithfully reported by him to the cardinal.

III

Of the Visit of the Two Guildford Merchants to the Forester's Hut

TRISTRAM LYNDWOOD did not return home till late in the evening; and when informed of the cardinal's visit, he shook his head gravely.

"I am sorry we went to the hunting-party," he observed. "Valentine Hagthorne said mischief would come of it, and I wish I had attended to his advice."

"I see no mischief in the matter, grandsire," cried Mabel. "On the contrary, I think I have met with excellent fortune. The good cardinal promises me a high destiny, and says the king himself noticed me."

"Would his regards had fallen anywhere else than on you, child," rejoined Tristram. "But I warrant me, you told the cardinal your history—all you know of it, at least."

"I did so," she replied—"nor did I know I was doing any harm."

"Answer no such inquiries in future," said Tristram angrily.

"But, grandfather, I could not refuse to answer the cardinal," she replied, in a deprecating voice.

"No more excuses, but attend to my injunctions," said Tristram. "Have you seen Morgan Fenwolf to-day?"

"No; and I care not if I never see him again," she replied pettishly.

"You dislike him strangely, Mabel" rejoined her grandfather; "he is the best keeper in the forest, and makes no secret of his love for you."

"The very reason why I dislike him," she returned.

"By the same rule, if what the cardinal stated be true—though, trust me, he was but jesting—you ought to dislike the king. But get me my supper. I have need of it, for I have fasted long."

Mabel hastened to obey, and set a mess of hot pottage and other viands before him. Little more conversation passed between them, for the old man was weary, and sought his couch early.

That night, Mabel did nothing but dream of the king —of stately chambers, rich apparel, and countless attendants. She awoke, and finding herself in a lowly cottage, and without a single attendant, was, like other dreamers of imaginary splendour, greatly discontented.

The next morning her grandsire went again to Bray Wood, and she was left to muse upon the event of the previous day. While busied about some trifling occupations, the door suddenly opened, and Morgan Fenwolf entered the cottage. He was followed by a tall man, with a countenance of extreme paleness, but a noble and commanding figure. There was something so striking in the appearance of the latter person, that it riveted the attention of Mabel. But no corresponding effect was produced on the stranger, for he scarcely bestowed a look upon her.

Morgan Fenwolf hastily asked whether her grandsire was at home, or near at hand, and being answered in the negative, appeared much disappointed. He then said that he must borrow the skiff for a short while, as he wished to visit some nets on the lake. Mabel readily assented, and the stranger quitted the house, while Fenwolf lingered to offer some attention to Mabel, which was so ill received that he was fain to hurry forth to the boathouse, where he embarked with his companion. As soon as the plash of oars announced their departure, Mabel went forth to watch them. The stranger, who was seated in the stern of the boat, for the first time fixed his large, melancholy eyes full upon her, and did not withdraw his gaze till an angle of the lake hid him from view.

Marvellling who he could be, and reproaching herself for not questioning Fenwolf on the subject, Mabel resolved to repair the error when the skiff was brought back. But the opportunity did not speedily occur. Hours flew by; the shades of evening drew on; but neither Fenwolf nor the stranger returned.

Soon after dusk, her grandfather came home. He did not express the least astonishment at Fenwolf's prolonged absence, but said he was sure to be back in the course of the evening, and the skiff was not wanted.

" He will bring us back a fine jack, or a carp for dinner to-morrow, I'll warrant me," he said. " If he had returned in time, we might have had fish for supper. No matter. I must make shift with the mutton pie and a rasher of bacon. Morgan did not mention the name of his companion, you say ? "

" He did not," replied Mabel; " but I hope he will bring him with him. He is the goodliest gentleman I ever beheld."

" What ! a goodlier gentleman than the king ? " cried Tristram.

" Nay, they should not be compared," replied Mabel; " the one is stout and burly; the other, slight, long-visaged, and pale, but handsome withal—very handsome."

" Well, I dare say I shall see him anon," said Tristram; " and now for supper, for I am as sharp-set as a wolf; and so is old Hubert," he added, glancing affectionately at the hound by which he was attended.

Mabel placed the better part of a huge pie before him, which the old forester attacked with great zeal. He then fell to work upon some slices of bacon, toasted over the embers by his grand-daughter, and having washed them down with a jug of mead, declared he had supped famously. While taking care of himself, he did not forget his hound. From time to time, he threw him morsels of the pie, and when he had done, he gave him a large platter full of bones.

" Old Hubert has served me faithfully nigh twenty years," he said, patting the hound's shaggy neck, " and must not be neglected."

Throwing a log of wood on the fire, he drew his chair into the ingle nook and disposed himself to slumber.

122

Meanwhile, Mabel busied herself about her household concerns, and was singing a lulling melody to her grandfather, in a voice of exquisite sweetness, when a loud tap was heard at the door. Tristram roused himself from his doze, and old Hubert growled menacingly.

" Quiet, Hubert—quiet ! " cried Tristram. " It cannot be Morgan Fenwolf," he added. " He would never knock thus. Come in, friend, whoever thou art."

At this invitation, two persons darkened the doorway. The foremost was a man of bulky frame, and burly demeanour. He was attired in a buff jerkin, over which he wore a loose, brown surcoat; had a flat velvet cap on his head; and carried a stout staff in his hand. His face was broad and handsome; though his features could scarcely be discerned in the doubtful light to which they were submitted. A reddish coloured beard clothed his chin. His companion, who appeared a trifle the taller of the two, and equally robust, was wrapped in a cloak of dark green camlet.

" Give you good-e'en, friend," said the foremost stranger to the forester. " We are belated travellers, on our way from Guildford to Windsor, and, seeing your cottage, have called to obtain some refreshment before we cross the Great Park. We do not ask you to bestow a meal upon us, but will gladly pay for the best your larder affords."

" You shall have it, and welcome, my master," replied Tristram; " but I am afraid my humble fare will scarcely suit you."

" Fear nothing," replied the other; " we have good appetites, and are not over dainty. Beshrew me, friend," he added, regarding Mabel, " you have a comely daughter."

" She is my grand-daughter, sir," replied Tristram.

" Well, your grand-daughter, then," said the other; " by the mass a lovely wench. We have none such in Guildford, and I doubt if the king hath such in Windsor Castle. What say you, Charles Brandon ? "

" It were treason to agree with you, Harry Le Roy,"

replied Brandon, laughing; " for they say the king visits with the halter all those who disparage the charms of the Lady Anne Boleyn. But, comparisons apart, this damsel is very fair."

" You will discompose her, my masters, if you praise her this to her face," said Tristram, somewhat testily. " Here, Mab, bring forth all my scanty larder affords, and put some rashers of bacon on the fire."

" Cold meat and bread will suffice for us," said Harry; " we will not trouble the damsel to play the cook."

With this, Mabel, who appeared a good deal embarrassed, by the presence of the strangers, spread a cloth of snow-white linen on the little table, and placed the remains of the pie and a large oven cake before them. The newcomers sat down, and ate heartily of the humble viands—he who had answered to the name of Harry frequently stopping in the course of his repast, to compliment his fair attendant.

" By our Lady, I have never been so waited on before," he added, rising and removing his stool towards the fire, while his companion took up a position, with his back against the wall, near the fireplace. " And now, my pretty Mabel, have you never a cup of ale to wash down the pie ? "

" I can offer you a draught of right good mead, master," said Tristram; " and that is the only liquor my cottage can furnish."

" Nothing can be better," replied Harry. " The mead, by all means."

While Mable went to draw the liquor, Tristram fixed his eyes on Harry, whose features were now fully revealed by the light of the fire.

" Why do you look at me so hard, friend ? " demanded Harry bluffly.

" I have seen some one very like you, mister," replied Trsitram; " and one whom it is no light honour to resemble."

" You mean the king," returned Harry, laughing.

" You are not the first person who has thought me like him."

" You are vain of the likeness, I see, master," replied Tristram, joining in the laugh. " How say you, Mab ? " he added to his grand-daughter, who at that moment returned with a jug and a couple of drinking horns. " Whom does this gentleman resemble ? "

" No one," returned Mabel, without raising her eyes.

" No one ! " echoed Harry, chucking her under the chin. " Look me full in the face, and you will find out your mistake. Marry, if I were the royal Henry, instead of what I am, a plain Guildford merchant, I should prefer you to Anne Boleyn."

" Is that said in good sooth, sir ? " asked Mabel, slightly raising her eyes, and instantly dropping them before the ardent gaze of the self-styled merchant.

" In good sooth and sober truth," replied Harry, rounding his arm, and placing his hand on his lusty thigh, in true royal fashion.

" Were you the royal Henry, I should not care for your preference," said Mabel, more confidently. " My grandsire says the king changes his love as often as the moon changes—nay, oftener."

" God's death !—your grandsire is a false knave to say so ! " cried Harry.

" Heaven help us ! you swear the king's oaths," said Mabel.

" And wherefore not, sweetheart ? " said Harry, checking himself. " It is enough to make one swear, and in royal fashion, too, to hear one's liege lord unjustly accused. I have ever heard the king styled a mirror of constancy. How say you, Charles Brandon ?—can you not give him a good character ? "

" Oh ! an excellent character," said Brandon. " He is constancy itself—while the fit lasts," he added, aside.

" You hear what my friend says, sweetheart," observed Harry ; " and I assure you he has the best opportunities of judging. But I'll be sworn you did not believe your grandsire when he thus maligned the king."

" She contradicted me flatly," said Tristram; " but pour out the mead, girl. Our guests are waiting for it."

While Mabel, in compliance with her grandsire's directions, filled the horn, the door of the cottage was noiselessly opened by Morgan Fenwolf, who stepped in, followed by Bawsey. He stared inquisitively at the strangers, but both were so much occupied by the damsel that he remained unnoticed. A sign from the old forester told him he had better retire. Jealous curiosity, however, detained him; and he tarried till Harry had received the cup from Mabel, and drained it to her health. He then drew back, closed the door softly, and joined a dark and mysterious figure, with hideous lineaments and an antlered helm upon its brows, lurking outside the cottage.

Meanwhile, a cup of mead having been offered to Brandon, he observed to his companion. " We must now be setting forth on our journey. Night is advancing, and we have five long miles to traverse across the Great Park."

" I would stay where I am," rejoined Harry, " and make a bench near the fire serve me in lieu of a couch, but the business requires our presence at the castle to-night. There is payment for our meal, friend," he added, giving a mark to Tristram, " and as we shall probably return to-morrow night, we will call and have another supper with you. Provide us a capon, and some fish from the lake."

" You pay as you swear, good sir, royally," replied Tristram. " You shall have a better supper to-morrow night."

" You have a dangerous journey before you, sir," said Mabel. " They say there are plunderers and evil spirits in the Great Park."

" I have no fear of any such, sweetheart," replied Harry; " I have a strong arm to defend myself, and so has my friend Charles Brandon. And as to evil spirits, a kiss from you will shield me from all ill."

And as he spoke, he drew her towards him, and clasping her in his arms, imprinted a score of rapid kisses on her lips.

" Hold ! hold, master ! " cried Tristram, rising angrily; " this may not be. 'Tis an arrant abuse of hospitality."

" Nay, be not offended, good friend," replied Harry, laughing, " I am on the look-out for a wife, and I know not but I may take your grand-daughter with me to Guildford."

" She is not to be so lightly won," cried Tristram; " for though I am but a poor forester, I rate her as highly as the haughtiest noble can rate his child."

" And with reason," said Harry. " Good-night, sweetheart ! By my crown ! Suffolk," he exclaimed to his companion, as he quitted the cottage, " she is an angel, and shall be mine."

" Not if my arm serves me truly," muttered Fenwolf, who, with his mysterious companion, had stationed himself at the window of the hut.

" Do him no injury," returned the other; " he is only to be made captive—mark that. And now to apprise Sir Thomas Wyat. We must intercept them before they reach their horses."

IV

How Herne the Hunter showed the Earl of Surrey the Fair
Geraldine in a vision

ON the third day after Surrey's imprisonment in the keep,
he was removed to the Norman Tower. The chamber
allotted him was square, tolerably lofty, and had two
narrow pointed windows on either side, looking on the
one hand into the upper quadrangle, and on the other
into the middle ward. At the same time, permission was
accorded him to take exercise on the battlements of the
Round Tower, or within the dry and grassy moat at
its foot.

The fair Geraldine, he was informed, had been sent
to the royal palace at Greenwich; but her absence
occasioned him little disquietude, because he knew, if she
had remained at Windsor, he would not have been allowed
to see her.

On the same day that Surrey was removed to the
Norman Tower, the Duke of Richmond quitted the castle
without assigning any motive for his departure, or even
taking leave of his friend. At first, some jealous mistrust
that he might be gone to renew his suit ot the fair
Geraldine troubled the earl; but he strongly combated
the feeling, as calculated, if indulged, to destroy his
tranquillity, and by fixing his thoughts sedulously on other
subjects, he speedily succeeded in overcoming it.

On that night, while occupied in a translation of the
Æneid, which he had commenced, he remained at his
task to a late hour. The midnight bell had tolled, when,
looking up, he was startled by perceiving a tall dark
figure standing silent and motionless beside him.

Independently of the difficulty of accounting for its
presence, the appearance of the figure was, in itself,
sufficiently appalling. It was above the ordinary stature,
and was enveloped in a long black cloak, while a tall,

conical black cap, which added to its height, and increased the hideousness of its features, covered its head.

For a few minutes, Surrey remained gazing at the figure in mute astonishment, during which it maintained the same motionless posture. At length, he was able to murmur forth the interrogation—" Who art thou ? "

" A friend," replied the figure, in a sepulchral tone.

" Are you man or spirit ? " demanded Surrey.

" It matters not—I am a friend," rejoined the figure.

" On what errand come you here ? " asked Surrey.

" To serve you," replied the figure; " to liberate you. You shall go hence with me, if you choose."

" On what condition ? " rejoined Surrey.

" We will speak of that when we are out of the castle, and on the green sod of the forest," returned the figure.

" You tempt in vain," cried Surrey. " I will not go with you. I recognise in you the demon-hunter Herne."

The figure laughed hollowly—so hollowly that Surrey's flesh crept upon his bones.

" You are right, Lord of Surrey," he said; " I *am* Herne the hunter. You must join me. Sir Thomas Wyat is already one of my band."

" You lie, false fiend ! " rejoined Surrey. " Sir Thomas Wyat is in France."

" It is you who lie, Lord of Surrey," replied Herne; " Sir Thomas Wyat is now in the Great Park. You shall see him in a few minutes, if you will come with me."

" I disbelieve you, tempter ! " cried Surrey indignantly. " Wyat is too good a Christian, and too worthy a knight, to league with a demon."

Again Herne laughed bitterly.

" Sir Thomas Wyat told you he would seek me out," said the demon. " He did so, and gave himself to me for Anne Boleyn."

" But you have no power over her, demon ? " cried Surrey, shuddering.

" You will learn whether I have or not, in due time," replied Herne. " Do you refuse to go with me ? "

"I refuse to deliver myself to perdition," rejoined the earl.

"An idle fear," rejoined Herne. "I care not for your soul—you will destroy it without my aid. I have need of you. You shall be back again in this chamber before the officer visits it in the morning, and no one shall be aware of your absence. Come, or I will bear you hence."

"You dare not touch me," replied Surrey, placing his hand upon his breast; "I am armed with a holy relic."

"I know it," said Herne; "and I feel its power, or I would not have trifled with you thus long. But it cannot shield you from a rival. You believe the fair Geraldine constant—ha?"

"I know her to be so," said Surrey.

A derisive laugh broke from Herne.

"Peace, mocking fiend!" cried Surrey furiously.

"I laugh to think how you are deceived," said Herne. "Would you behold your mistress now?—would you see how she conducts herself during your absence?"

"If you choose to try me, I will not oppose the attempt," replied Surrey; "but it will be futile."

"Remove the relic from your person," rejoined Herne. "Place it upon the table, within your grasp, and you shall see her."

Surrey hesitated; but he was not proof against the low mocking laugh of the demon.

"No harm can result from it," he cried, at length detaching the relic from his neck, and laying it on the table.

"Extinguish the light!" cried Herne, in a commanding voice.

Surrey instantly sprang to his feet, and dashed the lamp off the table.

"Behold!" cried the demon.

And instantly a vision, representing the form and lineaments of the fair Geraldine to the life, shone forth against the opposite wall of the chamber. At the feet of the visionary damsel knelt a shape resembling the Duke of Richmond. He was pressing the hand extended to

130

him by the fair Geraldine to his lips, and a smile of triumph irradiated his features.

" Such is man's friendship—such woman's constancy!" cried Herne. " Are you now satisfied ? "

" I am, that you have deceived me, false spirit ! " cried the earl. " I would not believe the fair Geraldine inconstant, though all hell told me so."

A terrible laugh broke from the demon, and the vision faded away. All became perfect darkness, and for a few moments the earl remained silent. He then called to the demon, but receiving no answer, put forth his hand towards the spot where he had stood. He was gone.

Confounded, Surrey returned to the table, and searched for the relic, but, with a feeling of indescribable anguish and self-reproach, found that it had likewise disappeared.

v

What befell Sir Thomas Wyat in the Sandstone Cave; and how he drank a maddening potion

THE cave in which Sir Thomas Wyat found himself, on the removal of the bandage from his eyes, was apparently —for it was only lighted by a single torch—of considerable width and extent, and hewn out of a bed of soft sandstone. The roof, which might be about ten feet high, was supported by the trunks of three large trees, rudely fashioned into pillars. There were several narrow lateral passages within it, apparently communicating with other caverns; and at the further end, which was almost buried in obscurity, there was a gleam seemingly occasioned by the reflection of the torchlight upon water. On the right hand stood a pile of huge stones, disposed somewhat in the form of a Druidical altar, on the top of which, as on a throne, sat the demon-hunter, surrounded by his satellites—one of whom, horned and bearded like a satyr, had clambered the roughened side of the central pillar, and held a torch over the captive's head.

Half-stifled by the noxious vapour he had inhaled, and blinded by the tightness of the bandage, it was some time before Wyat fully recovered his powers of sight and utterance.

" Why am I brought hither, false fiend ? " he demanded, at length.

" To join my band," replied the demon, harshly and imperiously.

" Never ! " rejoined Wyat. " I will have nought to do with you, except as regards our compact."

" What I require from you *is* part of our compact," rejoined the demon. " He who has once closed hands with Herne the hunter cannot retreat. But I mean you fairly, and will not delude you with false expectations. What you seek cannot be accomplished on the instant. Ere three days, Anne Boleyn shall be yours."

" Give me some proof that you are not deceiving me, spirit," said Wyat.

" Come, then ! " replied Herne. So saying, he sprang from the stones and, taking Wyat's hand, led him towards the lower end of the cave, which gradually declined till it reached the edge of a small but apparently deep pool of water, the level of which rose above the rock that formed its boundary.

" Remove the torch ! " thundered the demon to those behind. " Now summon your false love, Sir Thomas Wyat," he added, as his orders were obeyed, and the light was taken into one of the side passages, so that its gleam no longer fell upon the water.

" Appear, Anne Boleyn ! " cried Wyat.

Upon this, a shadowy resemblance of her he had invoked flitted over the surface of the water, with hands outstretched towards him. So moved was Wyat by the vision, that he would have flung himself into the pool to grasp it, if he had not been forcibly detained by the demon. During the struggle, the figure vanished, and all was buried in darkness.

" I have said she shall be yours," cried Herne; " but time is required for the accomplishment of my purpose. I have only power over her when evil is predominant in her heart. But such moments are not unfrequent," he added, with a bitter laugh. " And now to the chase. I promise you it will be a wilder and more exciting ride than you ever enjoyed in the king's company. To the chase !—to the chase, I say ! "

Sounding a call upon his horn, the light instantly reappeared. All was stir and confusion amid the impish troop—and presently afterwards a number of coal-black horses, and hounds of the same hue, leashed in couples, were brought out of one of the side passages. Among the latter were two large sable hounds of Saint Hubert's breed, whom Herne summoned to his side by the names of Saturn and Dragon.

A slight noise, as of a blow dealt against a tree, was now heard overhead, and Herne, imposing silence on the group by a hasty gesture, assumed an attitude of fixed attention. The stroke was repeated a second time.

" It is our brother, Morgan Fenwolf," cried the demon.

Catching hold of a chain hanging from the roof, which Wyat had not hitherto noticed, he swung himself into a crevice above, and disappeared from view. During the absence of their leader, the troop remained motionless and silent.

A few minutes afterwards Herne reappeared at the upper end of the cave. He was accompanied by Fenwolf, between whom and Wyat a slight glance of recognition passed.

The order being given by the demon to mount, Wyat, after an instant's hesitation, seized the flowing mane of the horse nearest him—for it was furnished neither with saddle nor bridle—and vaulted upon its back. At the same moment Herne uttered a wild cry, and plunging into the pool, sank within it. Wyat's steed followed, and swam swiftly forward beneath the water.

When Wyat rose to the surface he found himself in the open lake, which was gleaming in the moonlight.

Before him he beheld Herne clambering the bank, accompanied by his two favourite hounds, while a large white owl wheeled round his head, hooting loudly. Behind came the grisly cavalcade, with their hounds, swimming from beneath a bank covered by thick, overhanging trees, which completely screened the secret entrance to the cave. Having no control over his steed, Wyat was obliged to surrender himself to its guidance, and was soon placed by the side of the demon-hunter.

" Pledge me, Sir Thomas Wyat," said Herne, unslinging a gourd-shaped flask from his girdle, and offering it to him. " 'Tis a rare wine, and will prevent you from suffering from your bath, as well as give you spirits for the chase."

Chilled to the bone by the immersion he had undergone, Wyat did not refuse the offer, but placing the flask to his lips took a deep draught from it. The demon uttered a low, bitter laugh, as he received back the flask, and he slung it to his girdle without tasting it.

The effect of the potion upon Wyat was extraordinary. The whole scene seemed to dance around him;—the impish figures in the lake, or upon its bank, assumed forms yet more fantastic; the horses looked like monsters of the deep; the hounds like wolves and ferocious beasts; the branches of the trees writhed and shot forward like hissing serpents;—and though this effect speedily passed off, it left behind it a wild and maddening feeling of excitement.

" A noble hart is lying in yon glen," said Morgan Fenwolf, advancing towards his leader; " I tracked his slot thither this evening."

" Haste, and unharbour him," replied Herne, " and as soon as you rouse him, give the halloa."

Fenwolf obeyed; and, shortly afterwards, a cry was heard from the glen.

" List halloa! list halloa ! " cried Herne, " that's he ! that's he ! hyke, Saturn ! hyke, Dragon !—Away !—away, my merry men all."

VI

How Sir Thomas Wyat hunted with Herne

ACCOMPANIED by Wyat, and followed by the whole cavalcade, Herne dashed into the glen, where Fenwolf awaited him. Threading the hollow, the troop descried the hart, flying swiftly along a sweeping glade, at some two hundred yards distance. The glade was passed—a woody knoll skirted—a valley traversed—and the hart plunged into a thick grove clothing the side of Hawk's Hill. But it offered him no secure retreat. Dragon and Saturn were close upon him, and behind them came Herne, crashing through the branches of the trees, and heedless of all impediments. By and by the thicket became more open, and they entered Cranbourne Chase. But the hart soon quitted it to return to the Great Park, and darted down a declivity skirted by a line of noble oaks. Here he was so hotly pressed by his fierce opponents, whose fangs he could almost feel within his haunches, that he suddenly stopped, and stood at bay, receiving the foremost of his assailants, Saturn, on the points of his horns. But his defence, though gallant, was unavailing. In another instant, Herne came up, and dismounting, called off Dragon, who was about to take the place of his wounded companion. Drawing a knife from his girdle, the hunter threw himself on the ground, and, advancing on all fours towards the hart, could scarcely be distinguished himself from some denizen of the forest. As he approached, the hart snorted and bellowed fiercely, and dashed its horns against him; but the blow was received by the hunter upon his own antlered helm, and at the same moment his knife was thrust to the hilt into the stag's throat, and it fell to the ground.

Springing to his feet, Herne whooped joyfully, placed his bugle to his lips, and blew the dead mot. He then shouted to Fenwolf to call away and couple the hounds, and striking off the deer's right forefoot with his knife, presented it to Wyat. Several large leafy branches being gathered and laid upon the ground, the hart was placed upon them, and Herne commenced breaking him up, as the process of dismembering the deer is termed in the language of woodcraft. His first step was to cut off the animal's head, which he performed by a single blow with his heavy trenchant knife.

" Give the hounds the flesh," he said, delivering the trophy to Fenwolf; " but keep the antlers, for it is a great deer of head."

Placing the head on a hunting-pole, Fenwolf withdrew to an open space among the trees, and hallooing to the others, they immediately cast off the hounds, who rushed towards him, leaping and baying at the stag's head, which he alternately raised and lowered, until they were sufficiently excited, when he threw it on the ground before them.

While this was going forward, the rest of the band were occupied in various ways—some striking a light with flint and steel—some gathering together sticks and dried leaves to form a fire—others producing various strange-shaped cooking utensils—while others were assisting their leader in his butcherly task, which he executed with infinite skill and expedition.

As soon as the fire was kindled, Herne distributed certain portions of the venison among his followers which were instantly thrown upon the embers to broil; while a few choice morsels were stewed in a pan with wine, and subsequently offered to the leader and Wyat.

This hasty repast concluded, the demon ordered the fire to be extinguished, and the quarters of the deer to be carried to the cave. He then mounted his steed, and attended by Wyat and the rest of his troop, except those engaged in executing his orders, galloped towards Snow Hill, where he speedily succeeded in unharbouring another noble hart.

Away then went the whole party—stag, hounds, hunts-men, sweeping, like a dark cloud down the hill, and crossing the wide, moonlit glade, studded with noble trees, on the west of the great avenue.

For a while the hart held a course parallel with the avenue; he then dashed across it, threaded the intricate woods on the opposite side, tracked a long glen, and, leaping the pales, entered the Home Park. It almost seemed as if he designed to seek shelter within the castle, for he made straight towards it, and was only diverted by Herne himself, who, shooting past him with incredible swiftness, turned him towards the lower part of the park.

Here the chase continued with unabated ardour, until, reaching the banks of the Thames, the hart plunged into it, and suffered himself to be carried noiselessly down the current. But Herne followed him along the banks, and when sufficiently near dashed into the stream, and drove him again ashore.

Once more they flew across the Home Park—once more they leaped its pales—once more they entered the Great Park—by this time, the stag took the direction of Englefield Green. He was not, however, allowed to break forth into the open country; but, driven again into the thick woods, he held on with wondrous speed, till the lake appeared in view. In another instant he was swimming across it.

Before the eddies occasioned by the affrighted animal's plunge had described a wide ring, Herne had quitted his steed, and was cleaving with rapid strokes the waters of the lake. Finding escape impossible, the hart turned to meet him, and sought to strike him with his horns; but, as in the case of his ill-fated brother of the wood, the blow was warded by the antlered helm of the swimmer. The next moment the clear water was dyed with blood, and Herne, catching the gasping animal by the head, guided his body to shore. Again the process of breaking up the stag was gone through; and when Herne had concluded his task he once more offered his gourd to Sir Thomas Wyat. Reckless of the consequences, the knight placed the flask to his lips, and draining it to the last drop, fell from his horse insensible.

VII

How Wyat beheld Mabel Lyndwood; and how he was rowed by Morgan Fenwolf upon the lake

WHEN perfect consciousness returned to him, Wyat found himself lying upon a pallet in what he at first took to be the cell of an anchorite; but as recollection of recent events arose more distinctly before him he guessed it to be a chamber connected with the sandstone cave. A small lamp, placed in a recess, lighted the cell; and upon a footstool by his bed stood a jug of water, and a cup containing some drink, in which herbs had evidently been infused. Well-nigh emptying the jug, for he felt parched with thirst, Wyat attired himself, took up the lamp, and walked into the main cavern. No one was there, nor could he obtain any answer to his calls. Evidences, however, were not wanting to prove that a feast had recently been held there. On one side were the scarcely-extinguished embers of a large wood fire; and in the midst of the chamber was a rude table, covered with drinking horns and wooden platters, as well as with the remains of three or four haunches of venison. While contemplating this scene, Wyat heard footsteps in one of the lateral passages, and presently afterwards Morgan Fenwolf made his appearance.

" So you are come round at last, Sir Thomas," observed the keeper, in a slightly sarcastic tone.

" What has ailed me ? " asked Wyat, in surprise.

" You have had a fever for three days," returned Fenwolf, " and have been raving like a madman."

" Three days ! " muttered Wyat. " The false, juggling fiend promised her to me on the third day ! "

" Fear not;—Herne will be as good as his word," said Fenwolf; " but will you go forth with me ? I am about to visit my nets. It is a fine day, and a row on the lake will do you good."

Wyat acquiesced, and followed Fenwolf, who returned along the passage. It grew narrower at the sides, and lower in the roof, as they advanced, until at last they were compelled to move forward on their hands and knees. For some space, the passage, or rather hole (for it was nothing more), ran on a level. A steep and tortuous ascent then commenced, which brought them to an outlet concealed by a large stone. Pushing it aside, Fenwolf crept forth, and immediately afterwards Wyat emerged into a grove, through which, on one side, the gleaming waters of the lake were discernible. The keeper's first business was to replace the stone, which was so screened by brambles and bushes that it could not, unless careful search were made, be detected.

Making his way through the trees to the side of the lake, Fenwolf marched along the greensward, in the direction of Tristram Lyndwood's cottage. Wyat mechanically followed him; but he was so pre-occupied that he scarcely heeded the fair Mabel, nor was it till after his embarkation in the skiff with the keeper, when she came forth to look at them, that he was at all struck with her beauty. He then inquired her name from Fenwolf.

"She is called Mabel Lyndwood, and is an old forester's grand-daughter," replied the other, somewhat gruffly.

"And do you seek her love?" asked Wyat.

"Ay, and wherefore not?" asked Fenwolf, with a look of displeasure.

"Nay, I know not, friend," rejoined Wyat. "She is a comely damsel."

"What!—comelier than the Lady Anne?" demanded Fenwolf spitefully.

"I said not so," replied Wyat; "but she is very fair, and looks true-hearted."

Fenwolf glanced at him from under his brows; and, plunging his oars into the water, soon carried him out of sight of the maiden.

It was high noon, and the day was one of resplendent

139

loveliness. The lake sparkled in the sunshine, and as they shot past its tiny bays and woody headlands new beauties were every moment revealed to them. But while the scene softened Wyat's feelings, it filled him with intolerable remorse, and so poignant did his emotions become that he pressed his hands upon his eyes to shut out the lovely prospect. When he looked up again, the scene was changed. The skiff had entered a narrow creek, arched over by huge trees, and looking as dark and gloomy as the rest of the lake was fair and smiling. It was closed in by a high overhanging bank, crested by two tall trees, whose tangled roots protruded through it, like monstrous reptiles, while their branches cast a heavy shade over the deep, sluggish water.

" Why have you come here ? " demanded Wyat, looking uneasily round the forbidding spot.

" You will discover anon," replied Fenwolf moodily.

" Go back into the sunshine, and take me to some pleasant bank—I will not land here," said Wyat sternly.

" Needs must when—I need not remind you of the proverb," rejoined Fenwolf, with a sneer.

" Give me the oars, thou malapert knave ! " cried Wyat fiercely ; " and I will put myself ashore."

" Keep quiet," said Fenwolf; " you must, perforce, abide our master's coming."

Wyat gazed at the keeper for a moment, as if with the intention of throwing him overboard ; but, abandoning the idea, he rose up in the boat, and caught at what he took to be the root of the tree above. To his surprise and alarm, it closed upon him with an iron grasp, and he felt himself dragged upwards, while the skiff, impelled by a sudden stroke from Morgan Fenwolf, shot from beneath him. All Wyat's efforts to disengage himself were vain, and a wild, demoniacal laugh, echoed by a chorus of voices, proclaimed him in the power of Herne the hunter. The next moment he was set on the top of the bank, while the demon greeted him with a mocking laugh.

" So, you thought to escape me, Sir Thomas Wyat ! "

he cried, in a taunting tone—" but any such attempt will prove fruitless. The murderer may repent the blow when dealt; the thief may desire to restore the gold he has purloined; the barterer of his soul may rue his bargain; —but they are Satan's nevertheless. You are mine, and nothing can redeem you ! "

" Woe is me, that it should be so ! " groaned Wyat.

" Lamentation is useless and unworthy of you," rejoined Herne scornfully. " Your wish will be speedily accomplished. This very night your kingly rival shall be placed in your hands."

" Ha ! " exclaimed Wyat, the flame of jealousy again rising within his breast.

" You can make your own terms with him for the Lady Anne," pursued Herne. " His life will be at your disposal."

" Do you promise this ? " cried Wyat.

" Ay," replied Herne. " Put yourself under the conduct of Fenwolf, and all shall happen as you desire. We shall meet again at night. I have other business on hand now. Meschines," he added, to one of his attendants, " go with Sir Thomas to the skiff."

The personage who received the command, and who was wildly and fantastically habited, beckoned Wyat to follow him, and, after many twistings and turnings, brought them to the edge of the lake, where the skiff was lying, with Fenwolf reclining at full length upon its benches. He arose, however, quickly, on the appearance of Meschines, and asked him for some provisions, which the latter promised to bring; and while Wyat got into the skiff he disappeared, but returned, a few minutes afterwards, with a basket, which he gave to the keeper.

Crossing the lake, Fenwolf then shaped his course towards a verdant bank, enamelled with wild flowers, where he landed. The basket being opened was found to contain a flask of wine and the better part of a venison pasty, of which Wyat, whose appetite was keen enough after his long fasting, ate heartily. He then stretched himself on the velvet sod and dropped into a tranquil

141

slumber, which lasted to a late hour in the evening. He was roused from it by a hand laid on his shoulder, while a deep voice thundered in his ear—" Up, up, Sir Thomas, and follow me, and I will place the king in your hands ! "

VIII

How the King and the Duke of Suffolk were assailed by Herne's band ; and what followed the attack

HENRY and Suffolk, on leaving the forester's hut, took their way for a short space along the side of the lake, and then turned into a path leading through the trees up the eminence on the left. The king was in a joyous mood, and made no attempt to conceal the passion with which the fair damsel had inspired him.

" I'faith ! " he cried, " the cardinal has a quick eye for a pretty wench. I have heard that he loves one in secret; and I am therefore the more beholden to him for discovering Mabel to me."

" You forget, my liege, that it is his object to withdraw your regards from the Lady Anne Boleyn," remarked Suffolk.

" I care not what his motive may be, as long as the result is so satisfactory," returned Henry. " Confess now, Suffolk, you never beheld a figure so perfect—a complexion so blooming—or eyes so bright. As to her lips, by my soul, I never tasted such ! "

" And your majesty is not inexperienced in such matters," laughed Suffolk. " For my own part, I was as much struck by her grace as by her beauty, and can scarcely persuade myself she can be nothing more than a mere forester's grand-daughter."

" Wolsey told me there was a mystery about her birth," rejoined Henry ; " but, pest on it ! her beauty drove all recollections of the matter out of my head. I will go back, and question her now."

" Your majesty forgets that your absence from the castle will occasion surprise, if not alarm," said Suffolk. " The mystery will keep till to-morrow."

" Tut, tut—I *will* return," said the king perversely. And Suffolk, knowing his wilfulness, and that all remonstrance would prove fruitless, retraced his steps with him.

They had not proceeded far, when they perceived a female figure at the bottom of the ascent, just where the path turn off on the margin of the lake.

" As I live, there she is ! " exclaimed the king joyfully. " She has divined my wishes, and is come herself to tell me her history."

And he sprang forward, while Mabel advanced rapidly towards him.

They met half-way, and Henry would have caught her in his arms, but she avoided him, exclaiming in a tone of confusion and alarm—" Thank Heaven ! I have found you, sire ! "

" Thank Heaven, too, sweetheart ! " rejoined Henry. " I would not hide when you are the seeker. So you know me—ha ? "

" I knew you at first," replied Mabel confusedly. " I saw you at the great hunting party; and once beheld, your majesty is not easily forgotten."

" Ha ! by Saint George ! you turn a compliment as soothly as the most practised dame at court," cried Henry, catching her hand.

" Beseech your majesty, release me ! " returned Mabel, struggling to get free. " I did not follow you on the light errand you suppose, but to warn you of danger. Before you quitted my grandsire's cottage I told you this part of the forest was haunted by plunderers and evil beings, and apprehensive lest some mischance might befall you, I opened the window softly to look after you——"

" And you overheard me tell the Duke of Suffolk how much smitten I was with your beauty, ha ? " interrupted the king, squeezing her hand—" and how resolved I was to make you mine—ha ! sweetheart ? "

" The words I heard were of very different import, my

liege," rejoined Mabel. " You were menaced by mis-
creants who purposed to waylay you before you could
reach your steed."

" Let them come," replied Henry carelessly, " they
shall pay for their villainy. How many were there ? "

" Two, sire," answered Mabel; " but one of them was
Herne, the weird hunter, of the forest. He said he would
summon his band to make you captive. What can your
strong arm, even aided by that of the Duke of Suffolk,
avail against numbers ? "

" Captive ! ha ! " exclaimed the king. " Said the
knave so ? "

" He did, sire," replied Mabel; " and I knew it was
Herne by his antlered helm."

" There is reason in what the damsel says, my liege,"
interposed Suffolk. " If possible, you had better avoid
an encounter with the villains."

" My hands itch to give them a lesson," rejoined Henry.
" But I will be ruled by you. God's death ! I will return
to-morrow, and hunt them down like so many wolves."

" Where are your horses, sire ? " asked Mabel.

" Tied to a tree at the foot of the hill," replied Henry.
" But I have attendants midway between this spot and
Snow Hill."

" This way, then ! " said Mabel, breaking from him,
and darting into a narrow path among the trees.

Henry ran after her, but was not agile enough to over-
take her. At length she stopped.

" If your majesty will pursue this path," she cried,
" you will come to an open space amid the trees, when,
if you will direct your course towards a large beech-tree
on the opposite side, you will find another narrow path,
which will take you where you desire to go."

" But I cannot go alone," cried Henry.

Mabel, however, slipped past him, and was out of
sight in an instant.

Henry looked as if he meant to follow her, but Suffolk
ventured to arrest him.

" Do not tarry here longer, my gracious liege," said

the duke. " Danger is to be apprehended, and the sooner you rejoin your attendants the better. Return with them, if you please, but do not expose yourself further now."

Henry yielded, though reluctantly, and they walked on in silence. Ere long, they arrived at the open space described by Mabel, and immediately perceived the large beech-tree, behind which they found the path.

By this time the moon had arisen, and as they emerged upon the marsh they easily discovered a track, though not broader than a sheep-walk, leading along its edge. As they hurried across it, Suffolk occasionally cast a furtive glance over his shoulder, but he saw nothing to alarm him. The whole tract of marshy land on the left was hidden from view by a silvery mist.

In a few minutes, the king and his companion gained firmer ground, and, ascending the gentle elevation on the other side of the marsh, made their way to a little knoll crowned by a huge oak, which commanded a fine view of the lake, winding through the valley beyond. Henry, who was a few yards in advance of his companions, paused at a short distance from the tree, and, being somewhat overheated, took off his cap to wipe his brow, laughingly observing, " In good truth, Suffolk, we must henceforth be rated as miserable faineants, to be scared from our path by a silly wench's tale of deer-stealers and wild huntsmen. I am sorry I yielded to her entreaties. If Herne be still extant, he must be more than a century and a half old, unless the legend is false, he flourished in the time of my predecessor, Richard the Second. I would I could see him ! "

" Behold him, then ! " cried a harsh voice from behind. Turning at the sound, Henry perceived a tall, dark figure, of hideous physiognomy and strange attire, helmed with a huge pair of antlers, standing between him and the oak tree. So sudden was the appearance of the figure that, in spite of himself, the king slightly started.

" What art thou ?—ha ! " he demanded.

" What I have said," replied the demon. " I am Herne the hunter. Welcome to my domain, Harry of England.

You are lord of the castle, but I am lord of the forest. Ha ! ha ! "

" I am lord both of the forest and the castle—yea, of all this broad land, false fiend ! " cried the king, " and none shall dispute it with me. In the name of the most holy faith of which I am the defender, I command thee to avoid my path ! Get thee backwards, Satan ! "

The demon laughed derisively.

" Harry of England, advance towards me, and you advance at your peril," he rejoined.

" Avaunt, I say ! " cried the king. " In the name of the blessed Trinity, and of all holy angels and saints, I strike ! "

And he whirled the staff round his head. But ere the weapon could descend, a flash of dazzling fire encircled the demon, amidst which he vanished.

" Heaven protect us ! " exclaimed Henry, appalled.

At this juncture, the sound of a horn was heard, and a number of wild figures in fantastic garbs, some mounted on swarthy steeds, and accompanied by hounds, others on foot, issued from the adjoining covert, and hurried towards the spot occupied by the king.

" Aha," exclaimed Henry—" more of the same sort. Hell, it would seem, has let loose her hosts; but I have no fear of them. Stand by me, Suffolk."

" To the death, sire," replied the duke, drawing his sword.

By this time, one of the foremost of the impish crew had reached the king, and commanded him to yield himself prisoner.

" Dost know whom thou askest to yield, dog ? " cried Henry furiously.

" Yea," replied the other, " thou are the king ! "

" Then down on thy knees, traitor ! " roared Henry; " down all of ye and sue for mercy."

" For mercy—ha ! ha ! " rejoined the other; " it is thy turn to sue for mercy, tyrant ! We acknowledge no other ruler than Herne the hunter."

" Then seek him in hell ! " cried Henry, dealing the

speaker a tremendous blow on the head with his staff, which brought him senseless to the ground.

The others immediately closed round him, and endeavoured to seize the king.

" Ha ! dogs !—ha ! traitors ! " vociferated Henry, plying his staff with great activity, and bringing down an assailant at each stroke; " do you dare to lay hands upon our sacred person ? Back ! back ! "

The determined resistance offered by the king, supported as he was by Suffolk, paralysed his assailants, who seemed more bent upon securing his person than on doing him injury. But Suffolk's attention was presently diverted by the attack of a fierce black hound, set upon him by a stout fellow in a bearded mask. After a hard struggle, and not before he had been severely bitten in the arm, the duke contrived to despatch his assailant.

" This to avenge poor Bawsey ! " cried the man who had set on the hound, stabbing at Suffolk with his knife.

But the duke parried the blow, and, disarming his antagonist, forced him to the ground, and tearing off his mask, disclosed the features of Morgan Fenwolf.

Meanwhile, Henry had been placed in considerable jeopardy. Like Suffolk, he had slaughtered a hound, and, in aiming a blow at the villain who set it on, his foot slipped, and he lay at his mercy. The wretch raised his knife, and was in the act of striking, when a sword was passed through his body. The blow was decisive; the king instantly arose, and the rest of his assailants—horse as well as foot—disheartened by what had occurred, beat a hasty retreat. Harry turned to look for his deliverer, and uttered an exclamation of astonishment and anger.

" Ah ! God's death ! " he cried, " can I believe my eyes? Is it you, Sir Thomas Wyat ? "

" Ay," replied the other.

" What do you here ? ha ! " demanded the king. " You should be in Paris."

" I have tarried for revenge," replied Wyat.

" Revenge !—ha ! " cried Henry. " On whom ? "

" On you," replied Wyat.

" What ! " vociferated Henry, foaming with rage—
" Is it you, traitor, who have devised this damnable
plot ?—is it you would make your king a captive ?—you
who slay him ? Have you leagued yourself with fiends?"

But Wyat made no answer; and though he lowered
the point of his sword, he regarded the king sternly.

A female figure now rushed forward, and bending
before the king, cried, in an imploring voice—

" Spare him, sire—spare him ! He is no party to the
attack. I was near him in yon wood, and he stirred not
forth till he saw your life in danger. He then delivered
you from the assassin."

" I did so because I reserved him for my own hand,"
said Wyat.

" You hear him confess his treason," cried Henry;
" down on your knees, villain, or I will strike you to
my feet."

" He has just saved your life, my liege," cried the
supplicant. " Oh, spare him ! "

" What makes you here, Mabel ? " cried Henry
angrily.

" I followed your majesty unseen," she replied, in some
confusion, " and reached yon wood just as the attack
commenced. I did not dare to advance further."

" You should have gone home—gone home," rejoined
the king. " Wyat," he continued, in a tone of stern
reproach, " you were once a loyal subject. What means
this change ? "

" It means that you have robbed me of a mistress,"
replied Wyat; " and for this cause I have damned myself."

" Pardon him !—oh, pardon him, sire ! cried Mabel.

" I cannot understand you, Wyat," said Henry, after
a pause; " but I have myself suffered from the pangs of
jealousy. You have saved my life, and I will spare yours."

" Sire ! " cried Wyat.

" Suffolk ! " exclaimed Henry, looking towards the
duke, who was holding Fenwolf by the throat, " shall I
be justified in letting him go free ? "

" Strike !—strike ! " cried a deep voice in Wyat's ear ;
" your rival is now in your power."

" Far be it from me to thwart your majesty's generous
impulses," rejoined Suffolk. " It is true that Wyat has
saved your life ; and if he had been disposed to take it,
you have this moment exposed yourself to him."

" Sir Thomas Wyat," said the king, turning to him,
" you have my full and free pardon. Quit this forest
instantly and make your way to Paris. If you are found
within it to-morrow, you will be lodged in the Tower."

Wyat knelt down, and would have pressed Henry's
hand to his lips ; but the latter pushed him aside.

" No—no ! Not now—on your return."

Thus rebuffed, Wyat strode away, and as he passed
the tree, he heard a voice exclaim—

" You have escaped him, but think not to escape *me !* "

" And now, sweetheart," said Henry, turning to Mabel,
" since you are so far on the way, you shall go with me
to the castle."

" On no account, my liege, she returned ; " my grandsire
will wonder what has become of me. He must already be
in great alarm."

" But I will send an attendant to quiet his fears," urged
Henry.

" That would only serve to increase them, she rejoined.
" Nay, I must go."

And breaking from him, she darted swiftly down the
hill, and glanced across the marsh like a moonbeam.

" Plague on it ! " cried Henry—" I have again forgotten to question her about her birth."

" Shall I despatch this knave, my liege ? " cried Suffolk,
pointing with his sword to Fenwolf.

" By no means," said the king ; "something may be
learned from him. Hark thee, thou felon hound—if thou
indeed servest the fiend, thou seest he deserts thee, as he
does all who put faith in him."

" I see it," replied Fenwolf, who, finding resistance
vain, had folded his hands doggedly upon his breast.

" Then confess thy evil practices," said the king.

" Give me my life, and I will," replied Fenwolf. And as he uttered the words, he caught sight of the dark figure of Herne, stationed at the side of the oak, with its right arm raised menacingly.

" What seest thou ? " cried Henry, remarking his fixed gaze towards the tree, and glancing in that direction.

Fenwolf made no reply.

Henry went up to the tree, and walked round it, but he could see nothing.

" I will scour the forest to-morrow," he muttered, " and hang every knave I find within it who cannot give a good account of himself."

" Ho ! ho ! ho ! " laughed a voice, which seemed to proceed from the branches of the tree.

Henry looked up, but no one was visible.

" God's death !—derided ! " he roared. " Man or devil, thou shalt feel my wrath."

" Ho ! ho ! ho ! " again laughed the voice.

Stamping with rage, Henry swore a great oath and smote the trunk of the tree with his sword.

" Your majesty will search in vain," said Suffolk ; " it is clearly the fiend with whom you have to deal, and the aid of holy priests must be obtained to drive them from the forest."

" Ho ! ho ! ho ! " again laughed the voice.

A party of horsemen now appeared in view. They proved to be the royal attendants, who had ridden forward in search of the king, and were instantly hailed by Henry and Suffolk. They were headed by Captain Bouchier, who, at a sign from the king, instantly dismounted.

" Give me your horse, Bouchier," said Henry, " and do you and half a dozen of your men remain on guard at this tree till I send a troop of arquebusiers to relieve you. When they arrive, station them near it, and let them remain here till I return in the morning. If any one appears, make him a prisoner."

" Your majesty's orders shall be faithfully obeyed," replied Bouchier.

Bound hand and foot, Fenwolf was thrown upon the back of a horse, and guarded by two halberdiers, who were prepared to strike him dead on the slightest movement. In this way, he was conveyed to the castle, and placed in the guard-chamber of the lower gate, till further orders should be issued respecting him.

IX

Showing how Morgan Fenwolf escaped from the Garter Tower

HALF an hour afterwards, Fenwolf was visited by the Duke of Suffolk and a canon of the college; and the guard-chamber being cleared, the duke enjoined him to make clear his bosom by confession.

" I hold it my duty to tell you, prisoner," said Suffolk, " that there is no hope of your life. The king's highness is determined to make a fearful example of you and all your companions in crime; but he does not seek to destroy your soul, and has therefore sent this holy man to you, with the desire that you may open your heart to him, and by confession and repentance save yourself from eternal perdition."

" Confession will profit me nothing," said Fenwolf moodily. " I cannot pray if I would."

" You cannot be so utterly lost, my son," rejoined the canon. " Hell may have woven her dark chains round you, but not so firmly but that the hand of Heaven can burst them."

" You waste time in seeking to persuade me," returned Fenwolf.

" You are not ignorant of the punishment inflicted upon those condemned for sorcery, my son ? " demanded the canon.

" It is the stake, is it not ? " replied Fenwolf.

" Ay," replied the canon; " but even that fiery trial

will fail to purge out your offences without penitence. My Lord of Suffolk, this wretched man's condition demands special attention. It will profit the church much to win his soul from the fiend. Let him, I pray you, be removed to the dungeon beneath the Garter Tower, where a priest will visit him, and pray by his side till daybreak."

" It will be useless, father," said Fenwolf.

" I do not despair, my son," replied the canon; " and when I see you again in the morning, I trust to find you in a better frame of mind."

The duke then gave directions to the guard to remove the prisoner; and after some further conference with the canon, returned to the royal apartments.

Meanwhile, the canon shaped his course towards the Horse-shoe Cloisters—a range of buildings so designated from their form, and situated at the west end of St. George's Chapel, and he had scarcely entered them when he heard footsteps behind him, and, turning at the sound, beheld a Franciscan friar, for so his habit of the coarsest gray cloth, tied with a cord round the waist, proclaimed him. The friar was very tall and gaunt, and his cowl was drawn over his face so as to conceal his features.

" What would you, brother ? " inquired the canon, halting.

" I have a request to make of you, reverend sir," replied the friar, with a lowly inclination of the head. " I have just arrived from Chertsey Abbey, whither I have been tarrying for the last three days, and while conversing with the guard at the gate I saw a prisoner brought into the castle, charged with heinous offences, and amongst others with dealings with the fiend."

" You have been rightly informed, brother," rejoined the canon.

" And I have, also, been rightly informed that you desire a priest to pass the night with him, reverend sir ? " returned the friar. " If so, I would crave permission to undertake the office. Two souls, as deeply laden as that

152

of this poor wretch, have been snatched from the jaws of Satan by my efforts, and I do not despair of success now."

" Since you are so confident, brother," said the canon, " I commit him readily to your hands. I was about to seek other aid, but your offer comes opportunely. With Heaven's help, I doubt not you will achieve a victory over the Evil One."

As the latter words were uttered, a sudden pain seemed to seize the friar. Staggering slightly, he caught at the railing of the cloisters for support, but he instantly recovered himself.

" It is nothing, reverend sir," he said, seeing that the good canon regarded him anxiously. " Long vigils and fasting have made me liable to frequent attacks of giddiness, but they pass as quickly as they come. Will it please you to go with me, and direct the guard to admit me to the prisoner ? "

The canon assented; and, crossing the quadrangle, they returned to the gateway.

Meanwhile, the prisoner had been removed to the lower chamber of the Garter Tower. This fortification, one of the oldest in the castle, being coeval with the Curfew Tower, is now in a state of grievous neglect and ruin. Unroofed, unfloored, filled with rubbish, masked by the yard walls of the adjoining habitations, with one side entirely pulled down, and a great breach in front, it is solely owing to the solid and rock-like construction of its masonry that it is indebted for partial preservation. Still, notwithstanding its dilapidated condition, and that it is the mere shell of its former self, its appearance is highly picturesque. The walls are of prodigious thickness, and the deep embrasures within them are almost perfect; while a secret staircase may still be tracked partly round the building. Amid the rubbish choking up its lower chamber grows a young tree, green and flourishing— a type, it is to be hoped, of the restoration of the structure !

Conducted to a low vaulted chamber in this tower, the

prisoner was cast upon its floor—for he was still bound hand and foot—and left alone and in darkness. But he was not destined to continue in this state long. The door of the dungeon opened, and the guard ushered in the tall Franciscan friar.

"What ho! dog of a prisoner," he cried, "here is a holy man come to pass the night with you in prayer."

"He may take his Ave Maries and Paternosters elsewhere—I want them not," replied Fenwolf moodily.

"You would prefer my bringing Herne the hunter, no doubt," rejoined the guard, laughing at his own jest; "but this is a physician for your soul. The saints help you in your good work, father. You will have no easy task."

"Set down the light, my son," cried the friar harshly, "and leave us. My task will be easily accomplished."

Placing the lamp on the stone floor of the dungeon, the guard withdrew, and locked the door after him.

"Do you repent my son?" demanded the friar, as soon as they were alone.

"Certes, I repent having put faith in a treacherous fiend who has deserted me—but that is all," replied Fenwolf, with his face turned to the ground.

"Will you put faith in me, if I promise you deliverance?" demanded the friar.

"You promise more than you can perform, as most of your brethren do," rejoined the other.

"You will not say so if you look up," said the friar.

Fenwolf started at the words, which were pronounced in a different voice from that previously adopted by the speaker, and raised himself as far as his bonds would permit him. The friar had thrown back his cowl, and disclosed features of appalling hideousness, lighted up by a diabolical grin.

"You here?" cried Fenwolf.

"You doubted me," rejoined Herne; "but I never desert a follower. Besides, I wish to show the royal Harry that my power is equal to his own."

" But how are we to get out of this dungeon ? " asked
Fenwolf, gazing round apprehensively.

" My way out will be easy enough," replied Herne;
" but your escape is attended with more difficulty. You
remember how we went to the vaulted chamber, in the
Curfew Tower, on the night when Mark Fytton, the
butcher, was confined within it."

" I do," replied Fenwolf. " But I can think of nothing
while I am tied thus."

Herne instantly drew forth a hunting-knife, and cutting
Fenwolf's bonds asunder, the latter started to his feet.

" If that bull-headed butcher would have joined me, I
would have liberated him, as I am about to liberate
you," pursued Herne. " But to return to the matter in
hand. You recollect the secret passage we then tracked?
There is such another staircase in this tower."

And, stepping to the further side of the chamber, he
touched, a small knob in the wall, and a stone flew back,
disclosing an aperture just large enough to allow a man
to pass through it.

" There is your road to freedom," he said, pointing
to the hole; " creep along that narrow passage, and it
will bring you to a small loophole in the wall, not many
feet from the ground. The loophole is guarded by a bar
of iron, but it is moved by a spring in the upper part of
the stone in which it appears to be mortised. This
impediment removed, you will easily force your way
through the loophole. Drop cautiously, for fear of the
sentinels on the walls; then make your way to the forest,
and if you 'scape the arquebusiers who are scouting it,
conceal yourself in the sandstone cave below the beech-
tree."

" And what of you ? " asked Fenwolf.

" I have more to do here," replied Herne impatiently
—" away ! "

Thus dismissed, Fenwolf entered the aperture, which
was instantly closed after him by Herne. Carefully
following the instructions of his leader, the keeper passed
through the loophole, let himself drop softly down, and,

keeping close to the walls of the tower till he heard the sentinels move off, darted swiftly across the street and made good his escape.

Meanwhile, Herne drew the cowl over his head, and stepping to the door, knocked loudly against it.

" What would you, father ? " cried the guard from without.

" Enter, my son, and you shall know," replied Herne.

The next moment the door was unlocked, and the guard advanced into the dungeon.

" Ha ! " he exclaimed, snatching up the lamp and looking around—" Where is the prisoner ? "

" Gone," replied Herne.

" What ! has the fiend flown away with him ? " cried the man, in mixed astonishment and alarm.

" He has been set free by Herne the hunter ! " cried the demon. " Tell all who question thee so, and relate what thou now seest."

At the words, a bright blue flame illumined the chamber, in the midst of which was seen the tall dark figure of Herne. His Franciscan gown had dropped to his feet, and he appeared habited in his wild deerskin garb. With a loud cry, the guard fell senseless to the ground.

A few minutes after this, as was subsequently ascertained, a tall Franciscan friar threaded the cloisters behind Saint George's Chapel, and, giving the word to the sentinels, passed through the outer door communicating with the steep descent leading to the town.

X

How Herne the Hunter was Himself Hunted

On the guard's recovery, information of what had occurred was immediately conveyed to the king, who had not yet retired to rest, but was sitting in his private chamber with the Dukes of Suffolk and Norfolk. The intelligence threw him into a great fury; he buffeted the guard, and ordered him to be locked up in the dungeon whence the prisoner had escaped; reprimanded the canon; directed the Duke of Suffolk, with a patrol, to make search in the neighbourhood of the castle for the fugitive and the friar; and bade the Duke of Norfolk get together a band of arquebusiers; and as soon as the latter were assembled he put himself at their head, and again rode into the forest.

The cavalcade had proceeded about a mile along the great avenue, when one of the arquebusiers rode up and said that he heard some distant sounds on the right. Commanding a halt, Henry listened for a moment, and satisfied that the man was right, quitted the course he was pursuing, and dashed across the broad glade now traversed by the avenue called Queen Anne's Ride. As he advanced, the rapid trampling of horses was heard, accompanied by shouts, and presently afterwards a troop of wild-looking horsemen in fantastic garbs was seen galloping down the hill, pursued by Bouchier and his followers. The king immediately shaped his course so as to intercept the flying party, and being in some measure screened by the trees, he burst unexpectedly upon them at a turn of the road.

Henry called to the fugitives to surrender, but they refused; and brandishing their long knifes and spears, made a desperate resistance. But they were speedily surrounded and overpowered. Bouchier inquired from the king what should be done with the prisoners.

157

"Hang them all upon yon trees!" cried Henry, pointing to two sister oaks which stood near the scene of strife.

The terrible sentence was immediately carried into execution. Cords were produced, and in less than half an hour twenty breathless bodies were hanging from the branches of the two trees indicated by the king.

"This will serve to deter others from like offences," observed Henry, who had watched the whole proceedings with savage satisfaction. "And now, Bouchier, how came you to let the leader of these villains escape?"

"I did not know he had escaped, my liege," replied Bouchier, in astonishment.

"Yea, marry, but he has escaped," rejoined Henry; "and he has had the audacity to shew himself in the castle within this hour, and the cunning, moreover, to set the prisoner free."

And he proceeded to relate what had occurred.

"This is strange, indeed, my liege," replied Bouchier, at the close of the king's recital; "and to my thinking is proof convincing that we have to do with a supernatural being."

"Supernatural!—pshaw—banish the idle notion," rejoined Henry sternly. "We are all the dupes of some jugglery. The caitiff will doubtless return to the forest. Continue your search, therefore, for him throughout the night. If you catch him, I promise you a royal reward."

So saying, he rode back to the castle, somewhat appeased by the wholesale vengeance he had taken upon the offenders.

In obedience to the orders he had received, Bouchier with his followers continued riding about the forest during the whole night, but without finding anything to reward his search, until about dawn it occurred to him to return to the trees on which the bodies were suspended. As he approached them, he fancied he beheld a horse standing beneath the nearest tree and immediately ordered his followers to proceed as noiselessly as possible, and to keep under the cover of the wood. A nearer advance convinced him that his eyes had not deceived him. It was a swart, wild-looking horse that he beheld, with eyes that flamed like carbuncles, while a couple of bodies, evidently snatched from the branches, were laid across its back. A glance at the trees, too, showed Bouchier that they had been considerably lightened of their hideous spoil.

Seeing this, Bouchier dashed forward. Alarmed by the noise, the wild horse neighed loudly, and a dark figure instantly dropped from the tree upon its back, and proceeded to disencumber it of its load. But before this could be accomplished, a bolt from a cross-bow, shot by one of Bouchier's followers, pierced the animal's brain. Rearing aloft, it fell backwards, in such a manner as would have crushed an ordinary rider, but Herne slipped off uninjured, and with incredible swiftness darted among the trees. The others started in pursuit, and a chase commenced, in which the demon huntsman had to sustain the part of a deer—nor could any deer have afforded better sport.

Away flew the pursued and pursuers over broad glade and through tangled glen—the woods resounding with their cries. Bouchier did not lose sight of the fugitive for a moment, and urged his men to push on; but despite his alternate proffers and menaces, they gained but little on Herne, who, speeding towards the Home Park, cleared its high palings with a single bound.

Over went Bouchier and his followers, and they then descried him making his way to a large oak, standing almost alone in the centre of a wide glade. An instant afterwards, he reached the tree, shook his arm menacingly at his pursuers and vanished.

The next moment, Bouchier came up; flung himself from his panting steed, and, with his drawn sword in hand, forced himself, through a rift in its side, into the tree. There was a hollow within it large enough to allow a man to stand upright, and two funnel-like holes ran upwards into the branches. Finding nothing, Bouchier called for a hunting spear, and thrust it as far as he could into the holes above. The point encountered no obstruction except such as was offered by the wood itself. He stamped upon the ground—and sounded it on all sides with the spear, but with no better success.

Issuing forth, he next directed his attention to the upper part of the tree, which, while he was occupied inside, had been carefully watched by his followers; and not content with viewing it from below, he clambered into the branches. But they had nothing to show, except their own leafy covering.

The careful examination of the ground about the tree at length led to the discovery of a small hole among its roots, about half a dozen yards from the trunk, and though this hole seemed scarcely large enough to serve for an entrance to the burrow of a fox, Bouchier deemed it expedient to keep a careful watch over it.

His investigation completed, he despatched a sergeant of the guard to the castle, to acquaint the king with what had occurred.

Disturbed by the events of the night, Henry obtained little sleep, and at an early hour summoned an attendant, and demanded whether there were any tidings from the forest. The attendant replied that a sergeant of the guard was without, sent by Captain Bouchier, with a message for his majesty. The sergeant was immediately admitted to the royal presence, and on the close of his marvellous story the king, who had worked himself into a tremendous fury during its relation, roared out—" What ! foiled again—ha ! But he shall not escape, if I have to root up half the trees in the forest. Bouchier and his fellows must be bewitched. Hark ye, knaves, get together a dozen of the best woodmen and yeomen in the castle—instantly, as you value your lives—bid them bring axe and saw, pick and spade. D'ye mark me—ha ! Stay, I have not done. I must have fagots and straw, for I will burn this tree to the ground—burn it to a char. Summon the Dukes of Suffolk and Norfolk—the rascal archer I dubbed the Duke of Shoreditch, and his mates—the keepers of the forest and their hounds—summon them quickly, and bid a band of yeomen of the guard get ready." And he sprang from his couch.

The king's commands were executed with such alacrity, that by the time he was fully attired, the whole of the persons he had ordered to be summoned were assembled. Putting himself at their head, he rode forth to the Home Park, and found Bouchier and his followers grouped around the tree.

"We are still at fault, my liege," said Bouchier.

"So I see, sir," replied the king angrily. "Hew down the tree instantly, knaves," he added to the woodmen. "Fall to—fall to."

Ropes were then fastened to the head of the tree, and the welkin resounded with the rapid strokes of the hatchets. It was a task of some difficulty, but such zeal and energy were displayed by the woodmen, that ere long, the giant trunk lay prostrate on the ground. Its hollows were now fully exposed to view, but they were empty.

"Set fire to the accursed piece of timber ! " roared the king—" burn it to dust, and scatter it to the wind ! "

At these orders, two yeomen of the guard advanced, and, throwing down a heap of fagots, straw, and other combustibles, on the roots of the tree, soon kindled a fierce fire.

Meanwhile, a couple of woodmen, stripped of their jerkins, and with their brawny arms bared to the shoulder, mounted on the trunk, and strove to split it asunder. Some of the keepers likewise got into the branches, and peered into every crack and crevice, in the hope of making some discovery. Amongst the latter was Will Sommers, who had posted himself near a great arm of the tree, which he maintained, when lopped off, would be found to contain the demon.

Nor were other expedients neglected. A fierce hound had been sent into the hole near the roots of the tree, by Gabriel Lapp, but after a short absence he returned howling and terrified; nor could all the efforts of Gabriel, seconded by a severe scourging with his heavy dog-whip, induce him to enter it again.

When the hound had come forth, a couple of yeomen advanced to enlarge the opening, while a third with a pick endeavoured to remove the root, which formed an impediment to their efforts.

" They may dig, but they'll never catch him," observed Shoreditch, who stood by, to his companions. " Hunting a spirit is not the same thing as training and raising a wolf, or earthing and digging out a badger."

" Not so loud, duke," said Islington, " his majesty may think thy jest irreverent."

" I have an arrow blessed by a priest," said Paddington, " which I shall let fly at the spirit, if he appears."

" Here he is ! here he is ! " cried Will Sommers, as a great white-horned owl, which had been concealed in some part of the tree, flew forth.

" It may be the demon in that form—shoot !—shoot ! " cried Shoreditch.

Paddington bent his bow. The arrow whistled through the air, and in another moment the owl fell fluttering to the ground completely transfixed; but it underwent no change, as was expected by the credulous archer.

Meanwhile, the fire, being kept constantly supplied with fresh fagots, and stirred by the yeomen of the guard, burnt bravely. The lower part of the tree was already consumed, and the flames, roaring through the hollow within, with a sound like that of a furnace, promised soon to reduce it to charcoal.

The mouth of the hole having now been widened, another keeper, who had brought forward a couple of lurchers, sent them into it; but in a few moments they returned, as the hound had done, howling, and with scared looks. Without heeding their enraged master, they ran off with their tails between their legs, towards the castle.

" I see how it is, Rufus," said Gabriel, patting his hound, who looked wistfully and half-reproachfully at him. " Thou wert not to blame, poor fellow ! The best dog that ever was whelped cannot be expected to face the devil."

Though long ere this it had become the general opinion that it was useless to persevere further in the search, the king, with his characteristic obstinacy, would not give it up. In due time, the whole of the trunk of the enormous tree was consumed, and its branches cast into the fire. The roots were rent from the ground, and a wide and deep trench digged around the spot. The course of the hole was traced for some distance, but it was never of any size, and was suddenly lost by the falling in of the earth.

At length, after five hours' watching, Henry's patience was exhausted, and he ordered the pit to be filled up, and every crevice and fissure in the ground about to be carefully stopped.

" If we cannot unkennel the fox," he said, " we will at least earth him up."

" For all your care, gossip Henry," muttered Will Sommers, as he rode after his royal master to the castle, " the fox will work his way out."

Book the Third

THE HISTORY OF THE CASTLE

I

Comprising the First Two Epochs in the History of Windsor Castle

AMID the gloom hovering over the early history of Windsor Castle appear the mighty phantoms of the renowned King Arthur and his knights, for whom, it is said, Merlin reared a magic fortress upon its heights, in a great hall whereof, decorated with trophies of war and of the chase, was placed the famous Round Table. But if the antique tale is now worn out, and no longer part of our faith, it is pleasant at least to record it, and surrendering ourselves for awhile to the sway of fancy, to conjure up the old enchanted castle on the hill, to people its courts with warlike and lovely forms, its forests with fays and giants, and its stream with beauteous and benignant sprites.

Windsor, or Wyndleshore, so called from the winding banks of the river flowing past it, was the abode of the ancient Saxon monarchs; and a legend is related by William of Malmsbury, of a woodman named Wulwin, who being stricken with blindness, and having visited eighty-seven churches and vainly implored their tutelary saints for relief, was at last restored to sight by the touch of Edward the Confessor, who further enhanced the boon by making him keeper of his palace at Windsor. But though this story may be doubted, it is certain that the pious king above mentioned granted Windsor to the abbot and monks of St. Peter at Westminster, " for the hope of eternal reward, the remission of his sins, the sins of his father, mother, and all his ancestors, and to the praise of Almighty God, as a perpetual endowment and inheritance."

But the royal donation did not long remain in the hands of the priesthood. Struck by the extreme beauty of the spot, " for that it seemed exceeding profitable and commodious, because situate so near the Thames, the wood fit for game, and many other particulars lying there, meet and necessary for kings—yea, a place very convenient for his reception," William the Conqueror prevailed upon Abbot Edwin to accept in exchange for it Wakendune and Feringes, in Essex, together with three other tenements in Colchester; and having obtained possession of the coveted hill, he forthwith began to erect a castle upon it—occupying a space of about half a hide of land. Around it, he formed large parks, to enable him to pursue his favourite pastime of hunting; and he enacted and enforced severe laws for the preservation of the game.

As devoted to the chase as his father, William Rufus frequently hunted in the forests of Windsor, and solemnised some of the festivals of the church in the castle.

In the succeeding reign—namely, that of Henry the First—the castle was entirely rebuilt and greatly enlarged —assuming somewhat of the character of a palatial residence, having before been little more than a strong hunting-seat. The structure then erected, in all probability, occupied the same site as the upper and lower wards of the present pile; but nothing remains of it except, perhaps, the keep, and of that little beyond its form and position. In 1109, Henry celebrated the feast of Pentecost with great state and magnificence within the castle. In 1122, he there espoused his second wife, Adelicia, daughter of Godfrey, Duke of Louvaine; and failing in obtaining issue by her, assembled the barons at Windsor, and caused them together with David, King of Scotland, his sister Adela, and her son Stephen, afterwards King of England, to do homage to his daughter Maud, widow of the Emperor Henry the Fifth.

Proof that Windsor Castle was regarded as the second fortress in the realm is afforded by the treaty of peace between the usurper Stephen and the Empress Maud, in which it is coupled with the Tower of London under the designation of *Mota de Windsor*. At the signing of the treaty, it was committed to the custody of Richard de

Lucy, who was continued in the office of keeper by Henry the Second.

In the reign of this monarch many repairs were made in the castle, to which a vineyard was attached—the cultivation of the grape being at this time extensively practised throughout England. Strange as the circumstance may now appear, Stow mentions that vines grew in abundance in the Home Park in the reign of Richard the Second, the wine made from them being consumed at the king's table, and even sold.

It is related by Fabian, that Henry, stung by the disobedience and ingratitude of his sons, caused an allegorical picture to be painted, representing an old eagle assailed by four young ones, which he placed in one of the chambers of the castle. When asked the meaning of the device, he replied, " I am the old eagle, and the four eaglets are my sons, who cease not to pursue my death. The youngest bird, who is tearing out its parent's eyes, is my son John, my youngest and best-loved son, and who yet is the most eager for my destruction."

On his departure for the holy wars, Richard Cœur de Lion entrusted the government of the castle to Hugh de Pudsey, Bishop of Durham and Earl of Northumberland ; but a fierce dispute arising between the warrior-prelate and his ambitious colleague, William Longchamp, Bishop of Ely, he was seized and imprisoned by the latter, and compelled to surrender the castle. After an extraordinary display of ostentation, Longchamp was ousted in his turn. On the arrival of the news of Richard's capture and imprisonment in Austria, the castle was seized by Prince John ; but it was soon afterwards taken possession of in the king's behalf by the barons, and consigned to the custody of Eleanor, the queen-dowager.

In John's reign, the castle became the scene of a foul and terrible event. William de Braose, a powerful baron, having offended the king, his wife, Maud, was ordered to deliver up her son as a hostage for her husband. But, instead of complying with the injunction, she rashly returned for answer—" that she would not entrust her child to the person who could slay his own nephew." Upon which, the ruthless king seized her and her son, and enclosing them in a recess in the wall of the castle, built them up within it.

Sorely pressed by the barons in 1215, John sought refuge within the castle, and in the same year signed the two charters, Magna Charta and Charta de Foresta, at Runnymede—a plain between Windsor and Staines. A curious account of his frantic demeanour, after divesting himself of so much power, and extending so greatly the liberties of the subject, is given by Holinshed:—" Having acted so far contrary to his mind, the king was right sorrowful in heart, cursed his mother that bare him, and the hour in which he was born; wishing that he had received death by violence of sword or knife instead of natural nourishment. He whetted his teeth, and did bite now on one staff, now on another, as he walked, and oft break the same in pieces when he had done, and with such disordered behaviour and furious gestures he uttered his grief, that the noblemen very well perceived the inclination of his inward affection concerning these things before the breaking-up of the council, and therefore sore lamented the state of the realm, guessing what would follow of his impatience, and displeasant taking of the matter." The faithless king made an attempt to regain his lost power, and war breaking out afresh in the following year, a numerous army, under the command of William de Nivernois, besieged the castle, which was stoutly defended by Inglehard de Achie and sixty knights. The barons, however, learning that John was marching through Norfolk and Suffolk, and ravaging the country, hastily raised the siege, and advanced to meet him. But he avoided them, marched to Stamford and Lincoln, and from thence towards Wales. On his return from this expedition, he was seized with the distemper of which he died.

Henry the Third was an ardent encourager of architecture, and his reign marks the second great epoch in the annals of the castle. In 1223, eight hundred marks were paid to Englehard de Cygony, constable of the castle, John le Draper, and William, the clerk of Windsor, masters of the works, and others, for repairs and works within the castle; the latter, it is conjectured, referring to the erection of a new great hall within the lower ward, there being already a hall of small dimensions in the upper court. The windows of the new building were filled with painted glass, and at the upper end, upon a raised dais, was a gilt throne sustaining a statue of the king in his robes. Within this vast and richly decorated chamber, in 1240, on the day of the Nativity, an infinite number of poor persons were collected and fed by the king's command.

During the greater part of Henry's long and eventful reign the works within the castle proceeded with unabated activity. Carpenters were maintained on the royal establishment; the ditch between the hall and the lower ward was repaired; a new kitchen was built; the bridges were repaired with timber procured from the neighbouring forest; certain breaches in the wall facing the garden were stopped; the fortifications were surveyed, and the battlements repaired. At the same time, the queen's chamber was painted and wainscoted, and iron bars were placed before the windows of Prince Edward's chamber. In 1240, Henry commenced building an apartment for his own use near the wall of the castle sixty feet long, and twenty-eight high; another apartment for the queen continuous to it; and a chapel seventy feet long, and twenty-eight feet wide, along the same wall, but with a grassy space between it and the royal apartments. The chapel, as appears from an order to Walter de Grey, Archbishop of York, had a galilee, and a cloister, a lofty wooden roof covered with lead, and a stone turret in front holding three or four bells. Withinside, it was made to appear like stonework with good ceiling and painting, and it contained four gilded images.

This structure is supposed to have been in existence, under the designation of the Old College Church, in the latter part of the reign of Henry the Seventh, by whom it was pulled down to make way for the tombhouse. Traces of its architecture have been discovered by diligent antiquarian research in the south ambulatory of the Dean's Cloister, and in the door behind the altar in St. George's Chapel, the latter of which is conceived to have formed the principal entrance to the older structure, and has been described as exhibiting "one of the most beautiful specimens which time and innovation have respected of the elaborate ornamental work of the period."

In 1241, Henry commenced operations upon the out-works of the castle, and the three towers on the western side of the lower ward—now known as the Curfew, the Garter, and the Salisbury Towers—were erected by him. He also continued the walls along the south side of the lower ward, traces of the architecture of the period being discoverable in the inner walls of the houses of the alms-knights as far as the tower now bearing his name. From thence, it is concluded that the ramparts ran along the east side of the upper ward to a tower occupying the site of the Wykeham or Winchester Tower.

The three towers at the west end of the lower ward, though much dilapidated, present unquestionable features of the architecture of the thirteenth century. The lower storey of the Curfew Tower, which has been but little altered, consists of a large vaulted chamber, twenty-two feet wide, with walls of nearly thirteen feet in thickness, and having arched recesses terminated by loopholes. The walls are covered with the inscriptions of prisoners who have been confined within it. The Garter Tower, though in a most ruinous condition, exhibits high architectural beauty in its moulded arches and corbelled passages. The Salisbury Tower retains only externally, and on the side towards the town, its original aspect. The remains of a fourth tower are discernible in the Governor of the Alms-Knights' Tower; and Henry the Third's Tower, as before observed, completes what remains of the original chain of fortifications.

On the 24th of November, 1244, Henry issued a writ enjoining " the clerks of the works at Windsor to work day and night to wainscot the high chamber upon the wall of the castle near our chapel in the upper bailey, so that it may be ready and properly wainscoted on Friday next [the 24th occurring on a Tuesday, only two days were allowed for the task], when we come there, with boards radiated and coloured, so that nothing be found reprehensible in that wainscot; and also to make at each gable of the said chamber one glass window, on the outside of the inner window of each gable, so that when the inner window shall be closed, the glass windows may be seen outside."

The following year the works were suspended, but they were afterwards resumed and continued, with few interruptions; the keep was new constructed; a stone bench was fixed in the wall near the grass-plot by the king's chamber; a bridge was thrown across the ditch to the king's garden, which lay outside the walls; a barbican was erected, to which a portcullis was subsequently attached; the bridges were defended by strong iron chains; the old chambers in the upper ward were renovated; a conduit and lavatory were added; and a fountain was constructed in the garden.

In this reign, in all probability, the Norman Tower, which now forms a gateway between the middle and the upper ward, was erected. This tower was used as a prison-lodging during the civil wars of Charles the First's time; and many noble and gallant captives have left mementoes of their loyalty and ill fate upon its walls.

In 1260, Henry received a visit at Windsor, from his daughter Margaret, and her husband, Alexander the Third, King of Scotland. The queen gave birth to a daughter during her stay at the castle.

In 1264, during the contest between Henry and the barons, the valiant Prince Edward, his son, returning from a successful expedition into Wales, surprised the citizens of London, and carrying off their military chest, in which was much treasure, retired to Windsor Castle, and strongly garrisoned it. The Queen Eleanor, his mother, would fain have joined him there, but she was driven back by the citizens at London Bridge, and compelled to take sanctuary in the palace of the Bishop of London, at St. Paul's.

Compelled, at length, to surrender the castle to the barons, and to depart from it with his consort, Eleanor of Castile, the brave prince soon afterwards recovered it, but was again forced to deliver it up to Simon de Montford, Earl of Leicester, who appointed Geoffrey de Langele governor. But though frequently wrested from him at this period, Windsor Castle was never long out of Henry's possession; and in 1265, the chief citizens of London were imprisoned till they had paid the heavy fine imposed upon them for their adherence to Simon de Montford, who had been just before slain at the battle of Evesham.

During this reign, a terrific storm of wind and thunder occurred, which tore up several great trees in the park, shook the castle, and blew down a part of the building in which the queen and her family were lodged, but happily without doing them injury.

Four of the children of Edward the First, who was blessed with numerous offspring, were born at Windsor; and as he frequently resided at the castle, the town began to increase in importance and consideration. By a charter granted in 1276, it was created a free borough, and various privileges were conferred on its inhabitants. Stow tells us, that in 1295, " on the last day of February, there suddenly arose such a fire in the castle of Windsor, that many offices were therewith consumed, and many goodly images, made to beautify the buildings, defaced and deformed."

Edward the Second, and his beautiful but perfidious queen, Isabella of France, made Windsor Castle their frequent abode; and here, on the 13th day of November, 1312, at forty minutes past five in the morning, was born a prince, over whose nativity the wizard Merlin must have presided. Baptised within the old chapel by the name of

Edward, this prince became afterwards the third monarch of the name, and the greatest, and was also styled from the place of his birth, EDWARD OF WINDSOR.

II

Comprising the Third Great Epoch in the History of the Castle ; and Showing how the Most Noble Order of the Garter was Instituted

STRONGLY attached to the place of his birth, Edward the Third, by his letters patent, dated from Westminster, in the twenty-second year of his reign, new founded the ancient chapel established by Henry the First, and dedicated it to the Virgin, St. George of Cappadocia, and St. Edward the Confessor; ordaining that to the eight canons appointed by his predecessor, there should be added one custos, fifteen more canons, and twenty-four alms-knights; the whole to be maintained out of the revenues with which the chapel was to be endowed. The institution was confirmed by Pope Clement the Sixth, by a bull issued at Avignon, the 13th November, 1351.

In 1349, before the foundation of the college had been confirmed, as above related, Edward instituted the Order of the Garter. The origin of this illustrious order has been much disputed. By some writers it has been ascribed to Richard Cœur de Lion, who is said to have girded a leathern band round the legs of his bravest knights in Palestine. By others it has been asserted that it arose from the word " garter " having been used as a watchword by Edward at the battle of Cressy. Others again have stoutly maintained that its ring-like form bore mysterious reference to the Round Table. But the popular legend, to which, despite the doubts thrown upon it, credence still attaches, declares its origin to be as follows: Joan, Countess of Salisbury, a beautiful dame, of whom Edward was enamoured, while dancing at a high festival, accidentally slipped her garter, of blue embroidered velvet. It was picked up by her royal partner, who, noticing the significant looks of his courtiers on the occasion, used the words to them, which afterwards became the motto of the order, " *Honi soit qui mal y pense* " ; adding, that " in a short time they should see that garter advanced to so high honour and estimation, as to account themselves happy to wear it."

But whatever may have originated the order, it unquestionably owes its establishment to motives of policy. Wise as valiant, and bent upon prosecuting his claim to the crown of France, Edward, as a means of accomplishing his object, resolved to collect beneath his standard the best knights in Europe, and to lend a colour to the design, he gave fourth that he intended a restoration of King Arthur's Round Table, and accordingly commenced constructing within the castle a large circular building of two hundred feet in diameter, in which he placed a round table. On the completion of the work, he issued proclamations throughout England, Scotland, France, Burgundy, Flanders, Brabant, and the Empire, inviting all knights, desirous of approving their valour, to a solemn feast and jousts to be holden within the castle of Windsor, on St. George's Day, 1345. The scheme was completely successful. The flower of the chivalry of Europe—excepting that of Philip the Sixth of France, who, seeing through the design, interdicted the attendance of his knights—were present at the tournament, which was graced by Edward and his chief nobles, together with his queen and three hundred of her fairest dames, " adorned with all imaginable gallantry." At this chivalrous convocation the institution of the Order of the Garter was arranged; but before its final establishment Edward assembled his principal barons and knights, to determine upon the regulations, when it was decided that the number should be limited to twenty-six.

The first installation took place on the anniversary of St. George, the patron of the order, 1349, when the king, accompanied by the twenty-five knights-companions, attired in gowns of russet, with mantles of fine blue woollen cloth, powdered with garters, and bearing the other insignia of the order, marched, bareheaded, in solemn procession, to the chapel of St. George, then recently rebuilt, where mass was performed by William Edington, Bishop of Winchester, after which they partook of a magnificent banquet. The festivities were continued for several days. At the jousts held on this occasion, David, King of Scotland, the Lord Charles of Blois, and Ralph, Earl of Eu and Guisnes, and constable of France, to whom the chief prize of the day was adjudged, with others, then prisoners, attended. The harness of the King of Scotland, embroidered with a pale of red velvet, and beneath it a red rose, was provided at Edward's own charge. This suit of armour was, until a few years back, preserved in the Round Tower, where the royal prisoner was confined. Edward's device was a white swan, gorged or, with the " daring and inviting " motto—

> *Hay hay the wythe swan*
> *By God's soul I am thy man.*

The insignia of the order in the days of its founder were the garter, mantle, surcoat and hood; the George and collar being added by Henry the Eighth. The mantle, as before intimated, was originally of fine blue woollen cloth, but velvet, lined with taffeta, was substituted by Henry the Sixth, the left shoulder being adorned with the arms of St. George, embroidered within a garter. Little is known of the materials of which the early garter was composed; but it is supposed to have been adorned with gold, and fastened with a buckle of the same metal. The modern garter is of blue velvet, bordered with gold wire, and embroidered with the motto—" *Honi soit qui mal y pense.*" It is worn on the left leg, a little below the knee. The most magnificent garter that ever graced a sovereign was that presented to Charles the First by Gustavus Adolphus, King of Sweden, each letter in the motto of which was composed of diamonds. The collar is formed of pieces of gold fashioned like garters, with a blue enamelled ground. The letters of the motto are in gold, with a rose enamelled red in the centre of each garter. From the collar hangs the George, an ornament enriched with precious stones, and displaying the figure of the saint encountering the dragon.

The officers of the order are, the prelate, represented by the Bishop of Winchester; the chancellor, by the Bishop of Oxford; the registrar, dean, garter king-at-arms, and the usher of the black rod. Among the foreign potentates who have been invested with the order are, eight emperors of Germany; two of Russia; five kings of France; three of Spain; one of Arragon; seven of Portugal; one of Poland; two of Sweden; six of Denmark; two of Naples; one of Sicily and Jerusalem; one of Bohemia; two of Scotland; seven princes of Orange; and many of the most illustrious personages of different ages in Europe.

Truly hath the learned Selden written, " that the Order of the Garter hath not only precedency of antiquity before the eldest rank of honour of that kind anywhere established, but it exceeds in majesty, honour, and fame, all chivalrous orders in the world." Well, also, hath glorious Dryden, in the " Flower and the Leaf," sung the praises of the illustrious institution :—

" Behold an order yet of newer date,
 Doubling their number, equal in their state;
 Our England's ornament, the crown's defence,
 In battle brave, protectors of their prince;
 Unchanged by fortune, to their sovereign true.
 For which their manly legs are bound with blue.
 These of the Garter call'd, of faith unstain'd,
 In fighting fields the laurel have obtain'd,
 And well repaid the laurels which they gain'd."

In 1357, John, King of France, defeated at the battle of Poitiers by Edward the Black Prince, was brought captive to Windsor; and on the festival of St. George in the following year, 1358, Edward outshone all his former splendid doings by a tournament which he gave in honour of his royal prisoner. Proclamation having been made as before, and letters of safe-conduct issued, the nobles and knighthood of Almayne, Gascoigne, Scotland, and other countries, flocked to attend it. The Queen of Scotland, Edward's sister, was present at the jousts; and it is said that John, commenting upon the splendour of the spectacle, shrewdly observed " that he never saw or knew such royal shows and feastings without some after reckoning." The same monarch replied to his kingly captor, who sought to rouse him from dejection, on another occasion—" Quomodo cantabimus canticum in terra aliena ! "

That his works might not be retarded for want of hands, Edward, in the twenty-fourth year of his reign, appointed John de Sponlee master of the stonehewers, with a power not only " to take and keep, as well within the liberties as without, as many persons and other artificers as were necessary, and to convey them to Windsor, but to arrest and imprison such as should disobey or refuse; with a command to all sheriffs, mayors, bailiffs, etc., to assist him." These powers were fully acted upon at a later period, when some of the workmen, having left their employment, were thrown into Newgate; while the place of others, who had been carried off by a pestilence then raging in the castle, was supplied by impressment.

In 1356, WILLIAM OF WYKEHAM was constituted superintendent of the works, with the same powers as John de Sponlee, and his appointment marks an important era in the annals of the castle. Originally secretary to Edward the Third, this remarkable man became Bishop of Winchester, and prelate of the Garter. When he solicited the bishopric, it is said that Edward told him that he was neither a priest nor a scholar; to which he replied that he would soon be the one, and in regard to the other, he would make more scholars than all the bishops of England ever did. He made good his word by founding the collegiate school at Winchester, and erecting New College at Oxford. When the Winchester Tower was finished, he caused the words HOC FECIT WYKEHAM, to be carved upon it; and the king, offended at his presumption, Wykeham turned away his displeasure by declaring that the inscription meant that the castle had made *him*, and not that *he* had made the castle. It is a curious coincidence, that this tower, after a lapse of four centuries and a half, should become the residence of an architect, possessing the genius of Wykeham, and who, like him, had rebuilt the kingly edifice—SIR JEFFRY WYATVILLE.

William of Wykeham retired from office, loaded with honours, in 1362, and was succeeded by William de Mulso. He was interred in the cathedral at Winchester. His arms were argent, two chevrons, sable, between three roses, gules, with the motto—" Manners maketh man."

In 1359, Holinshed relates, that the king " set workmen in hand to take down much old buildings belonging to the castle, and caused divers other fine and sumptuous works to be set up in and about the same castle, so that almost all the masons and carpenters that were of any account in the land were sent for and employed about the same works." The old buildings here referred to were probably the remains of the palace and the keep of Henry the First, in the middle ward.

As the original chapel dedicated to St. George was demolished by Edward the Fourth, its position and form cannot be clearly determined. But a conjecture has been hazarded that it occupied the same ground as the choir of the present chapel, and extended further eastward. " Upon the question of its style," says Mr. Poynter, from whose valuable account of the castle much information has been derived, " there is the evidence of two fragments discovered near this site, a corbel and a piscina, ornamented with foliage strongly characteristic of the *decorated English* Gothic, and indicating, by the remains of colour on their surfaces, that they belonged to an edifice adorned in the polychromatic style, so elaborately developed in the chapel already built by Edward the Third at Westminster."

The royal lodgings, St. George's Hall, the buildings on the east and north sides of the upper ward, the Round Tower, the canons' houses in the lower ward, and the whole circumference of the castle, exclusive of the towers erected in Henry the Third's reign, were now built. Among the earlier works in Edward's reign is the Dean's Cloister. The square of the upper ward, added by this monarch, occupied a space of four hundred and twenty feet, and encroached somewhat upon the middle ward. Externally, the walls presented a grim, regular appearance, broken only by the buttresses, and offering no other apertures than the narrow loopholes and gateways. Some traces of the architecture of the period may still be discerned in the archway and machecoulis of the principal gateway adjoining the Round Tower; the basement chamber of the Devil Tower, or Edward the Third's Tower; and in the range of groined and four-centred vaulting, extending along the north side of the upper quadrangle, from the kitchen gateway to King John's Tower.

In 1359, Queen Philippa, consort of Edward the Third, breathed her last in Windsor Castle.

Richard the Second, grandson of Edward the Third, frequently kept his court at Windsor. Here, in 1382, it was determined by council that war should be declared against France; and here, sixteen years later, on a scaffold erected within the castle, the famous appeal for high treason was made by Henry of Lancaster, Duke of Hereford, against Thomas Mowbray, Duke of Norfolk, the latter of whom defied his accuser to mortal combat. The duel was stopped by the king, and the adversaries banished; but the Duke of Lancaster afterwards returned to depose his banisher. About the same time, the citizens of London, having refused Richard a large loan, he summoned the lord mayor, sheriffs, aldermen, and twenty-four of the principal citizens, to his presence, and after rating them soundly, ordered them all into custody, imprisoning the lord mayor in the castle. In this reign, " Geoffrey Chaucer, the father of English poetry," was appointed clerk to the works of St. George's Chapel, at a salary of two shillings per day (a sum equal to 657*l.* per annum of modern money), with the same arbitrary power as had been granted to previous surveyors, to impress carpenters and masons. Chaucer did not retain his appointment more than twenty months, and was succeeded by John Gedney.

It was at Windsor that Henry the Fourth, scarcely assured of the crown he had seized, received intelligence of a conspiracy against his life from the traitorous Aumerle, who purchased his own safety at the expense of his confederates. The timely warning enabled the king to baffle the design. It was in Windsor, also, that the children of Mortimer, Earl of March, the rightful successor to the throne, were detained as hostages for their father. Liberated by the countess dowager of Gloucester, who contrived to open their prison-door with false keys, the youthful captives escaped to the marches of Wales, where, however, they were overtaken by the emissaries of Henry, and brought back to their former place of confinement.

A few years later, another illustrious prisoner was brought to Windsor—namely, Prince James, the son of King Robert the Third, and afterwards James the First of Scotland. This prince remained a captive for upwards of eighteen years; not being released till 1424, in the second of Henry the Sixth, by the Duke of Bedford, then regent. James's captivity, and his love for Jane of Beaufort, daughter of the Duke of Somerset, and grand-daughter to John of Gaunt, to whom he was united, have breathed a charm over the Round Tower, where he was confined; and his memory, like that of the chivalrous and poetical Surrey, whom he resembled in character and accomplishments, will be ever associated with it.

In the " King's Quair," the royal poet has left an exquisite picture of a garden nook, contrived within the dry moat of the dungeon.

" Now was there made, fast by the tower's wall,
    A garden faire, and in the corners set
An arbour green with wandis long and small
    Railed about, and so with leaves beset
Was all the place and hawthorn hedges knet,
    That lyf was none, walking there forbye,
    That might within scarce any wight espy.

" So thick the branches and the leavés green
    Beshaded all the alleys that there were,
And midst of every arbour might be seen
    The sharpe, green, sweet juniper,
Growing so fair with branches here and there,
    That as it seeméd to a lyf without
    The boughs did spread the arbour all about."

And he thus describes the first appearance of the lovely
Jane, and the effect produced upon him by her charms :—

" And therewith cast I down mine eye again,
    Where as I saw walking under the tower,
Full secretly, new comyn her to plain,
    The fairest and the freshest youngé flower
That e'er I saw, methought, before that hour ;
    For which sudden abate, anon did start
    The blood of all my body to my heart."

Henry the Fifth occasionally kept his court at Windsor,
and in 1416 entertained with great magnificence the
Emperor Sigismund, who brought with him an invaluable
relic—the heart of St. George, which he bestowed upon
the chapter. The emperor was at the same time invested
with the order.

In 1421, the unfortunate Henry the Sixth was born
within the castle : and, in 1484, he was interred within it.

III

Comprising the Fourth Epoch in the History of the Castle ; and showing how St. George's Chapel was Rebuilt by King Edward the Fourth

FINDING the foundation and walls of St. George's Chapel much dilapidated and decayed, Edward the Fourth resolved to pull down the pile, and build a larger and statelier structure in its place. With this view, he constituted Richard Beauchamp, Bishop of Salisbury, surveyor of the works, from whose designs arose the present beautiful edifice. To enable the bishop to accomplish the work, power was given him to remove all obstructions, and to enlarge the space by the demolition of the three buildings then commonly called Clure's Tower, Berner's Tower, and the Almoner's Tower.

The zeal and assiduity with which Beauchamp prosecuted his task is adverted to in the patent of his appointment to the office of chancellor of the Garter, the preamble whereof recites, " that out of mere love towards the order, he had given himself the leisure daily to attend the advancement and progress of this goodly fabric."

The chapel, however, was not completed in one reign, or by one architect. Sir Reginald Bray, prime minister of Henry the Seventh, succeeded Bishop Beauchamp as surveyor of the works, and it was by him that the matchless roof of the choir and other parts of the fabric were built. Indeed, the frequent appearance of Bray's arms, sometimes single, sometimes impaling his alliances, in many parts of the ceiling and windows, has led to the supposition that he himself contributed largely to the expense of the work. The groined ceiling of the chapel was not commenced till the twenty-seventh year of the reign of Henry the Seventh, when the pinnacles of the roof were decorated with vanes, supported by gilt figures of lions, antelopes, greyhounds, and dragons—the want of which is still a detriment to the external beauty of the structure.

"The main vaulting of St. George's Chapel," says Mr. Poynter, "is perhaps, without exception, the most beautiful specimen of the Gothic stone roof in existence; but it has been very improperly classed with those of the same architectural period in the chapels of King's College, Cambridge, and Henry the Seventh, at Westminster. The roofing of the aisle and the centre compartment of the body of the building are indeed in that style, but the vault of the nave and choir differ essentially from *fan* vaulting, both in drawing and construction. It is, in fact, a *wagon-headed* vault, broken by *Welsh groins*—that is to say, groins which cut into the main arch below the apex. It is not singular in the principle of its design, but it is unique in its proportions, in which the exact mean seems to be attained between the poverty and monotony of a wagon-headed ceiling, and the ungraceful effect of a mere groined roof with a depressed roof or large span. To which may be added, that with a richness of effect scarcely if at all inferior to fan tracery, it is free from those abrupt junctions of the lines and other defects of drawing inevitable when the length and breadth of the compartments of fan vaulting differ very much, of which King's College Chapel exhibits some notable instances."

Supported by these exquisite ribs and groins, the ceiling is decorated with heraldic insignia, displaying the arms of Edward the Confessor, Edward the Third, Edward the Black Prince, Henry the Sixth, Edward the Fourth, Henry the Seventh, and Henry the Eighth; with the arms of England and France quartered, the holy cross, the shield or cross of St. George, the rose, portcullis, lion rampant, unicorn, fluer-de-lis, dragon, and prince's feathers, together with the arms of a multitude of noble families. In the nave are emblazoned the arms of Henry the Eighth, and of several knights-companions, among which are those of Charles the Fifth, Francis the First, and Ferdinand, Infant of Spain. The extreme lightness and graceful proportions of the pillars lining the aisles contribute greatly to the effect of this part of the structure.

Beautiful, however, as is the body of the chapel, it is not comparable to the choir. Here, and on either side, are ranged the stalls of the knights, formerly twenty-six in number, but now increased to thirty-two, elaborately carved in black oak, and covered by canopies of the richest tabernacle-work, supported by slender pillars. On the pedestals is represented the history of the Saviour, and on the front of the stalls, at the west end of the choir, is carved the legend of St. George; while the outside of the upper seat is cut, in old Saxon characters, the twentieth psalm, in Latin. On the canopies of the stalls are placed the mantle, helmet, coat, and sword of the knights-companions; and above them are hung their emblazoned banners. On the back of each stall are fixed small enamelled plates, graven with the titles of the knights who have occupied it. The ancient stall of the sovereign was removed in 1788, and a new seat erected.

The altar was formerly adorned with costly hangings of crimson velvet and gold, but these, together with the consecrated vessels, of great value, were seized by order of parliament in 1642, and the general plunder of the foundation. The service of the altar was replaced by Charles the Second.

The sovereign's stall is immediately on the right on the entrance to the choir, and the prince's on the left. The queen's closet is on the north side, above the altar. Beneath it is a beautiful and elaborately-wrought framework of iron, representing a pair of gates between two Gothic towers, designed as a screen to the tomb of Edward the Fourth, and which, though popularly attributed to Quintin Matsys, has with more justice been assigned to Master John Tressilian.

One great blemish to the chapel exists in the window over the altar, the mullions and tracery of which have been removed to make way for dull, colourless copies in painted glass of West's designs. Instead of

——————blushing with the blood of kings,
And twilight saints and dim emblazonings

steeping the altar in rich suffusion, chequering the walls
and pavement with variegated hues, and filling the whole
sacred spot with a warm and congenial glow—these panes
produce a cold, cheerless, and most disagreeable effect.

The removal of this objectionable feature, and the
restoration of framework and compartments in the style
of the original, and enriched with ancient mellow-toned
and many-hued glass in keeping with the place, are
absolutely indispensable to the completeness and unity
of character of the chapel. Two clerestory windows at
the east end of the choir, adjoining the larger window,
have been recently filled with stained glass in much
better taste.

The objections above made may be urged with equal
force against the east and west windows, of the south
aisle of the body of the fane, and the west window of
the north aisle. The glorious west window, composed of
eighty compartments, embellished with figures of knights,
patriarchs, and bishops, together with the ensignia of the
Garter and the arms of the prelates—the wreck gathered
from all the other windows—and streaming with the
radiance of the setting sun upon the broad nave and
graceful pillars of the aisles—this superb window—an
admirable specimen of the architecture of the age in
which it was designed—had well-nigh shared the fate of
the others, and was only preserved from desecration by
the circumstance of the death of the glass-painter. The
mullions of this window being found much decayed, were
carefully and consistently restored by Mr. Blore, and the
ancient stained glass replaced.

Not only does St. George's Chapel form a house of
prayer and a temple of chivalry, but it is also the burial-
place of kings. At the east end of the north aisle of the
choir is a plain flag, bearing the words :—

King Edward IIII, and his Queen Elizabeth Widville

The coat of mail, and surcoat, decorated with rubies and precious stones, together with other rich trophies once ornamenting this tomb, were carried off by the parliamentary plunderers. Edward's queen, Elizabeth Woodville, it was thought slept beside him; but when the royal tomb was opened in 1789, and the two coffins within it examined, the smaller one was found empty. The queen's body was subsequently discovered in a stone coffin by the workmen employed in excavating the vault for George the Third. Edward's coffin was seven feet long, and contained a perfect skeleton. On the opposite aisle, near the choir door, as already mentioned, rests the ill-fated Henry the Sixth, beneath an arch sumptuously embellished by Henry the Eighth, on the keystone of which may still be seen his arms, supported by two antelopes connected by a golden chain. Henry's body was removed from Chertsey, where it was first interred, and reburied in 1484, with much solemnity, in this spot. Such was the opinion entertained of his sanctity, that miracles were supposed to be wrought upon his tomb, and Henry the Seventh applied to have him canonised, but the demands of the pope were too exorbitant. The proximity of Henry and Edward in death suggested the following lines to Pope:—

> " Here, o'er the martyr-king the marble weeps,
>   And fast beside him once-fear'd Edward sleeps;
>   The grave unites, where e'en the grave finds rest,
>   And mingled lie the oppressor and the opprest."

In the royal vault in the choir repose Henry the Eighth and his third queen, Jane Seymour, together with the martyred Charles the First.

Space only permits the hasty enumeration of the different beautiful chapels and chantries adorning this splendid fane. These are, Lincoln Chapel, near which Richard Beauchamp, Bishop of Salisbury, is buried; Oxenbridge Chapel; Aldworth Chapel; Bray Chapel, where rests the body of Sir Reginald de Bray, the architect of the pile; Beaufort Chapel, containing sumptuous monuments of the noble family of that name; Rutland Chapel; Hastings Chapel; and Urswick Chapel, in which is now placed the cenotaph of the Princess Charlotte, sculptured by Matthew Wyatt.

In a vault near the sovereign's stall lie the remains of the Duke of Gloucester, who died in 1805, and of his duchess, who died two years after him. And near the entrance of the south door is a slab of gray marble, beneath which lies one who in his day filled the highest offices of the realm, and was the brother of a king and the husband of a queen. It is inscribed with the great name of CHARLES BRANDON.

At the east end of the north aisle is the chapter-house, in which is a portrait and the sword of state of Edward the Third.

Adjoining the chapel, on the east, stands the royal tomb-house. Commenced by Henry the Seventh as a mausoleum, but abandoned for the chapel in Westminster Abbey, this structure was granted by Henry the Eighth to Wolsey, who, intending it as a place of burial for himself, erected within it a sumptuous monument of black and white marble, with eight large brazen columns placed around it, and four others in the form of candlesticks. At the time of the cardinal's disgrace, when the building reverted to the crown, the monument was far advanced towards completion—the vast sum of 4280 ducats having been paid to Benedetto, a Florentine sculptor, for work, and nearly four hundred pounds for gilding part of it. This tomb was stripped of its ornaments, and destroyed by the parliamentary rebels in 1646; but the black marble sarcophagus forming part of it, and intended as a receptacle for Wolsey's own remains, escaped destruction, and now covers the grave of Nelson in a crypt of St. Paul's Cathedral.

Henry the Eighth was not interred in this mausoleum, but in St. George's Chapel, as has just been mentioned, and as he himself directed, " midway between the state and the high altar." Full instructions were left by him for the erection of a monument, which, if it had been completed, would have been truly magnificent. The pavement was to be of oriental stones, with two great steps upon it of the same material. The two pillars of the church between which the tomb was to be set were to be covered with bas-reliefs, representing the chief events of the Old Testament, angels with gilt garlands, fourteen images of the prophets, the apostles, the evangelists, and the four doctors of the church, and at the foot of every image a little child with a basket full of red and white roses enamelled and gilt. Between these pillars, on a basement of white marble, the epitaphs of the king and queen were to be written in letters of gold. On the same basement were to be two tombs of black touchstone supporting the images of the king and queen, not as dead, but sleeping, " to show," so runs the order " that famous princes leaving behind them great fame do never die." On the right hand, at either corner of the tomb, was to be an angel holding the king's arms, with a great candlestick, and at the opposite corners, two other angels bearing the queen's arms and candlesticks. Between the two black tombs was to rise a high basement like a sepulchre, surmounted by a statue of the king on horseback, in armour—both figures to be " of the whole stature of a goodly man and a large horse." Over this statue was to be a canopy, like a triumphal arch, of white marble, garnished with oriental stones of divers colours, with the story of St. John the Baptist wrought in gilt brass upon it, with a crowning group of the Father holding the soul of the king in his right hand and the soul of the queen in his left, and blessing them. The height of the monument was to be twenty-eight feet. The number of statues was to be one hundred and thirty-four, with fortyfour bas-reliefs. It would be matter of infinite regret that this great design was never executed, if its destruction by the parliamentary plunderers would not in that case have been, also, matter of certainty.

Charles the First intended to fit up this structure as a royal mausoleum, but was diverted from the plan by the outbreak of the civil war. It was afterwards used as a chapel by James the Second, and mass was publicly performed in it. The ceiling was painted by Verrio, and the walls highly ornamented; but the decorations were greatly injured by the fury of an anti-catholic mob, who assailed the building, and destroyed its windows, on the occasion of a banquet given to the pope's nuncio by the king. In this state it continued till the commencement of the present century, when the exterior was repaired by George the Third, and a vault, seventy feet in length, twenty-eight in width, and fourteen in depth, constructed within it, for the reception of the royal family. Catacombs, formed of massive octangular pillars, and supporting ranges of shelves, line the walls on either side. At the eastern extremity, there are five niches, and in the middle twelve low tombs. A subterranean passage leads from the vault beneath the choir of St. George's altar to the sepulchre. Within it are deposited the bodies of George the Third and Queen Charlotte, the Princesses Amelia and Charlotte, the Dukes of Kent and of York, and the two last sovereigns, George the Fourth and William the Fourth.

But to return to the reign of Edward the Fourth, from which the desire to bring down the history of St. George's Chapel to the present time has led to the foregoing digression. About the same time that the chapel was built, habitations for the dean and canons were erected on the north-east of the fane, while another range of dwellings for the minor canons was built at its west end, disposed in the form of a fetter-lock, one of the badges of Edward the Fourth, and since called the Horse-shoe Cloisters. The ambulatory of these cloisters once displayed a fine specimen of the timber architecture of Henry the Seventh's time, when they were repaired, but little of their original character can now be discerned.

In 1482, Edward, desirous of advancing his popularity with the citizens of London, invited the lord mayor and aldermen to Windsor, where he feasted them royally, and treated them to the pleasures of the chase, sending them back to their spouses loaded with game.

In 1484, Richard the Third kept the feast of St. George at Windsor, and the building of the chapel was continued during his reign.

The picturesque portion of the castle on the north side of the upper ward, near the Norman gateway, and which is one of the noblest Gothic features of the proud pile, was built by Henry the Seventh, whose name it still bears. The side of this building looking towards the terrace was originally decorated with two rich windows, but one of them has disappeared, and the other has suffered much damage.

In 1500, the deanery was rebuilt by Dean Urswick. At the lower end of the court, adjoining the canons' houses behind the Horse-shoe Cloisters, stands the Collegiate Library, the date of which is uncertain, though it may perhaps be referred to this period. The establishment was enriched in later times by a valuable library, bequeathed to it by the Earl of Ranelagh.

In 1506, Windsor was the scene of great festivity, in consequence of the unexpected arrival of Philip, King of Castile, and his queen, who had been driven by stress of weather into Weymouth. The royal visitors remained for several weeks at the castle, during which it continued a scene of revelry, intermixed with the sports of the chase. At the same time, Philip was invested with the Order of the Garter, and installed in the chapel of St. George.

The great gateway to the lower ward was built in the commencement of the reign of Henry the Eighth; it is decorated with his arms and devices—the rose, portcullis, and fleur-de-lis, and with the bearings of Catharine of Arragon. In 1522, Charles the Fifth visited Windsor, and was installed knight of the Garter.

During a period of dissension in the council, Edward the Sixth was removed for safety to Windsor, by the lord protector, Somerset; and here, at a later period, the youthful monarch received a letter from the council urging the dismissal of Somerset, with which, by the advice of the Archbishop of Canterbury, he complied.

In this reign, an undertaking to convey water to the castle from Blackmore Park, near Wingfield, a distance of five miles, was commenced, though it was not till 1555, in the time of Mary, that the plan was accomplished, when a pipe was brought into the upper ward, " and there the water plenteously did rise thirteen feet high." In the middle of the court was erected a magnificent fountain, consisting of a canopy raised upon columns, gorgeously decorated with heraldic ornaments, and surmounted by a great vane, with the arms of Philip and Mary impaled upon it, and supported by a lion and an eagle, gilt and painted. The water was discharged by a great dragon, one of the supporters of the Tudor arms, into the cistern beneath, whence it was conveyed by pipes to every part of the castle.

Mary held her court at Windsor soon after her union with Philip of Spain. About this period, the old habitations of the alms-knights on the south side of the lower quadrangle were taken down, and others erected in their stead.

Fewer additions were made to Windsor Castle by Elizabeth than might have been expected from her predilection for it as a place of residence. She extended and widened the north terrace, where, when lodging within the castle, she daily took exercise, whatever might be the weather. The terrace at this time, as it is described by Paul Hentzner, and as it appears in Norden's view, was a sort of balcony projecting beyond the scarp of the hill, and supported by great cantilevers of wood.

In 1576, the gallery still bearing her name, and lying between Henry the Seventh's buildings and the Norman Tower, was erected by Elizabeth. This portion of the castle had the good fortune to escape the alterations and modifications made in almost every other part of the upper ward after the restoration of Charles the Second. It now forms the Library. A large garden was laid out by the same queen, and a small gateway on Castle Hill, built by her—which afterwards became one of the greatest obstructions to the approach, and it was taken down by George the Fourth.

Elizabeth often hunted in the parks, and exhibited her skill in archery, which was by no means inconsiderable, at the butts. Her fondness for dramatic performances likewise induced her to erect a stage within the castle, on which plays and interludes were performed. And to her admiration of the character of Falstaff, and her love of the locality, the world is indebted for the *Merry Wives of Windsor*.

James the First favoured Windsor as much as his predecessors; caroused within its halls, and chased the deer in its parks; Christian the Fourth of Denmark was sumptuously entertained by him at Windsor. In this reign a curious dispute occurred between the king and the dean and chapter respecting the repair of a breach in the wall, which was not brought to issue for three years, when, after much argument, it was decided in favour of the clergy.

Little was done at Windsor by Charles the First until the tenth year of his reign, when a banqueting-house erected by Elizabeth was taken down, and the magnificent fountain constructed by Queen Mary demolished. Two years afterwards, " a pyramid or lantern," with a clock, bell, and dial, was ordered to be set up in the front of the castle, and a balcony was erected before the room where Henry the Sixth was born.

In the early part of the year 1642, Charles retired to Windsor, to shield himself from the insults of the populace, and was followed by a committee of the House of Commons, who prevailed upon him to desist from the prosecution of the impeached members. On the 23rd of October, in the same year, Captain Fogg, at the head of a parliamentarian force, demanded the keys of the college treasury, and not being able to obtain them, forced open the doors, and carried off the whole of the plate.

The plunder of the college was completed by Vane, the parliamentary governor of the castle, who seized upon the whole of the furniture and decorations of the choir; rifled the tomb of Edward the Fourth; stripped off all the costly ornaments from Wolsey's tomb; defaced the emblazonings over Henry the Sixth's grave; broke the rich painted glass of the windows, and wantonly destroyed the exquisite woodwork of the choir.

Towards the close of the year 1648, the ill-fated Charles was brought a prisoner to Windsor, where he remained while preparations were made for the execrable tragedy soon afterwards enacted. After the slaughter of the martyr-monarch, the castle became the prison of the Earl of Norwich, Lord Capel, and the Duke of Hamilton, and other royalists and cavaliers.

Cromwell frequently resided within the castle, and often took a moody and distrustful walk upon the terrace. It was during the Protectorate, in 1657, that the ugly buildings, appropriated to the naval knights, standing between the Garter Tower and Chancellor's Tower, were erected by Sir Francis Crane.

I V

Containing the History of the Castle from the Reign of Charles the Second to that of George the Third; with a few particulars concerning the Parks and the Forest

ON the Restoration, the castle resumed its splendour, and presented a striking contrast to the previous gloomy period. The terrace, with its festive groups, resembled a picture by Watteau; the courts resounded with laughter; and the velvet sod of the Home Park was as often pressed by the foot of frolic beauty as by that of the tripping deer.

Seventeen state apartments were erected by Sir Christopher Wren, under the direction of Sir John Denham; the ceilings were painted by Verrio; and the walls decorated with exquisite carvings by Grinling Gibbons. A grand staircase was added at the same time.

195

Most of the chambers were hung with tapestry, and all adorned with pictures and costly furniture. The addition made to the castle by Charles was the part of the north front, then called the Star Building, from the star of the Order of the Garter worked in colours in the front of it, but now denominated the Stuart Building, extending eastward along the terrace from Henry the Seventh's building, one hundred and sevety feet. In 1676, the ditch was filled up, and the terrace carried along the south and east fronts of the castle.

Meanwhile, the original character of the castle was completely destroyed and Italianised. The beautiful and picturesque irregularities of the walls were removed; the towers shaved off; the windows transformed into commonplace circular-headed apertures. And so the castle remained for more than a century.

Edward the Third's Tower, indifferently called the Earl Marshal's Tower and the Devil Tower, and used as a place of confinement for state prisoners, was now allotted to the maids of honour. It was intended by Charles to erect a monument in honour of his martyred father on the site of the tomb-house, which he proposed to remove, and 70,000*l*. were voted by parliament for this purpose. The design, however, was abandoned under the plea that the body could not be found, though it was perfectly well known where it lay. The real motive probably was that Charles had already spent the money.

In 1680, an equestrian statue of Charles the Second, executed by Strada, at the expense of Tobias Rustat, formerly housekeeper at Hampton Court, was placed in the centre of the upper ward. It now stands at the lower end of the same court. The sculptures on the pedestal were designed by Grinling Gibbons; and Horace Walpole pleasantly declared that the statue had no other merit than to attract attention to them.

In old times, a road, forming a narrow irregular avenue, ran through the woods from the foot of the castle to Snow Hill. But this road having been neglected, during a long series of years, the branches of the trees and underwood had so much encroached upon it as to render it wholly impassable. A grand avenue, 240 feet wide, was planned by Charles in its place; and the magnificent approach called the Long Walk laid out and planted.

The only material incident connected with the castle during the reign of James the Second has been already related.

Windsor was not so much favoured as Hampton Court by William the Third, though he contemplated alterations within it during the latter part of his life, which it may be matter of rejoicing were never accomplished.

Queen Anne's operations were chiefly directed towards the parks, in improving which nearly 40,000*l.* were expended. In 1707, the extensive avenue running almost parallel with the Long Walk, and called the Queen's Walk, was planted by her; and three years afterwards, a carriage road was formed through the Long Walk. A garden was also planned on the north side of the castle. In this reign, Sir James Thornhill commenced painting Charles the Second's staircase with designs from Ovid's Metamorphoses, but did not complete his task till after the accession of George the First. This staircase was removed in 1800, to make way for the present Gothic entrance erected by the elder Wyatt.

The first two monarchs of the House of Hanover rarely used Windsor as a residence, preferring Hampton Court and Kensington; and even George the Third did not actually live in the castle, but in the Queen's Lodge—a large detached building, with no pretension to architectural beauty, which he himself erected opposite the south terrace, at a cost of nearly 44,000*l.* With most praiseworthy zeal, and almost entirely at his own expense, this monarch undertook the restoration of St. George's Chapel. The work was commenced in 1787, occupied three years, and was executed by Mr. Emlyn, a local architect. The whole building was repaved, a new altar-screen and organ added, and the carving restored.

In 1796, Mr. James Wyatt was appointed surveyor-general of the royal buildings, and effected many internal arrangements. Externally, he restored Wren's round-headed windows to their original form, and at the same time Gothicised a large portion of the north and south sides of the upper ward.

Before proceeding further, a word must be said about the parks. The Home Park, which lies on the east and north sides of the castle, is about four miles in circumference, and was enlarged and enclosed with a brick wall by William the Third. On the east, and nearly on the site of the present sunk garden, a bowling-green was laid out by Charles the Second. Below, on the north, were Queen Anne's gardens, since whose time the declivity of the hill has been planted with forest trees. At the east angle of the north terrace are the beautiful slopes, with a path skirting the north side of the Home Park, and leading through charming plantations in the direction of the royal farm and dairy, the ranger's lodge, and the kennel for the queen's harriers. This park contains many noble trees; and the grove of elms in the south-east, near the spot where the scathed oak assigned to Herne stands, is traditionally asserted to have been the favourite walk of Queen Elizabeth. It still retains her name.

The Great Park is approached by the magnificent avenue, called the Long Walk, laid out, as has been stated, by Charles the Second, and extending to the foot of Snow Hill, the summit of which is crowned by the colossal equestrian statue of George the Third, by Westmacott. Not far from this point stands Cumberland Lodge, which derives its name from William, Duke of Cumberland, to whom it was granted in 1744. According to Norden's survey, in 1607, this park contained 3050 acres; but when surveyed by George the Third it was found to consist of 3800 acres, of which 200 were covered with water. At that time the park was overgrown with fern and rushes, and abounded in bogs and swamps, which in many places were dangerous and almost impassable. It contained about three thousand head of deer in bad condition. The Park has since been thoroughly drained, smoothed, and new planted in parts, and two farms have been introduced upon it.

Boasting every variety of forest scenery, and commanding from its knolls and acclivities magnificent views of the Great Park is traversed in all directions, by green drives threading its long vistas, or crossing its open glades, laid out by George the Fourth. Amid the groves at the back of Spring Hill, in a charmingly-sequestered situation, stands a small private chapel, built in the Gothic style, and which was used as a place of devotion by George the Fourth during the progress of the improvements at the castle, and is sometimes attended by the present queen.

Not the least of the attractions of the park is Virginia Water, with its bright and beautiful expanse, its cincture of green banks, soft and smooth as velvet, its screen of noble woods, its Chinese fishing-temple, its frigates, its ruins, its cascade, cave, and Druidical temple, its obelisk and bridges, with numberless beauties besides, which it would be superfluous to describe here. This artificial mere covers pretty nearly the same surface of ground as that occupied by the great lake of olden times.

Windsor Forest once comprehended a circumference of a hundred and twenty miles, and comprised part of Buckinghamshire, a considerable portion of Surrey, and the whole south-east side of Berkshire, as far as Hungerford. On the Surrey side it included Chobham and Chertsey, and extended along the side of the Wey, which marked its limits as far as Guildford. In the reign of James the First, when it was surveyed by Norden, its circuit was estimated at seventy-seven miles and a half, exclusive of the liberties extending into Buckinghamshire. There were fifteen walks within it, each under the charge of a head keeper, and the whole contained upwards of three thousand head of deer. It is now almost wholly enclosed.

V

The Last Great Epoch in the History of the Castle

A PRINCE of consummate taste and fine conceptions, George the Fourth meditated, and what is better, accomplished, the restoration of the castle to more than its original grandeur. He was singularly fortunate in his architect. Sir Jeffry Wyatville was to him what William of Wykeham had been to Edward the Third. All the incongruities of successive reigns were removed; all, or nearly all, the injuries inflicted by time repaired; and when the work so well commenced was finished, the structure took its place as the noblest and most majestic palatial residence in existence.

To enter into a full detail of Wyatville's achievements is beyond the scope of the present work; but a brief survey may be taken of them. Never was lofty design more fully realised. View the castle on the north, with its grand terrace of nearly a thousand feet in length, and high embattled walls; its superb façade, comprehending the stately Brunswick Tower; the Cornwall Tower, with its gorgeous window; George the Fourth's Tower, including the great oriel window of the state drawing-room; the restored Stuart buildings, and those of Henry the Seventh and of Elizabeth; the renovated Norman Tower; the Powder Tower, with the line of walls as far as the Winchester Tower; view this, and then turn to the east, and behold another front of marvellous beauty extending more than four hundred feet from north to south, and displaying the Prince of Wales's Tower, the Chester, Clarence, and Victoria Towers—all of which have been raised above their former level, and enriched by great projecting windows; behold also the beautiful sunken garden, with its fountain and orangery, its flight of steps, and charming pentagonal terrace; proceed to the south front, of which the Victoria Tower, with its machicolated battlements and oriel window, forms so superb a feature at the eastern corner, the magnificent gateway receiving its name from George the Fourth, flanked by the York and Lancaster Towers, and opening in a continued line from the Long Walk; look at St. George's Gate, Edward the Third's renovated tower, and the octagon tower beyond it; look at all these, and if they fail to excite a due appreciation of the genius that conceived them, gaze at the triumph of the whole, and which lords over all the rest—the Round Tower—gaze at it, and not here alone, but from the heights of the Great Park, from the vistas of the Home Park, from the bowers of Eton, the meads of Clewer and Datchet, from the Brocas, the gardens of the naval knights—from a hundred points; view it at sunrise when the royal standard is hoisted, or at sunset when it is lowered, near or at a distance, and it will be admitted to be the work of a prodigious architect!

But Wyatville's alterations have not yet been fully considered. Pass through St. George's gateway, and enter the grand quadrangle to which it leads. Let your eye wander round it, beginning with the inner sides of Edward the Third's Tower, and George the Fourth's gateway, and proceeding to the beautiful private entrance to the sovereign's apartments, the grand range of windows of the eastern corridor, the proud towers of the gateway to the household, the tall pointed windows of St. George's Hall, the state entrance tower, with its noble windows, until it finally rests upon the Stuart buildings, and King John's Tower, at the angle of the pile.

Internally, the alterations made by the architect have been of corresponding splendour and importance. Around the south and east sides of the court at which you are gazing, a spacious corridor has been constructed, five hundred and fifty feet in length, and connected with the different suites of apartments on these sides of the quadrangle; extensive alterations have been made in the domestic offices; the state apartments have been repaired and rearranged; St. George's Hall has been enlarged by the addition of the private chapel (the only questionable change), and restored to the Gothic style; and the Waterloo chamber built to contain George the Fourth's munificent gift to the nation of the splendid collection of portraits now occupying it.

" The first and most remarkable characteristic of the operations of Sir Jeffry Wyatville on the exterior," observes Mr. Poynter, " is the judgment with which he has preserved the castle of Edward the Third. Some additions have been made to it, and with striking effect— as the Brunswick Tower, and the western tower of George the Fourth's gateway, which so nobly terminates the approach from the Great Park. The more modern buildings on the north side have also been assimilated to the rest; but the architect has yielded to no temptation to substitute his own design for that of William of Wykeham, and no small difficulties have been combated and overcome for the sake of preserving the outline of the edifice, and maintaining the towers in their original position."

The Winchester Tower, originally inhabited by William of Wykeham, was bestowed upon Sir Jeffry Wyatville as a residence by George the Fourth; and, on the resignation of the distinguished architect, was continued to him for life by Queen Victoria.

The works within the castle were continued during the reign of William the Fourth, and at its close the actual cost of the buildings had reached the sum of 771,000*l*., and it has been asserted that the general expenditure up to the present time has exceeded a million and a half of money.

The view from the summit of the Round Tower is beyond description magnificent, and commands twelve counties—namely, Middlesex, Essex, Hertford, Berks, Bucks, Oxford, Wilts, Hants, Surrey, Sussex, Kent, and Bedford; while, on a clear day, the dome of St. Paul's may be distinguished from it. This tower was raised thirty-three feet by Sir Jeffry Wyatville, crowned with a machicolated battlement, and surmounted with a flag-tower.

The circumference of the castle is 4180 feet; the length from east to west, 1480 feet; and the area, exclusive of the terraces, about twelve acres.

For the present the works are suspended. But it is to be hoped that the design of Sir Jeffry Wyatville will be fully carried out in the lower ward, by the removal of such houses on the north as would lay St. George's Chapel open to view from this side; by the demolition of the old incongruous buildings lying westward of the bastion near the "hundred steps," by the opening out of the pointed roof of the library; the repair and reconstruction in their original style of the Curfew, the Garter, and the Salisbury Towers; and the erection of a lower terrace extending outside the castle, from the bastion above mentioned to the point of termination of the improvements, and accessible from the town; the construction of which terrace would necessitate the removal of the disfiguring and encroaching houses on the east side of Thames Street. This accomplished, Crane's ugly buildings removed, and the three western towers laid open to the court, the Horse-shoe Cloisters consistently repaired, Windsor Castle would indeed be complete. And fervently do we hope that this desirable event may be identified with the reign of VICTORIA.

Book the Fourth

CARDINAL WOLSEY

I

*Of the Interview between Henry and Catharine of Arragon
in the Urswick Chapel; and how it was Interrupted*

IT was now the joyous month of June; and where is
June so joyous as within the courts and halls of peerless
Windsor? Where does the summer sun shine so brightly
as upon its stately gardens and broad terraces, its matchless parks, its silver belting river, and its circumference of
proud and regal towers? Nowhere in the world. At all
seasons, Windsor is magnificent; whether, in winter, she
looks upon her garniture of woods stripped of their
foliage—her river covered with ice—or the wide expanse
of country around her, sheeted with snow—or, in
autumn, gazes on the same scene—a world of golden-
tinted leaves, brown meadows, or glowing corn-fields.
But summer is her season of beauty—June is the month
when her woods are fullest and greenest; when her
groves are shadiest; her avenues most delicious; when
her river sparkles like a diamond zone; when town and
village, mansion and cot, church and tower, hill and vale,
the distant capital itself—all within view—are seen to the
highest advantage. At such a season, it is impossible to
behold from afar the heights of Windsor, crowned, like
the Phrygian goddess, by a castled diadem, and backed
by lordly woods, and withhold a burst of enthusiasm and
delight. And it is equally impossible, at such a season,
to stand on the grand northern terrace and gaze first at
the proud pile enshrining the sovereign mistress of the
land, and then gaze on the unequalled prospect spread
out before it, embracing in its wide range every kind of
beauty that the country can boast, and not be struck with
the thought that the perfect and majestic castle—

In state as wholesome as in state 'tis fit,
Worthy the owner, and the owner it—

together with the wide, and smiling, and populous district around it, form an apt representation of the British sovereign and her dominions. There stands the castle, dating back as far as the Conquest, and boasting since its foundation a succession of royal inmates, while at its foot lies a region of unequalled fertility and beauty —full of happy homes, and loving, loyal hearts—a miniature of the whole country and its inhabitants. What though the smiling landscape may be darkened by a passing cloud !—what though a momentary gloom may gather round the august brow of the proud pile !—the cloud will speedily vanish, the gloom disperse, and the bright and sunny scene look yet brighter and sunnier from the contrast.

But it was, as has been said, the merry month of June, and Windsor Castle looked down in all its magnificence upon the pomp of woods, and upon the twelve fair and smiling counties lying within its ken. A joyous stir was within its courts—the gleam of arms and the fluttering of banners were seen upon its battlements and towers, and the ringing of bells, the beating of drums, and the fanfares of trumpets, mingled with the shouting of crowds and the discharge of ordnance.

Amidst this tumult, a grave procession issued from the deanery, and took its way across the lower quadrangle, which was thronged with officers and men-at-arms, in the direction of the lower gate. Just as it arrived there, a distant gun was heard, and an answering peal was instantly fired from the culverins of the Curfew Tower, while a broad standard, emblazoned with the arms of France and England within the garter, and having for supporters the English lion, crowned, and the red dragon, sinister, was reared upon the keep. All these preparations betokened the approach of the king, who was returning to the castle, after six weeks' absence.

Though information of the king's visit to the castle had only preceded him by a few hours, everything was ready for his reception—and the greatest exertions were used to give splendour to it.

In spite of his stubborn and tyrannical nature, Henry was a popular monarch, and never showed himself before his subjects but he gained their applauses; his love of pomp, his handsome person and manly deportment, always winning him homage from the multitude. But at no period was he in a more critical position than the present. The meditated divorce from Catharine of Arragon was a step which found no sympathy from the better portion of his subjects, while the ill-assorted union of Anne Boleyn, an avowed Lutheran, which it was known would follow it, was equally objectionable. The seeds of discontent had been widely sown in the capital; and tumults had occurred which, though promptly checked, had nevertheless alarmed the king, coupled as they were with the disapprobation of his ministers, the sneering remonstrances of France, the menaces of the Papal see, and the open hostilities of Spain. But the characteristic obstinacy of his nature kept him firm to his point, and he resolved to carry it, be the consequences what they might.

All his efforts to win over Campeggio proved fruitless. The legate was deaf to his menaces or promises, well knowing that to aid Anne Boleyn would be to seriously affect the interests of the Church of Rome.

The affair, however, so long and so artfully delayed, was now drawing to a close. A court was appointed by the legatees to be holden on the 18th of June, at Black-friars, to try the question. Gardiner had been recalled from Rome to act as counsel for Henry; and the monarch, determining to appear by proxy at the trial, left his palace at Bridewell the day before it was to come on, and set out with Anne Boleyn and his chief attendants for Windsor Castle.

Whatever secret feelings might be entertained against him, Henry was received by the inhabitants of Windsor with every demonstration of loyalty and affection. Deafening shouts rent the air as he approached; blessings and good wishes were showered upon him; and hundreds of caps were flung into the air. But noticing that Anne

Boleyn was received with evil looks and in stern silence, and construing this into an affront to himself, Henry not only made slight and haughty acknowledgment of the welcome given him, but looked out for some pretext to manifest his displeasure. Luckily none was afforded him, and he entered the castle in a sullen mood.

The day was spent in gentle exercise within the Home Park and on the terrace, and the king affected the utmost gaiety and indifference; but those acquainted with him could readily perceive he was ill at ease. In the evening, he remained for some time alone in his closet penning despatches, and then summoning an attendant, ordered him to bring Captain Bouchier into his presence.

" Well, Bouchier," he said, as the officer made his appearance, " have you obeyed my instructions in regard to Mabel Lyndwood ? "

" I have, my liege," replied Bouchier. " In obedience to your majesty's commands, immediately after your arrival at the castle, I rode to the forester's hut, and ascertained that the damsel was still there."

" And looking as beautiful as ever, I'll be sworn ! " said the king.

" It was the first time I had seen her, my liege," replied Bouchier; " but I do not think she could have ever looked more beautiful."

" I am well assured of it," replied Henry. " The pressure of affairs during my absence from the castle had banished her image from my mind: but now it returns as forcibly as before. And you have so arranged it that she will be brought hither to-morrow night ? "

Bouchier replied in the affirmative.

" It is well," pursued Henry; " but what more ?—for you look as if you had something further to declare."

" Your majesty will not have forgotten how you exterminated the band of Herne the Hunter ? " said Bouchier.

" Mother of Heaven, no ! " cried the king, starting up—" I have not forgotten it. What of them ?—Ha ! have they come to life again ?—do they scour the parks once more ?—That were indeed a marvel ! "

"What I have to relate is almost as great a marvel," returned Bouchier. "I have not heard of the resurrection of the band, though for aught I know it may have occurred. But Herne has been seen again in the forest. Several of the keepers have been scared by him—travellers have been affrightened and plundered—and no one will now cross the Great Park after nightfall."

"Amazement!" cried Henry, again seating himself; "once let the divorce be settled, and I will effectually check the career of this lawless and mysterious being."

"Pray Heaven your majesty may be able to do so!" replied Bouchier. "But I have always been of opinion that the only way to get rid of the demon would be by the aid of the church. He is unassailable by mortal weapons."

"It would almost seem so," said the king. "And yet I do not like to yield to the notion."

"I shrewdly suspect that old Tristram Lyndwood, the grandsire of the damsel upon whom your majesty has deigned to cast your regards, is in some way or other leagued with Herne," said Bouchier. "At all events, I saw him with a tall, hideous-looking personage, whose name I understood to be Valentine Hagthorne, and who, I feel persuaded, must be one of the remnants of the demon-hunter's band."

"Why did you not arrest him?" inquired Henry.

"I did not like to do so without your majesty's authority," replied Bouchier. "Besides, I could scarcely arrest Hagthorne without at the same time securing the old forester, which might have alarmed the damsel. But I am ready to execute your injunctions now."

"Let a party of men go in search of Hagthorne to-night," replied Henry; "and while Mabel is brought to the castle to-morrow, do you arrest old Tristram, and keep him in custody till I have leisure to examine him."

"It shall be done as you desire, my liege," replied Bouchier, bowing and departing.

Shortly after this, Henry, accompanied by Anne Boleyn, proceeded with his attendants to St. George's

Chapel, and heard vespers performed. Just as he was about to return, an usher advanced towards him, and making a profound reverence, said that a masked dame, whose habiliments proclaimed her of the highest rank, craved a moment's audience of him.

"Where is she?" demanded Henry.

"In the north aisle, an please your majesty," replied the usher, "near the Urswick Chapel. I told her that this was not the place for an audience of your majesty, nor the time; but she would not be said nay, and therefore, at the risk of incurring your sovereign displeasure, I have ventured to proffer her request."

The usher omitted to state that his chief inducement to incur the risk was a valuable ring given him by the lady.

"Well, I will go to her," said the king. "I pray you, excuse me for a short space, fair mistress," he added, to Anne Boleyn.

And quitting the choir, he entered the northern aisle, and casting his eyes down the line of noble columns by which it is flanked, and seeing no one, he concluded that the lady must have retired into the Urswick Chapel. And so it proved; for on reaching this exquisite little shrine he perceived a tall, masked dame within it, clad in robes of the richest black velvet. As he entered the chapel, the lady advanced towards him, and throwing herself on her knees, removed her mask—disclosing features stamped with sorrow and suffering, but still retaining an expression of the greatest dignity. They were those of Catharine of Arragon.

Uttering an angry exclamation, Henry turned on his heel, and would have left her, but she clung to the skirts of his robe.

"Hear me a moment, Henry—my king—my husband —one single moment—hear me!" cried Catharine, in tones of such passionate anguish, that he could not resist the appeal.

"Be brief, then, Kate," he rejoined, taking her hand to raise her.

"Blessings on you for the word!" cried the queen,

covering his hand with kisses. " I am indeed your own true Kate—your faithful, loving, lawful wife ! "

" Rise, madam ! " cried Henry coldly, " this posture beseems not Catharine of Arragon."

" I obey you now as I have ever done," she replied, rising; " though if I followed the prompting of my heart, I should not quit my knees till I had gained my suit."

" You have done wrong in coming here, Catharine, at this juncture," said Henry, " and may compel me to some harsh measure which I would willingly have avoided."

" No one knows I am here," replied the queen, " except two faithful attendants, who are vowed to secrecy; and I shall depart as I came."

" I am glad you have taken these precautions," replied Henry. " Now speak freely, but again I must bid you be brief."

" I will be as brief as I can," replied the queen; " but I pray you bear with me, Henry, if I unhappily weary you. I am full of misery and affliction, and never was daughter and wife of king wretched as I am. Pity me, Henry—pity me ! But that I restrain myself, I should pour forth my soul in tears before you. Oh, Henry, after twenty years' duty and love, to be brought to this unspeakable shame—to be cast from you with dishonour —to be supplanted by another—it is terrible ! "

" If you have only come here to utter reproaches, madam, I must put an end to the interview," said Henry, frowning.

" I do not reproach you, Henry," replied Catharine meekly—" I only wish to show you the depth and extent of my affection. I only implore you to do me right and justice—not to bring shame upon me to cover your own wrongful action. Have compassion upon the princess, our daughter—spare her, if you will not spare me ! "

" You sue in vain, Catharine," replied Henry. " I lament your condition, but my eyes are fully opened to the sinful state in which I have so long lived, and I am resolved to abandon it."

" An unworthy prevarication," replied Catharine, " by

which you seek to work my ruin, and accomplish your union with Anne Boleyn. And you will no doubt succeed; for what can I, a feeble woman, and a stranger in your country, do to prevent it ? You will succeed, I say—you will divorce me, and place her upon the throne. But mark my words, Henry, she will not long remain there."

The king smiled bitterly.

" She will bring dishonour upon you," pursued Catharine. " The woman who has no regard for ties so sacred as those which bind us will not respect other obligations."

" No more of this ! " cried Henry. " You suffer your resentment to carry you too far."

" Too far ! " exclaimed Catharine. " Too far !—is to warn you that you are about to take a wanton to your bed—and that you will bitterly repent your folly, when too late, going too far ! It is my duty, Henry, no less than my desire, thus to warn you ere the irrevocable step be taken."

" Have you said all you wish to say, madam ? " demanded the king.

" No, my dear liege, not a hundredth part of what my heart prompts me to utter," replied Catharine. " I conjure you, by my strong and tried affection—by the tenderness that has for years subsisted between us—by your hopes of temporal prosperity and spiritual welfare —by all you hold dear and sacred—to pause while there is yet time. Let the legates meet to-morrow—let them pronounce sentence against me—and as surely as those fatal words are uttered, my heart will break."

" Tut, tut ! " exclaimed Henry impatiently—" you will live many years in happy retirement."

" I will die as I have lived—a queen," replied Catharine; " but my life will not be long. Now, answer me truly— if Anne Boleyn plays you false——"

" She never will play me false ! " interrupted Henry.

" I say, if she does," pursued Catharine, " and you are satisfied of her guilt, will you be content with divorcing her as you divorce me ? "

214

" No, by my father's head ! " cried Henry fiercely. " If such a thing were to happen, which I hold impossible, she should expiate her offence on the scaffold."

" Give me your hand on that," said Catharine.

" I give you my hand upon it," he replied.

" Enough," said the queen—" if I cannot have right and justice, I shall at least have vengeance, though it will come when I am in my tomb. But it *will* come, and that is sufficient."

" This is the frenzy of jealousy, Catharine," said Henry.

" No, Henry; it is not jealousy," replied the queen, with dignity. " The daughter of Ferdinand of Spain and Isabella of Castile, with the best blood of Europe in her veins, would despise herself if she could entertain so paltry a feeling towards one born so much beneath her as Anne Boleyn."

" As you will, madam," rejoined Henry. " It is time our interview terminated."

" Not yet, Henry—for the love of Heaven, not yet ! " implored Catharine. " Oh, bethink you by whom we were joined together !—by your father, Henry the Seventh—one of the wisest princes that ever sat upon a throne ; and by the sanction of my own father, Ferdinand the Fifth, one of the justest. Would they have sanctioned the match if it had been unlawful ? Were they destitute of good counsellors? Were they indifferent to the future ? "

" You had better reserve these arguments for the legate's ears to-morrow, madam," said Henry sternly.

" I shall urge them there with all the force I can," replied Catharine, " for I will leave nought untried to hinder an event so fraught with misery. But I feel the struggle will be hopeless."

" Then why make it ? " rejoined Henry.

" Because it is due to you—to myself—to the princess our daughter—to our illustrious progenitors—and to our people, to make it," replied Catharine. " I should be unworthy to be your consort if I acted otherwise—and

215

I will never, in thought, word, or deed, do aught derogatory to that title. You may divorce me, but I will never assent to it; you may wed Anne Boleyn, but she will never be your lawful spouse; and you may cast me from your palace, but I will never go willingly."

" I know you to be contumacious, madam," replied Henry. " And now, I pray you, resume your mask, and withdraw. What I have said will convince you that your stay is useless."

" I perceive it," replied Catharine. " Farewell, Henry —farewell, loved husband of my heart—farewell, for ever ! "

" Your mask—your mask, madam ! " cried Henry impatiently. " God's death ! footsteps are approaching. Let no one enter here ! " he cried aloud.

" I *will* come in," said Anne Boleyn, stepping into the chapel, just as Catharine had replaced her mask. " Ah ! your majesty looks confused. I fear I have interrupted some amorous conference."

" Come with me, Anne," said Henry, taking her arm, and trying to draw her away—" come with me."

" Not till I learn who your lady-love is," replied Anne pettishly. " You affect to be jealous of me, my liege, but I have much more reason to be jealous of you. When you were last at Windsor, I heard you paid a secret visit to a fair maiden near the lake in the park, and now you are holding an interview with a masked dame here. Nay, I care not for your gestures of silence. I will speak."

" You are distraught, sweetheart," cried the king. " Come away."

" No," replied Anne. " Let this dame be dismissed."

" I shall not go at your bidding, minion ! " cried Catharine fiercely.

" Ah ! " cried Anne, starting; " whom have we here ? "

" One you had better have avoided," whispered Henry.

" The queen ! " exclaimed Anne, with a look of dismay.

" Ay, the queen ! " echoed Catharine, unmasking.

" Henry, if you have any respect left for me, I pray you, order this woman from my presence. Let me depart in peace."

" Lady Anne, I pray you retire," said Henry.

But Anne stood her ground resolutely.

" Nay, let her stay, then," said the queen ; " and I promise you she shall repent her rashness. And do you stay too, Henry, and regard well her whom you are about to make your spouse. Question your sister Mary, somewhile consort to Louis the Twelfth and now Duchess of Suffolk—question her as to the character and conduct of Anne Boleyn when she was her attendant at the court of France—ask whether she had never to reprove her for levity—question the Lord Percy as to her love for him—question Sir Thomas Wyat, and a host of others."

" All these charges are false and calumnious," cried Anne Boleyn.

" Let the king inquire and judge for himself," rejoined Catharine, " and if he weds you, let him look well to you, or you will make him a scoff to all honourable men. And now, as you have come between him and me—as you have divided husband and wife—for the intent, whether successful or not, I denounce you before Heaven, and invoke its wrath upon your head. Night and day I will pray that you may be brought to shame; and when I shall be called hence, as I may be soon, I will appear before the throne of the Most High, and summon you to judgment."

" Take her from me, Henry ! " cried Anne faintly; " her violence affrights me."

" No, you shall stay," said Catharine, grasping her arm, and detaining her, " you shall hear your doom. You imagine your career will be a brilliant one, and that you will be able to wield the sceptre you wrongfully wrest from me, but it will moulder into dust in your hand —the crown unjustly placed upon your brow will fall to the ground, and it will bring the head with it."

" Take me away, Henry, I implore you ! " cried Anne.

" You *shall* hear me out," pursued Catharine, exerting

all her strength, and maintaining her grasp—" or I will follow you down yon aisles, and pour forth my malediction against you in the hearing of all your attendants. You have braved me, and shall feel my power. Look at her, Henry—see how she shrinks before the gaze of an injured woman. Look me in the face, minion—you cannot !—you dare not ! "

" Oh, Henry ! " sobbed Anne.

" You have brought it upon yourself," said the king.

"She has," replied Catharine; " and unless she pauses and repents, she will bring yet more upon her head. You suffer now, minion, but how will you feel when, in your turn, you are despised, neglected, and supplanted by a rival—when the false glitter of your charms having passed away, Henry will see only your faults—and will open his eyes to all I now tell him ? "

A sob was all the answer Anne could return.

" You will feel as I feel towards you," pursued the queen—" hatred towards her; but you will not have the consolations I enjoy. You will have merited your fate; and you will then think upon me and my woes, and will bitterly, but unavailingly, repent your conduct. And now, Henry," she exclaimed, turning solemnly to him, " you have pledged your royal word to me, and given me your hand upon it, that if you find this woman false to you, she shall expiate her offence on the block. I call upon you to ratify the pledge in her presence."

" I do so, Catharine," replied the king. " The mere suspicion of her guilt shall be enough."

" Henry ! " exclaimed Anne.

" I have said it ! " replied the king.

" Tremble, then, Anne Boleyn ! " cried Catharine, " tremble ! and when you are adjudged to die the death of an adulteress, bethink you of the prediction of the queen you have injured. I may not live to witness your fate, but we shall meet before the throne of an eternal Judge."

" Oh, Henry, this is too much ! " gasped Anne. And she sank fainting into his arms.

"Begone!" cried the king furiously. "You have killed her!"

"It were well for us both if I had done so," replied Catharine. "But she will recover to work my misery and her own. To your hands I commit her punishment. May God bless you, Henry!" With this she replaced her mask, and quitted the chapel.

Henry, meanwhile, anxious to avoid the comments of his attendants, exerted himself to restore Anne Boleyn to sensibility, and his efforts were speedily successful.

"Is it, then, reality?" gasped Anne, as she gazed around. "I hoped it was a hideous dream. Oh, Henry, this has been frightful! But you will not kill me, as she predicted? Swear to me you will not!"

"Why should you be alarmed?" rejoined the king. "If you are faithful, you have nothing to fear."

"But you said suspicion, Henry—you said suspicion!" cried Anne.

"You must put the greater guard upon your conduct," rejoined the king moodily. "I begin to think there is some truth in Catharine's insinuations."

"Oh! no; I swear to you there is not," said Anne. "I have trifled with the gallants of Francis's court, and have listened, perhaps too complacently, to the love-vows of Percy and Wyat, but when your majesty deigned to cast eyes upon me, all others vanished as the stars of night before the rising of the god of day. Henry, I love you deeply, devotedly—but Catharine's terrible imprecations make me feel more keely than I have ever done before the extent of the wrong I am about to inflict upon her—and I fear that retributive punishment will follow it."

"You will do her no wrong," replied Henry. "I am satisfied of the justice of the divorce, and of its necessity; and if my purposed union with you were out of the question, I should demand it. Be the fault on my head."

"Your words restore me, in some measure, my liege," said Anne. "I love you too well not to risk body and soul for you. I am yours for ever—ha ! " she exclaimed, with a fearful look.

" What ails you, sweetheart ! " exclaimed the king.

" I thought I saw a face at the window," she replied— " a black and hideous face like that of a fiend."

" It was mere fancy," replied the king. " Your mind is disturbed by what has occurred. You had better join your attendants, and retire to your own apartments."

" Oh, Henry ! " cried Anne—" do not judge me unheard—do not believe what any false tongue may utter against me. I love only you—and can love only you. I would not wrong you, even in thought, for worlds."

" I believe you, sweetheart," replied the king tenderly.

So saying, he led her down the aisle to her attendants. They then proceeded together to the royal lodgings, where Anne retired to her own apartments, and Henry withdrew to his private chamber.

II

How Herne the Hunter appeared to Henry on the Terrace

HENRY again sat down to his despatches, and employed himself upon them to a late hour. At length, feeling heated and oppressed, he arose, and opened a window. As he did so, he was almost blinded by a vivid flash of forked lightning. Ever ready to court danger, and convinced, from the intense gloom without, that a fearful storm was coming on, Henry resolved to go forth to witness it. With this view, he quitted the closet, and passed through a small door opening upon the northern terrace. The castle clock tolled the hour of midnight, as he issued forth, and the darkness was so profound that he could scarcely see a foot before him. But he went on.

" Who goes there ? " cried a voice, as he advanced, and a partisan was placed at his breast.

" The king ! " replied Henry, in tones that would have

left no doubt of the truth of the assertion, even if a gleam of lightning had not at that moment revealed his figure and countenance to the sentinel.

"I did not look for your majesty at such a time," replied the man, lowering his pike. "Has your majesty no apprehension of the storm? I have watched it gathering in the valley, and it will be a dreadful one. If I might make bold to counsel you, I would advise you to seek instant shelter in the castle."

"I have no fear, good fellow," laughed the king. "Get thee into yon porch, and leave the terrace to me. I will warn thee when I leave it."

As he spoke, a tremendous peal of thunder broke overhead, and seemed to shake the strong pile to its foundations. Again the lightning rent the black canopy of heaven in various places, and shot down in forked flashes of the most dazzling brightness. A rack of clouds, heavily charged with electric fluid, hung right over the castle, and poured down all their fires upon it.

Henry paced slowly to and fro, utterly indifferent to the peril he ran—now watching the lightning as it shivered some oak in the Home Park, or lighted up the wide expanse of country around him—now listening to the roar of heaven's artillery; and he had just quitted the western extremity of the terrace, when the most terrific crash he had yet heard burst over him. The next instant a dozen forked flashes shot from the sky, while fiery coruscations blazed athwart it; and at the same moment a bolt struck the Wykeham Tower, beside which he had been recently standing. Startled by the appalling sound, he turned and beheld upon the battlemented parapet on his left a tall ghostly figure, whose antlered helm told him it was Herne the hunter. Dilated against the flaming sky, the proportions of the demon seemed gigantic. His right hand was stretched forth towards the king, and in left he held a rusty chain. Henry grasped the handle of his sword, and partly drew it, keeping his gaze fixed upon the figure.

"You thought you had got rid of me, Harry of England," cried Herne,—" but were you to lay the weight of this vast fabric upon me, I would break from under it—ho ! ho ! "

" What wouldst thou, infernal spirit ? " cried Henry.

" I am come to keep company with you, Harry," replied the demon; " this is a night when only you and I should be abroad. We know how to enjoy it. We like the music of the loud thunder, and the dance of the blithe lightning."

" Avaunt, fiend ! " cried Henry, " I will hold no converse with thee. Back to thy native hell ! "

" You have no power over me, Harry," rejoined the demon, his words mingling with the rolling of the thunder, " for your thoughts are evil, and you are about to do an accursed deed. You cannot dismiss me. Before the commission of every great crime—and many great crimes you will commit—I will always appear to you. And my last appearance shall be three days before your end—ha ! ha ! "

" Darest thou say this to me ? " cried Henry furiously.

" I laugh at thy menaces," rejoined Herne, amid another peal of thunder—" but I have not yet done. Harry of England ! your career shall be stained in blood. Your wrath shall descend upon the heads of those who love you, and your love shall be fatal. Better Anne Boleyn had fled this castle, and sought shelter in the lowliest hovel in the land, than become your spouse. For you will slay her—and not her alone. Another shall fall by your hand; and so, if you had your own will, would all ! "

" What meanest thou by all ? " demanded the king.

" You will learn in due season," laughed the fiend. " But now mark me, Harry of England, thou fierce and bloody king !—thou shall be drunken with the blood of thy wives; and thy end shall be a fearful one. Thou shalt linger out a living death—a mass of breathing corruption shalt thou become—and when dead, the very hounds with which thou huntedst me shall lick thy blood ! "

These awful words, involving a fearful prophecy, which was afterwards, as will be shown, strangely fulfilled, were so mixed up with the rolling of the thunder, that Henry could scarcely distinguish one sound from the other. At the close of the latter speech, a flash of lightning of such dazzling brilliancy shot down past him, that he remained for some moments almost blinded; and when he recovered his powers of vision, the demon had vanished.

III

How Mabel Lyndwood was taken to the Castle by Nicholas Clamp; and how they encountered Morgan Fenwolf by the way

THE storm which had fallen so heavily on the castle had likewise visited the lake, and alarmed the inmates of the little dwelling on its banks. Both the forester and his grand-daughter were roused from their beds, and they sat together in the chief apartment of the cottage listening to the awful rolling of the thunder, and watching the blue flashing of the lightning. The storm was of unusually long duration, and continued for more than an hour with unintermitted violence. It then paused; the thunder rolled off, and the flashes of lightning grew fainter and less frequent. During the storm, Mabel continued on her knees, addressing the most earnest prayers to the Virgin for her preservation and that of her grandfather; but the old forester, though evidently much alarmed, uttered not a single supplication, but remained sitting in his chair with a sullen, scared look. As the thunder died away, he recovered his composure, and addressed himself to soothe the fears of his grand-daughter. In this he had partially succeeded, and was urging her again to seek her couch, when the storm recommenced with fresh fury. Mabel once more fell on her knees, and the old man resumed his sullen posture. Another dreadful half-hour, marked by a succession of terrible peals and vivid flashes, succeeded, when, amidst an awful pause, Mabel ventured to address her old relative.

"Why do you not pray, grandfather?" she said, regarding him uneasily. "Sister Anastasia and good Father Anselm always taught me to utter an Ave and cross myself during a thunderstorm. Why do you not pray, grandfather?"

"Do not trouble me," replied Tristram. "I have no fear."

"But your cheeks and lips are blanched," rejoined Mabel; "and I observed you shudder during that last awful crash. Pray, grandfather, pray!"

"Peace, wench, and mind your own business!" returned the old man angrily. "The storm will soon be over—it cannot last long in this way."

"The saints preserve us!" cried Mabel, as a tremendous concussion was heard overhead, followed by a strong sulphurous smell. "The cottage is struck!"

"It is—it is!" cried Tristram, springing to his feet, and rushing forth.

For a few minutes Mabel continued in a state of stupefaction. She then staggered to the door, and beheld her grandfather occupied with two dark figures, whom she recognised as Valentine Hagthorne and Morgan Fenwolf, in extinguishing the flames, which were bursting from the thatched roof of the hut. Surprise and terror held her silent; and the others were so busily engaged that they did not notice her. At last, by their united efforts, the fire was got under without material damage to the little building, and Mabel retired, expecting her grandsire to return; but as he did not do so, and as almost instantly afterwards the splash of oars was heard on the lake, she flew to the window, and beheld him, by the gleam of the lightning, seated in the skiff with Morgan Fenwolf, while Valentine Hagthorne had mounted a black horse, and was galloping swiftly away. Mabel saw no more. Overcome by fright, she sank on the ground insensible. When she recovered, the storm had entirely ceased. A heavy shower had fallen, but the sky was now perfectly clear, and day had begun to dawn. Mabel went to the door of the hut, and looked forth for her grandfather, but he was nowhere to be seen. She remained gazing at the now peaceful lake till the sun had fairly risen, when feeling more composed, she retired to rest, and sleep, which had been banished from them during the greater part of the night, now fell upon her lovely eyelids.

When she awoke, the day was far advanced, but still old Tristram had not returned; and with a heavy heart she set about her household concerns. The thought, however, of her anticipated visit to the castle speedily dispelled her anxiety, and she began to make preparations for setting out, attiring herself with unusual care. Bouchier had not experienced much difficulty in persuading her to obey the king's behest, and by his artful representations, he had likewise induced her grandfather to give his consent to the visit—the old forester only stipulating that she should be escorted there and back by a falconer, named Nicholas Clamp, in whom he could put trust; to which proposition Bouchier readily assented.

At length, five o'clock, the appointed hour, arrived, and with it came Nicholas Clamp. He was a tall, middle-aged man, with yellow hair, clipped closely over his brows, and a beard and moustaches to match. His attire resembled that of a keeper of the forest, and consisted of a doublet and hose of green cloth; but he did not carry a bugle or hunting-knife. His sole weapon was a stout quarter-staff. After some little hesitation, Mabel consented to accompany the falconer, and they set forth together.

The evening was delightful, and their way through the woods was marked by numberless points of beauty. Mabel said little, for her thoughts were running upon her grandfather, and upon his prolonged and mysterious absence; but the falconer talked of the damage done by the thunder-storm, which he declared was the most awful he had ever witnessed; and he pointed out to her several trees struck by the lightning. Proceeding in this way they gained a road leading from Blacknest, when, from behind a large oak, the trunk of which had concealed him from view, Morgan Fenwolf started forth, and planted himself in their path. The gear of the proscribed keeper was wild and ragged, his locks matted and disordered, his demeanour savage, and his whole appearance forbidding and alarming.

"I have been waiting for you for some time, Mabel Lyndwood," he said. "You must go with me to your grandfather."

"My grandfather would never send you for me," replied Mabel; "but if he did, I will not trust myself with you."

"The saints preserve us!" cried Nicholas Clamp. "Can I believe my eyes!—Do I behold Morgan Fenwolf!"

"Come with me, Mabel," cried Fenwolf, disregarding him. But she returned a peremptory refusal.

"She shall not stir an inch!" cried the falconer. "It is thou, Morgan Fenwolf, who must go with me. Thou art a proscribed felon, and thy life is forfeit to the king. Yield thee, dog, as my prisoner!"

"Thy prisoner!" echoed Fenwolf scornfully. "It would take three such as thou art to make me captive! Mabel Lyndwood, in your grandfather's name, I command you to come with me, and let Nick Clamp look to himself if he dares to hinder you."

"Nick will do something more than hinder her," rejoined the falconer, brandishing his staff, and rushing upon the other. "Felon hound! I command thee to yield!"

Before the falconer could reach him, Morgan Fenwolf plucked a long hunting-knife from his girdle, and made a desperate stab at his assailant. But Clamp avoided the blow, and striking Fenwolf on the shins, immediately afterwards closed with him.

The result was still doubtful, when the struggle was suddenly interrupted by the trampling of horse approaching from the side of Windsor; and at the sound, Morgan Fenwolf disengaged himself from his antagonist, and plunged into the adjoining wood. The next moment, Captain Bouchier rode up, followed by a small band of halberdiers, and receiving information from the falconer of what had occurred, darted with his men into the wood in search of the fugitive. Nicholas Clamp and his companion did not await the issue of the search, but proceeded on their way.

As they walked at a brisk pace, they reached the long avenue in about half an hour, and took their way down it. When within a mile of the castle, they were overtaken by Bouchier and his followers, and the falconer was much disappointed to learn that they had failed in tracking Morgan Fenwolf to his lair. After addressing a few complimentary words to the maiden, Bouchier rode on.

Soon after this, the pair quitted the Great Park, and passing through a row of straggling houses, divided by gardens and closes, which skirted the foot of Castle Hill, presently reached the lower gate. They were admitted without difficulty; but just as they entered the lower ward, the falconer was hailed by Shoreditch and Paddington, who at the moment issued from the doorway of the guard-room.

Clamp obeyed the call, and went towards them; and it was evident, from the gestures of the archers, that they were making inquiries about Mabel, whose appearance seemed to interest them greatly. After a brief conversation with the falconer, they approached her, and respectfully addressing her, begged leave to attend her to the royal lodgings, whither they understood she was going. No objection being made to the proposal by Mabel, the party directed their course towards the middle ward.

Passing through the gateway of the Norman Tower, they stopped before a low portal in a picturesque Gothic wing of the castle, with projecting walls and bay-windows, which had been erected in the preceding reign of Henry the Seventh, and was, consequently, still in all its freshness and beauty.

IV

How Mabel was received by the Party in the Kitchen ; and of the Quarrel between the Two Jesters

ADDRESSING himself to a stout-built yeoman of the guard, who was standing within the doorway, Nicholas Clamp demanded admittance to the kitchen, and the man having detained them for a few moments, during which he regarded Mabel with a very offensive stare, ushered them into a small hall, and from thence into a narrow passage connected with it. Lighted by narrow loopholes, pierced through the walls, which were of immense thickness, this passage described the outer side of the whole upper quadrangle, and communicated with many other lateral passages and winding stairs leading to the chambers allotted to the household, or to the state apartments. Tracking it for some time, Nicholas Clamp at length turned off on the right, and crossing a sort of ante-room, led the way into a large chamber with stone walls and a covered and groined roof, lighted by a great window at the lower end. This was the royal kitchen, and in it yawned no fewer than seven huge arched fireplaces, in which fires were burning, and before which various goodly joints were being roasted, while a number of cooks and scullions were congregated round them. At a large table, in the centre of the kitchen, were seated some half-dozen yeomen of the guard, together with the clerk of the kitchen, the chief bargeman, and the royal cutler, or blade-smith, as he was termed. These worthies were doing ample justice to a chine of beef, a wild boar pie, a couple of fat capons, a peacock pasty, a mess of pickled lobsters, and other excellent and inviting dishes with which the board was loaded. Neither did they neglect to wash down the viands with copious draughts of ale and mead, from great pots and flagons placed beside them. Behind this party stood Giovanni Joungevello, an Italian minstrel, much in favour with Anne Boleyn, and Domingo Lamellino, or Lamelyn—as he was familiarly termed—a Lombard, who pretended to some knowledge of chirurgery, astrology, and alchemy, and who was a constant attendant on Henry. At the head of the bench, on the right of the table, sat Will Sommers. The jester was not partaking of the repast, but was chatting with Simon Quanden, the chief cook, a good-humoured personage, round-bellied as a tun, and blessed with a spouse, yclept Deborah, as fond of good cheer, as fat, and as good-humoured as himself. Behind the cook stood the cellarman, known by the appellation of Jack of the Bottles, and at his feet were two playful little turnspits, with long backs, and short forelegs, as crooked almost as sickles.

On seeing Mabel, Will Sommers immediately arose, and advancing towards her with a mincing step, bowed with an air of mock ceremony, and said in an affected tone,—" Welcome, fair mistress, to the king's kitchen. We are all right glad to see you; are we not, mates ? "

" Ay, that we are ! " replied a chorus of voices.

" By my troth, the wench is wondrously beautiful ! " said Kit Coo, one of the yeomen of the guard.

" No wonder the king is smitten with her," said Launcelot Rutter, the blade-smith; " her eyes shine like a dagger's point."

" And she carries herself like a wafter on the river," said the bargeman.

" Her complexion is as good as if I had given her some of my sovereign balsam of beauty," said Domingo Lamelyn.

" Much better," observed Joungevello, the minstrel; " I shall write a canzonet in her praise, and sing it before the king."

" And get flouted for thy pains by the Lady Anne," said Kit Coo.

" The damsel is not so comely as I expected to find her," observed Amice Lovekyn, one of the serving women, to Hector Cutbeard, the clerk of the kitchen.

" Why, if you come to that, she is not to be compared

to you, pretty Amice ! " said Cutbeard, who was a red-nosed, red-faced fellow, with a twinkling merry eye.

" Nay, I meant not that," replied Amice, retreating.

" Excuse my getting up to receive you, fair mistress," cried Simon Quanden, who seemed fixed to his chair; " I have been bustling about all day, and am sore fatigued—sore fatigued. But will you not take something ? A sugared cate, and a glass of hippocras jelly—or a slice of capon. Go to the damsel, dame, and prevail on her to eat."

" That will I," replied Deborah. " What shall it be, sweetheart ? We have a well-stored larder here. You have only to ask and have."

" I thank you, but I am in want of nothing," replied Mabel.

" Nay, that is against all rule, sweetheart," said Deborah; " no one enters the king's kitchen without tasting his royal cheer."

" I am sorry I must prove an exception, then," returned Mabel smiling; " for I have no appetite."

" Well, well, I will not force you to eat against your will," replied the good dame. " But a cup of wine will do you good after your walk."

" I will wait upon her," said the Duke of Shoreditch, who vied with Paddington and Nick Clamp in attention to the damsel.

" Let me pray you to cast your eyes upon these two dogs, fair Mabel," said Will Sommers, pointing to the two turnspits, " they are special favourites of the king's highness. They are much attached to the cook, their master; but their chief love is towards each other, and nothing can keep them apart."

" Will Sommers speaks the truth," rejoined Simon Quanden. " Hob and Nob, for so they are named, are fast friends. When Hob gets into the box to turn the spit, Nob will watch beside it till his brother is tired, and then he will take his place. They always eat out of the same platter, and drink out of the same cup. I once separated them for a few hours to see what would happen, but they howled so piteously, that I was forced to bring them together again. It would have done your heart good to witness their meeting, and to see how they leaped and rolled with delight ! Here, Hob," he added, taking a cake from his apron pocket, " divide this with thy brother."

Placing his paws on his master's knees, the nearest turnspit took the cake in his mouth, and proceeding towards Nob, broke it into two pieces, and pushed the larger portion towards him.

While Mabel was admiring this display of sagacity and affection, a bustling step was heard behind her, and turning, she beheld a strange figure, in a parti-coloured gown and hose, with a fool's cap and bells on his head, whom she immediately recognised as the cardinal's jester, Patch. The new-comer recognised her too ; stared in astonishment ; and gave a leering look at Will Sommers.

" What brings you here, gossip Patch ? " cried Will Sommers. " I thought you were in attendance upon your master, at the court of Blackfriars."

" So I have been," replied Patch—" and I am only just arrived with his grace."

" What ! is the decision pronounced ? " cried Will Sommers eagerly. " Is the queen divorced ? Is the king single again ? Let us hear the sentence."

" Ay, the sentence !—the sentence ! " resounded on all hands.

Stimulated by curiosity, the whole of the party rose from the table ; Simon Quanden got out of his chair ; the other cooks left their joints to scorch at the fire ; the scullions suspended their work ; and Hob and Nob fixed their large inquiring black eyes upon the jester.

" I never talk thirsting," said Patch, marching to the table, and filling himself a flagon of mead. " Here's to you, fair maiden," he added, kissing the cup to Mabel, and swallowing its contents at a draught. " And now be seated, my masters, and you shall hear all I have to relate, and it will be told in a few words. The court is adjourned for three days—Queen Catharine having

231

demanded that time to prepare her allegations, and the delay has been granted her."

" Pest on it !—the delay is some trick of your crafty and double-dealing master," cried Will Sommers. " Were I the king, I know how I would deal with him."

" What wouldst thou do, thou scurril knave ? " cried Patch angrily.

" I would strip him of his ill-gotten wealth, and leave him only thee—a fitting attendant—of all his thousand servitors," replied Will.

" This shall to his grace's ears," screamed Patch, amid the laughter of the company,—" and see whether your back does not smart for it."

" I fear him not," replied Will Sommers. " I have not yet told the king my master of the rare wine we found in his cellar."

" What wine was that, Will ? " cried Jack of the Bottles.

" You shall hear," replied Will Sommers, enjoying the disconcerted look of the other jester. " I was at the palace at Hampton, when this scant-witted knave invited me to taste some of his master's wine, and accordingly to the cellar we went. ' This wine will surprise you,' quoth he, as we broached the first hogshead. And truly it did surprise me, for no wine followed the gimlet. So we went to another, and another, and another, till we had tried half a score of them, and all with the same result. Upon this, I seized a hammer, which was lying by, and sounded the casks, but none of them seeming empty, I at last broke the lid of one—and what do you think it contained ? "

A variety of responses were returned by the laughing assemblage, during which Patch sought to impose silence upon his opponent. But Will Sommers was not to be checked.

" It contained neither vinegar, nor oil, nor lead," he said, " but gold ; ay, solid bars of gold—ingots. Every hogshead was worth ten thousand pounds, and more."

" Credit him not, my masters," cried Patch, amid the

roars of the company; " the whole is a mere fable—an invention. His grace has no such treasure. The truth is, Will Sommers got drunk upon some choice Malmsey, and then dreamed he had been broaching casks of gold."

" It is no fable, as you and your master will find, when the king comes to sift the matter," replied Will. " This will be a richer result to him than was ever produced by your alchemical experiments, good Signor Domingo Lamelyn."

" It is false ! I say, false ! " screamed Patch. " Let the cellars be searched, and I will stake my head nothing is found."

" Stake thy cap, and there may be some meaning in it," said Will, plucking Patch's cap from his head, and elevating it on his truncheon—" here is an emblem of the Cardinal of York," he cried, pointing to it.

A roar of laughter from the company followed this sally, and Hob and Nob looked up in placid wonderment.

" I shall die with laughing," cried Simon Quanden, holding his fat sides, and addressing his spouse, who was leaning upon his shoulder.

In the meantime, Patch sprang to his feet, and gesticulating with rage and fury, cried, " Thou hast done well to steal my cap and bells, for they belong of right to thee. Add my folly to thy own, and thou wilt be a fitting servant to thy master; or e'en give him the cap, and then there will be a pair of ye."

" Who is the fool now, I should like to know ? " rejoined Will Sommers gravely. " I call you all to witness that he has spoken treason."

While this was passing, Shoreditch had advanced with a flagon of Malmsey to Mabel, but she was so interested in the quarrel between the two jesters that she heeded him not; neither did she attend to Nicholas Clamp, who was trying to explain to her what was going forward.

But just as Patch's indiscreet speech was uttered, an usher entered the kitchen and announced the approach of the king.

V

Of the Combat between Will Sommers and Patch; and how it Terminated

MABEL'S heart fluttered violently at the usher's announcement, and for a moment the colour deserted her cheek, while the next instant she was covered with blushes. As to poor Patch, feeling that his indiscretion might place him in great jeopardy, and seriously affect his master, to whom he was devotedly attached, he cast a piteous and imploring look at his antagonist, but was answered only by a derisive laugh, coupled with an expressive gesture to imitate that a halter would be his fate. Fearful that mischief might ensure, the good-natured Simon Quanden got out of his chair, and earnestly besought Will not to carry matters too far; but the jester remained implacable.

It was not unusual with Henry to visit the different offices of the castle, and converse freely and familiarly with the members of his household; but it was by no means safe to trust to the continuance of his good humour, or in the slightest degree to presume upon it. It is well known that his taste for variety of character often led him, like the renowned Caliph Haroun Al Reschid, to mix with the lower classes of his subjects in disguise; at which times many extraordinary adventures are said to have befallen him. His present visit to the kitchen, therefore, would have occasioned no surprise to its occupants, if it had not occurred so soon after the cardinal's arrival. But it was this circumstance, in fact, that sent him thither. The intelligence brought by Wolsey of the adjournment of the court for three days, under the plea of giving the queen time for her allegations, was so unlooked for by Henry, that he quitted the cardinal in his displeasure, and was about to repair to Anne Boleyn, when he encountered Bouchier, who told him that Mabel Lyndwood had been brought to the castle, and her grandsire arrested. The information changed Henry's intentions at once, and he proceeded with Bouchier and some other attendants to the kitchen, where he was given to understand he should find the damsel.

Many a furtive glance was thrown at the king, for no one dared openly to regard him, as he approached the forester's fair grand-daughter. But he tarried only a moment beside her, chucked her under the chin, and whispering a word or two in her ear that heightened her blushes, passed on to the spot where the two jesters were standing.

"What dost thou here, knave?" he said to Will Sommers.

"I might rather ask that question of your majesty," replied Will; "and I would do so, but that I require not to be told."

"I have come to see what passeth in my household," replied the king, throwing himself into the chair lately occupied by the chief cook. "Ah! Hob and Nob, my merry rascals," he cried, patting the turnspits who ran towards him, and thrust their noses against his hand, "ye are as gamesone and loving as ever, I see. Give me a manchet for them, master cook, and let not the proceedings in the kitchen be stayed for my presence. I would not have my supper delayed, or the roasts spoiled, for any false ceremony. And now, Will, what hast thou to say that thou lookest so hard at me?"

"I have a heavy charge to bring against this knave, an please your majesty," replied Will Sommers, pointing to Patch.

"What! hath he returned upon thee too sharply?" replied the king, laughing. "If so, challenge him to the combat, and settle the grievance with thy lathen dagger, but refer not the matter to me. I am no judge in fools' quarrels."

"Your own excepted," muttered Will. "This is not a quarrel that can be so adjusted," he added aloud. "I charge this rascal Patch with speaking disrespectfully of your highness in the hearing of the whole kitchen. And

I also charge his master, the cardinal, with having secreted in his cellars at Hampton a vast amount of treasure, obtained by extortion, privy dealings with foreign powers, and other iniquitous practices, and which aught of right to find its way to your royal exchequer."

"And which *shall* find its way thither, if thou dost not avouch a fable," replied the king.

"Your majesty shall judge," rejoined Will. And he repeated the story which he had just before related.

"Can this be true ! " exclaimed Henry, at its close.

"It is false, your highness, every word of it," cried Patch, throwing himself at the king's feet, "except so far as relates to our visits to the cellar, where, I shame to speak it, we drank so much that our senses clean forsook us. As to my indiscreet speech touching your majesty, neither disrespect nor disloyalty were intended by it. I was goaded to the rejoinder by the sharp sting of this hornet."

"The matter of the treasure shall be inquired, into without delay," said Henry. "As to the quarrel, it shall be thus settled. Get both of you upon that table. A flour bag shall be given to each; and he who is first knocked off shall be held vanquished."

The king's judgment was received with as much applause as dared be exhibited by the hearers ; and in an instant the board was cleared, and a couple of flour bags, partly filled, delivered to the combatants by Simon Quanden, who bestirred himself with unwonted activity on the occasion.

Leaping upon the table, amid the smothered mirth of the assemblage, the two jesters placed themselves opposite each other, and grinned such comical defiance that the king roared with laughter. After a variety of odd movements and feints on either side, Patch tried to bring down his adversary by a tremendous two-handed blow; but in dealing it, the weight of the bag dragged him forward, and well-nigh pitched him head foremost upon the floor. As it was, he fell on his face upon the table, and in this position received several heavy blows upon the prominent part of his back from Will Sommers. Ere long, however, he managed to regain his legs; and smarting with pain, attacked his opponent furiously in his turn. For a short space, fortune seemed to favour him. His bag had slightly burst, and the flour showering from it with every blow, well-nigh blinded his adversary, whom he drove to the very edge of the table. At this critical juncture, Will managed to bring down his bag full upon his opponent's sconce, and the force of the blow bursting it, Patch was covered from crown to foot with flour, and blinded in his turn. The appearance of the combatants was now so exquisitely ridiculous, that the king leaned back in his chair to indulge his laughter, and the mirth of the spectators could no longer be kept within decorous limits. The very turnspits barked in laughing concert.

" Well fought on both sides ! " cried Henry; " it were hard to say which will prove the victor. Now, knaves, to it again—ha ! ha !—to it again ! "

Once more the bags were wielded, descended, and the blows were so well directed on either side, that both combatants fell backwards. Again the king's laughter rose loud and long. Again the merriment of the other beholders was redoubled. Again Hob and Nob barked joyously and tried to spring on to the table to take part in the conflict. Amid the general glee, the combatants rose and renewed the fight, dealing blows thick and fast —for the bags were now considerably lightened of their contents—until they were completely hidden from view by a cloud of white dust.

" We cannot see the fray," remarked Henry; " but we can hear the din of battle. Which will prove the victor, I marvel ? "

" I am for Will Sommers," cried Bouchier.

" And I for Patch," said Simon Quanden. " Latterly, he hath seemed to me to have the advantage."

" It is decided ! " cried the king, rising, as one of the combatants was knocked off the table, and fell to the floor with a great noise. " Who is it ? "

" Patch," replied a faint voice. And through the cloud

of dust struggled forth the forlorn figure of the cardinal's jester, while Will Sommers leaped triumphantly to the ground.

" Get thee to a wash-tub, knave, and cleanse thyself," said Henry, laughing. " In consideration of the punishment thou hast undergone, I pardon thee thy treasonable speech."

So saying, he rose and walked towards Mabel, who had been quite as much alarmed as amused by the scene which had just taken place.

" I hope you have been as well cared for, damsel," he said, " since your arrival at the castle, as you cared for the Duke of Suffolk and myself when we visited your cottage ? "

" I have had everything I require, my liege," replied Mabel timidly.

" Dame Quanden will take charge of you till to-morrow," rejoined the king, " when you will enter upon the service of one of our dames."

" Your majesty is very considerate," said Mabel— " but I would rather go back at early dawn to my grandsire."

" That is needless," rejoined the king sternly. " Your grandsire is in the castle."

" I am glad to hear it ! " exclaimed Mabel. And then, altering her tone, for she did not like the expression of the king's countenance, she added, " I hope he has not incurred your majesty's displeasure."

" I trust he will be able to clear himself, Mabel," said Henry, " but he labours under the grave suspicion of leaguing with lawless men."

Mabel shuddered ; for the thought of what she had witnessed on the previous night during the storm rushed forcibly to her recollection. The king noticed her uneasiness, and added, in a gentler tone—" If he makes such confession as will bring the others to justice, he has nothing to fear. Dame Quanden, I commit this maiden to your charge. To-morrow she will take her place as attendant to the Lady Elizabeth Fitzgerald."

So saying, he moved off with Bouchier and the rest of his attendants, leaving Mabel to the care of the cook's good-humoured spouse, who seeing her eyes filled with tears, strove to cheer her, and led her towards a small side-table, where she pressed wine and cates upon her.

" Be of good cheer, sweetheart," she said, in a soothing tone, " no harm will befall your grandfather. You are much too high in favour with the king for that."

" I liked the king better as I saw him at our cottage, good dame," replied Mabel, smiling through her tears—" in the guise of a Guildford merchant. He seemed scarcely to notice me just now."

" That was because so many eyes were upon you, sweetheart," replied Deborah; " but sooth to say, I should be better pleased if he did not notice you at all."

Mabel blushed, and hung her head.

" I am glad you are to be an attendant on the Lady Elizabeth Fitzgerald," pursued Deborah, " for she is the fairest young lady at court, and as good and gentle as she is fair, and I am sure you will find her a kind mistress. I will tell you something about her. She is beloved by the king's son, the Duke of Richmond, but she requites not his passion, for her heart is fixed on the youthful Earl of Surrey. Alack a day ! the noble rivals quarrelled, and crossed swords about her; but as luck would have it, they were separated before any mischief was done. The king was very wroth with Lord Surrey, and ordered him to be imprisoned for two months in the Round Tower, in this castle, where he is now, though his term has very nearly expired."

" How I pity him, to be thus harshly treated," remarked Mabel, her eyes swimming with tears, " and the Lady Elizabeth, too ! I shall delight to serve her."

" I am told the earl passes the whole of his time in poring over books, and writing love verses and sonnets," said Deborah. " It seems strange that one so young should be a poet; but I suppose he caught the art from his friend Sir Thomas Wyat."

"Is he a friend of Sir Thomas Wyat?" asked Mabel quickly.

"His close friend," replied Deborah; "except the Duke of Richmond, now his rival, he had none closer. Have you ever seen Sir Thomas, sweetheart?"

"Yes, for a few moments," replied Mabel confusedly.

"I heard that he lingered for a short time in the forest before his departure for Paris," said Dame Quanden. "There was a strange rumour that he had joined the band of Herne the hunter. But that must have been untrue."

"Is he returned from France?" inquired Mabel, without heeding the remark.

"I fancy not," replied the good dame. "At all events, he is not come to the castle. Know you not," she added, in a low, confidential tone, "that the king is jealous of him? He was a former suitor to the Lady Anne Boleyn, and desperately in love with her; and it is supposed that his mission to France was only a pretext to get him out of the way."

"I suspected as much," replied Mabel. "Alas! for Sir Thomas; and alas! for the Earl of Surrey."

"And alas! for Mabel Lyndwood, if she allows her heart to be fixed upon the king," said Deborah.

While this was passing, the business of the kitchen, which had been interrupted by the various incidents above related, and especially by the conflict between the two jesters, was hurried forward, and for some time all was bustle and confusion.

But as soon as the supper was served, and all his duties were fully discharged, Simon Quanden, who had been bustling about, sat down in his easy chair, and recruited himself with a toast and a sack posset. Hob and Nob had their supper at the same time, and the party at the table, which had been increased by the two archers and Nicholas Clamp, attacked with renewed vigour a fresh supply of mead and ale, which had been provided for them by Jack of the Bottles.

The conversation then turned upon Herne the hunter; and as all had heard more or less about him, and some had seen him, while few knew the legend connected with him, Hector Cutbeard volunteered to relate it; upon which all the party gathered closer together, and Mabel and Deborah left off talking, and drew near to listen.

VI

The Legend of Herne the Hunter

"NEARLY a century and a half ago," commenced Cutbeard, " about the middle of the reign of Richard the Second, there was among the keepers of the forest a young man named Herne. He was expert beyond his fellows in all matters of woodcraft, and consequently in great favour with the king, who was himself devoted to the chase. Whenever he stayed at the castle, King Richard, like our own royal Harry, would pass his time in hunting, hawking, or shooting with the long bow; and on all these occasions the young keeper was his constant attendant. If a hart was to be chased, Herne and his two black hounds of Saint Hubert's breed would hunt him down with marvellous speed; if a wild boar was to be reared, a badger digged out, a fox unkennelled, a marten bayed, or an otter vented, Herne was chosen for the task. No one could fly a falcon so well as Herne— no one could break up a deer so quickly or so skilfully as him. But in proportion as he grew in favour with the king, the young keeper was hated by his comrades, and they concerted together how to ruin him. All their efforts, however, were ineffectual, and rather tended to his advantage than injury.

" One day, it chanced that the king hunted in the forest with his favourite, the Earl of Oxford, when a great deer of head was unharboured, and a tremendous chase ensued, the hart leading his pursuers within a few miles of Hungerford, whither the borders of the forest then extended. All the followers of the king, even the Earl of Oxford, had by this time dropped off, and the royal huntsman was only attended by Herne, who kept close behind him. At last, the hart, driven to desperation, stood at bay, and gored the king's horse as he came up in such manner that it reared and threw its rider. Another instant, and the horns of the infuriated animal would have been plunged into the body of the king, if Herne had not flung himself between the prostrate monarch and his assailant, and received the stroke intended for him. Though desperately wounded, the young hunter contrived slightly to raise himself, and plunge his knife into the hart's throat, while the king regained his feet.

" Gazing with the utmost concern at his unfortunate deliverer, King Richard demanded what he could do for him.

" ' Nothing, sire—nothing,' replied Herne, with a groan. ' I shall require nothing but a grave from you, for I have received a wound that will speedily bring me to it.'

" ' Not so, I trust, good fellow,' replied the king, in a tone meant to be encouraging, though his looks showed that his heart misgave him; ' my best leech shall attend you.'

" ' No skill will avail me now,' replied Herne sadly. ' A hurt from hart's horn bringeth to the bier.'

" ' I hope the proverb will not be justified in thy case ' rejoined the king; ' and I promise thee, if thou dost recover, thou shalt have the post of head keeper of the forest, with twenty nobles a year for wages. If, unhappily, thy forebodings are realised, I will give the same sum to be laid out in masses for thy soul.'

" ' I humbly thank your highness,' replied the young man, ' and I accept the latter offer, seeing it is the only one likely to profit me.'

" With this he put his horn to his lips, and winding the dead mot feebly, fell back senseless. Much moved, the king rode off for succour; and blowing a lusty call on his bugle, was presently joined by the Earl of Oxford and some of his followers, among whom were the keepers. The latter were secretly rejoiced on hearing what had befallen Herne, but they feigned the greatest affliction, and hastened with the king to the spot, where the body was lying stretched out beside that of the hart.

" ' It is almost a pity his soul cannot pass away thus,' said King Richard, gazing compassionately at him, ' for he will only revive to anguish and speedy death.'

" ' Your highness is right," replied the chief keeper, a grim old man, named Osmond Crooke, kneeling beside him, and half drawing his hunting knife, ' it were better to put him out of his misery.'

" ' What ! slay the man who has just saved my own life ! ' cried the king. ' I will consent to no such infamous deed. I would give a large reward to any one who could cure him.'

" As the words were uttered, a tall dark man, in a strange garb, and mounted on a black, wild-looking steed, whom no one had hitherto observed, sprang to the ground, and advanced towards the king.

" ' I take your offer, sire,' said this personage, in a harsh voice. ' I will cure him.'

" ' Who are thou, fellow ? ' demanded King Richard doubtfully.

" ' I am a forester,' replied the tall man, ' but I understand somewhat of chirurgery and leechcraft.'

" ' And woodcraft, too, I'll be sworn, fellow,' said the king. ' Thou hast, or I am mistaken, made free with some of my venison.'

" ' He looks marvellously like Arnold Sheafe, who was outlawed for deer-stealing,' said Osmond Crooke, regarding him steadfastly.

" ' I am no outlaw, neither am I called Arnold Sheafe,' replied the other. ' My name is Philip Urswick, and I can render a good account of myself when it shall please the King's highness to interrogate me. I dwell on the heath near Bagshot, which you passed to-day in the chase, and where I joined you.'

" ' I noted you not,' said Osmond.

" ' Nor I—nor I ! ' cried the other keepers.

" ' That may be; but I saw you,' rejoined Urswick contemptuously; ' and I tell you there is not one among you to be compared with the brave hunter who lies there. You have all pronounced his case hopeless. I repeat I can cure him if the king will make it worth my while.'

" ' Make good thy words, fellow,' replied the king; ' and thou shalt not only be amply rewarded, but shalt have a free pardon for any offence thou mayst have committed.'

" ' Enough,' replied Urswick. And taking a large, keen-edged hunting-knife from his girdle, he cut off the head of the hart close to the point where the neck joins the skull, and then laid it open from the extremity of the under-lip to the nuke. ' This must be bound on the head of the wounded man,' he said.

" The keepers stared in astonishment. But the king commanded that the strange order should be obeyed. Upon which the bleeding skull was fastened upon the head of the keeper with leathern thongs.

" ' I will now answer for his perfect cure in a month's time,' said Urswick to the king; ' but I shall require to watch over him myself till all danger is at an end. I pray your highness to command these keepers to transport him to my hut.'

" ' You hear, what he says, knaves,' cried the king— ' do his bidding, and carefully, or ye shall answer to me with your lives.'

" Accordingly, a litter was formed with branches of trees, and on this the body of Herne, with the hart's head still bound to it, was conveyed by the keepers to Urswick's hut—a small dwelling, situated in the wildest part of Bagshot Heath. After placing the body upon a bed of dried fern, the keepers were about to depart, when Osmond Crooke observed to the forester, ' I am now certain thou art Arnold Sheafe.'

" ' It matters not who I am, since I have the king's pardon,' replied the other, laughing disdainfully.

" ' Thou hast yet to earn it,' said Osmond.

" ' Leave that to me,' replied Urswick. ' There is more

fear that thou wilt lose thy post as chief keeper, which the king has promised to Herne, than that I should fail.'

" ' Would the deer had killed him outright,' growled Osmond.

" And the savage wish was echoed by the other keepers.

" ' I see you all hate him, bitterly,' said Urswick. ' What will you give me for revenge ? '

" ' We have little to give, save a fat buck on occasions,' replied Osmond ; ' and, in all likelihood, thou canst help thyself to venison.'

" ' Will you swear to grant the first request I may make of you—provided it shall be in your power ? ' demanded Urswick.

" ' Readily,' they replied.

" ' Enough,' said Urswick. ' I must keep faith with the king. Herne will recover, but he will lose all his skill as an archer—all his craft as a hunter.'

" ' If thou canst accomplish this thou art the fiend himself ! ' cried Osmond, trembling.

" ' Fiend or not,' replied Urswick, with a triumphant laugh—' ye have made a compact with me, and must fulfil it. Now begone. I must attend to the wounded man.'

" And the keepers, full of secret misgiving, departed.

" At the precise time promised, Herne, attended by Urswick presented himself to the king. He looked thin and pale, but all danger was past. King Richard gave the forester a purse full of nobles, and added a silver bugle to the gift. He then appointed Herne his chief keeper ; hung a chain of gold round his neck ; and ordered him to be lodged in the castle.

" About a week after this, Herne, having entirely regained his strength, accompanied the king on a hunting expedition to the forest, and they had scarcely entered it, when his horse started, and threw him. Up to that moment, such an accident had never happened to him, for he was an excellent horseman ; and he arose greatly discomfited, while the keepers eyed each other askance. Soon after this, a buck was started ; and though Herne was bravely mounted on a black steed bestowed on him on account of its swiftness by the king, he was the last in the chase.

" ' Thou art out of practice,' said the king, laughing as he came up.

" ' I know not what ails me,' replied Herne gloomily.

" ' It cannot be thy steed's fault,' said the king; ' for he is usually as fleet as the wind. But I will give thee an opportunity of gaining credit in another way. Thou seest yon buck. He cannot be seventy yards off; and I have seen thee hit the mark at twice the distance. Bring him down.'

" Herne raised his crossbow, and let fly the bolt; but it missed its mark, and the buck, startled by the noise, dashed down the brake, wholly uninjured.

" King Richard's brow grew dark, and Herne uttered an exclamation of rage and despair.

" ' Thou shalt have a third, and yet easier trial,' said the king. ' Old Osmond Crooke shall lend thee his bow, and thy quarry shall be yon maggot-pie.'

" As he spoke, the arrow sped. But it quivered in the trunk of the tree some yards from the bird. The unfortunate shooter looked distracted; but King Richard made no remark, until, towards the close of the day, he said to him, ' Thou must regain thy craft, friend Herne, or I cannot continue thee as my chief keeper.

" The keepers congratulated each other in secret, for they felt that their malice was about to be gratified.

" The next day, Herne went forth, as he thought, alone, but he was watched by his enemies. Not a shaft would go true, and he found that he had completely lost his mastery over hound and horse. The day after that, he again rode forth to hunt with the king, and his failure made him the laughing-stock of the party. Richard, at length, dismissed him with these words:—' Take repose for a week, and then thou shalt have a further trial. If thou dost not then succeed, I must, perforce, discharge thee from thy post.'

" Instead of returning to the castle, Herne rode off

wildly into the forest, where he remained till eventide. He then returned with ghastly looks and a strange appearance,—having the links of a rusty chain which he had plucked from a gibbet hanging from his left arm, and the hart's antlered skull, which he had procured from Urswick, fixed like a helm upon his head. His whole demeanour showed that he was crazed; and his condition, which might have moved the compassion of his foes, only provoked their laughter. After committing the wildest extravagances, he burst from all restraint, and disappeared among the trees of the Home Park.

" An hour after this, a pedlar, who was crossing the park from Datchet, found him suspended by a rope from a branch of the oak-tree which you have all seen, and which bears his name. Despair had driven him to the dreadful deed. Instead of cutting him down, the pedlar ran to the castle to relate what he had witnessed; and the keepers, satisfied that their revenge was now fully accomplished, hastened with him to the tree. But the body was gone; and all that proclaimed it had been there, was the rope hanging from the branch. Search was everywhere made for the missing body, but without effect. When the matter was related to the king, he was much troubled, and would fain have had masses said for the repose of the soul of the unfortunate keeper, but the priests refused to perform them, alleging that he had committed self-destruction, and was therefore out of the pale of the church.

" On that night, a terrible thunder-storm occurred—as terrible, it may be, as that of last night—and during its continuance, the oak on which Herne had hanged himself was blasted by the lightning.

" Old Osmond was immediately reinstated in his post of chief keeper; but he had little time for rejoicing, for he found that the same spell that had bound Herne had fallen upon him. His bolts and arrows went wide of their mark, his hounds lost their scent, and his falcon would not be lured back. Half frantic, and afraid of exposing himself to the taunts of his companions, he feigned illness, and left his comrade, Roger Barfoot, to take his place. But the same ill luck befell Barfoot, and he returned in woeful plight, without a single head of game. Four others were equally unfortunate, and it was now clear that the whole party was bewitched.

" Luckily, the king had quitted the castle, but they felt certain they should be dismissed on his return, if not more severely punished. At last, after taking counsel together, they resolved to consult Urswick, who they doubted not could remove the spell. Accordingly, they went to Bag-shot Heath, and related their story to him. When they had done, he said, ' The curse of Herne's blood is upon you, and can only be removed in one way. As you return to the castle, go to the tree on which he destroyed himself, and you may learn how to act.'

" The keepers would have questioned him further, but he refused to answer, and dismissed them.

" The shades of evening had fallen as they quitted Bagshot; and it was midnight as they entered the Home Park, and proceeded towards the fatal oak. It was pitchy dark; and they could only distinguish the tree by its white, scathed trunk. All at once, a blue flame, like a will-o'-the-wisp, appeared, flitted thrice round the tree, and then remained stationary, its light falling upon a figure in a wild garb, with a rusty chain hanging from its left arm and an antlered helm upon its head. They knew it to be Herne, and instantly fell down before him, while a burst of terrible laughter sounded in their ears.

" Without heeding them further, the spirit darted round the tree, rattling its chain, and uttering appalling imprecations. It then stopped, and turning to the terrified beholders, bade them, in a hollow voice, bring hounds and horses as for the chase on the following night, and vanished.

" Filled with dread, the keepers returned home, and the next day old Osmond again sought the forester, and told him what had occurred.

" ' You must obey the spirit's injunctions, or worse mischief will befall you,' said Urswick. ' Go to the tree, mounted as for a hunting-party, and take the black steed given to Herne by the king, and the two black hounds with you. You will see what will ensue.' And without another word he dismissed him.

" Osmond told his comrades what the forester had said, and though they were filled with alarm, they resolved upon compliance. At midnight, therefore, they rode towards the tree with the black hounds in leash, and leading Herne's favourite horse, saddled and bridled. As they drew near, they again saw the terrible shape stalking round the tree, and heard the fearful imprecations.

" His spells ended, Herne called to Osmond to bring him his steed; and the old man tremblingly obeyed. In an instant, the mysterious being vaulted on its back, and in a voice of resistless authority cried,' To the forest !— to the forest !' With this, he dashed forward, and the whole party, hounds and men, hurried after him.

" They rode at a furious pace for five or six miles over the Great Park, the keepers wondering where their un-earthly leader was taking them, and almost fancying they were hurrying to perdition, when they descended a hill-side leading to the marsh, and halted before a huge beech-tree, where Herne dismounted and pronounced certain mystic words, accompanying them with strange gestures.

" Presently, he became silent and motionless. A flash of fire then burst from the roots of the tree, and the forester Urswick stood before him. But his aspect was more terrible and commanding than it had seemed heretofore to the keepers.

" ' Welcome, Herne,' he cried; ' welcome, lord of the forest. And you his comrades, and soon to be his followers, welcome too. The time is come for the fulfil-ment of your promise to me. I require you to form a band for Herne the hunter, and to serve him as leader. Swear to obey him, and the spell that hangs over you shall be broken. If not I leave you to the king's justice.'

" Not daring to refuse compliance, the keepers took the oath proposed—and a fearful one it was! As soon it was uttered, Urswick vanished, as he came, in a flash of fire. Herne then commanded the others to dismount, and made them prostrate themselves before him, and pay him homage. This done, he blew a strike on his horn, rode swiftly up the hill-side, and a stag being unharboured, the chase commenced. Many a fat buck was hunted and slaughtered that night; and an hour before daybreak, Herne commanded them to lay the four finest and fattest at the foot of the beech-tree, and then dismissed them, bidding them meet him at midnight at the scathed oak in the Home Park.

"They came as they were commanded; but fearful of detection, they adopted strange disguises, not unlike those worn by the caitiffs who were put to death, a few weeks ago, by the king, in the Great Park. Night after night, they thus went forth, thinning the herds of deer, and committing other outrages and depradations. Nor were their dark proceedings altogether unnoticed. Belated travellers crossing the forest beheld them, and related what they had seen; others watched for them, but they were so effectually disguised that they escaped detection.

"At last, however, the king returned to the castle, and accounts of the strange doings in the forest were instantly brought him. Astonished at what he heard, and determined to ascertain the truth of the statement, he ordered the keepers to attend him that night in an expedition to the forest, when he hoped to encounter the demon huntsman and his band. Much alarmed, Osmond Crooke, who acted as spokesman, endeavoured by representing the risk he would incur, to dissuade the king from the enterprise; but he would not be deterred, and they now gave themselves up for lost.

"As the castle clock tolled forth the hour of midnight, Richard, accompanied by a numerous guard, and attended by the keepers, issued from the gates, and rode towards the scathed oak. As they drew near the tree, the figure of Herne, mounted on his black steed, was discerned beneath it. Deep fear fell upon all the beholders, but chiefly upon the guilty keepers, at the sight. The king, however, pressed forward, and cried, ' Why dost thou disturb the quietude of night, accursed spirit ? '

" ' Because I desire vengeance ! ' replied Herne, in a hollow voice. ' I was brought to my present woeful condition by Osmond Crooke and his comrades.'

" ' But you died by your own hand—did you not ? ' demanded King Richard.

" ' Yea,' replied Herne; ' but I was driven to the deed by an infernal spell laid upon me by the malice of the wretches I have denounced. Hang them upon this tree, and I will trouble these woods no longer while thou reignest ! ''

" The king looked round at the keepers. They all remained obdurate, except Roger Barfoot, who, falling on his knees, confessed his guilt, and accused the others.

" ' It is enough,' cried the king to Herne; ' they shall all suffer for their offence.'

" Upon this, a flash of fire enveloped the spirit and his horse, and he vanished.

" The king kept his word. Osmond and his comrades were all hanged upon the scathed tree, nor was Herne seen again in the forest while Richard sat upon the throne. But he reappeared with a new band at the commencement of the rule of Henry the Fourth, and again hunted the deer at night. His band was destroyed, but he defied all attempts at capture; and so it has continued to our own time, for not one of the seven monarchs who have held the castle since Richard's day, have been able to drive him from the forest.''

" Nor will the present monarch be able to drive him thence," said a deep voice. " As long as Windsor Forest endures, Herne the hunter will haunt it."

All turned at the exclamation, and saw that it proceeded from a tall dark man, in an archer's garb, standing behind Simon Quanden's chair.

" Thou has told thy legend fairly enough, good clerk of the kitchen," continued this personage; " but thou art wrong on many material points."

" I have related the story as it was related to me," said

Cutbeard, somewhat nettled at the remark; " but perhaps you will set me right where I have erred."

" It is true that Herne was a keeper in the reign of Richard the Second," replied the tall archer. " It is true also that he was expert in all matters of woodcraft, and that he was in high favour with the king; but he was bewitched by a lovely damsel, and not by a weird forester. He carried off a nun, and dwelt with her in a cave in the forest, where he assembled his brother keepers, and treated them to the king's venison and the king's wine."

" A sacrilegious villain and a reprobate ! " exclaimed Launcelot Rutter.

" His mistress was fair enough, I will warrant her," said Kit Coo.

" She was the very image of this damsel," rejoined the tall archer, pointing to Mabel, " and fair enough to work his ruin, for it was through her that the fiend tempted him. The charms that proved his undoing were fatal to her also, for in a fit of jealousy he slew her. The remorse occasioned by this deed made him destroy himself."

" Well, your version of the legend may be the correct one, for aught I know, worthy sir," said Cutbeard; " But I see not that it accounts for Herne's antlers so well as mine; unless indeed he were wedded to the nun, who you say played him false. But how come you to know she resembled Mabel Lyndwood ? "

" Ay, I was thinking of that myself," said Simon Quanden. " How do you know that, master ? "

" Because I have seen her picture," replied the tall archer.

" Painted by Satan's chief limner, I suppose ? " rejoined Cutbeard.

" He who painted it had seen her," replied the tall archer sternly. " But as I have said, it was the very image of this damsel."

And as he uttered the words, he quitted the kitchen.

" Who is that archer ? " demanded Cutbeard, looking after him.

But no one could answer the question, nor could any one tell when he had entered the kitchen.

"Strange!" exclaimed Simon Quanden, crossing himself. "Have you ever seen him before, Mabel?"

"I almost think I have," she replied, with a slight shudder.

"I half suspect he is Herne himself," whispered Shoreditch to Paddington.

"It may be," responded the other; "his glance made my blood run cold."

"You look somewhat fatigued, sweetheart," said Deborah, observed Mabel's uneasiness. "Come with me, and I will show you to a chamber."

Glad to escape, Mabel followed the good dame out of the kitchen, and they ascended a winding staircase, which brought them to a commodious chamber in the upper part of Henry the Seventh's buildings, where Deborah sat down with her young charge, and volunteered a great deal of good advice to her, which the other listened to with becoming attention, and promised to profit by it.

VII

Of the Mysterious Noise heard in the Curfew Tower

On quitting the kitchen, Henry, having been informed by Bouchier that Tristram Lyndwood was lodged in the prison-chamber in the lower gateway, proceeded thither to question him. He found the old man seated on a bench, with his hands tied behind him: but though evidently much alarmed at his situation, he could not be brought either by threats or proffers, to make any confession.

Out of patience, at length, the king ordered him to be conveyed to the dungeon beneath the Curfew Tower, and personally superintended his removal.

" I will find a means of shaking his obstinacy," said Henry, as he quitted the vault with Bouchier. " If I cannot move him by other means, I may through his grand-daughter. I will interrogate him in her presence to-night."

" To-night, sire ! " exclaimed Bouchier.

" Ay, to-night," repeated the king. " I am resolved, even if it should cost the life of this maiden, whose charms have moved me so, to break the infernal machinery woven around me. And now as I think it not unlikely the miscreant Herne may attempt the prisoner's deliverance, let the strictest watch be kept over the tower. Station an arquebusier throughout the night at the door of the dungeon, and another at the entrance to the chamber on the ground floor. Your own post must be on the roof of the fortification, that you may watch if any attempt is made to scale it from the town side, or to get in through the loopholes. Keep a sharp look-out, Bouchier, for I shall hold you responsible if any mischance occurs."

" I will do my best, my liege," replied Bouchier; " and

were it with a mortal foe I had to contend, I should have
no fear. But what vigilance can avail against a fiend ? "

" You have heard my injunctions, and will attend to
them," rejoined the king harshly. " I shall return anon
to the examination."

So saying, he departed.

Brave as a lion on ordinary occasions, Bouchier
entered upon his present duty with reluctance and misgiving; and he found the arquebusiers, by whom he was
attended, albeit stout soldiers, equally uneasy. Herne
had now become an object of general dread throughout
the castle; and the possibility of an encounter with him
was enough to daunt the boldest breast. Disguising his
alarm, Bouchier issued his directions in an authoritative
tone, and then mounted with three arquebusiers to the
summit of the tower. It was now dark, but the moon
soon arose, and her beams rendered every object as
distinguishable as daylight would have done, so that
watch was easily kept. But nothing occurred to occasion
alarm, until all at once, a noise, like that of a hammer
stricken against a board, was heard in the chamber
below.

Drawing his sword, Bouchier hurried down the steps
leading into this chamber, which was buried in darkness,
and advanced so precipitately and incautiously in the
gloom, that he struck his head against a cross-beam. The
violence of the blow stunned him for a moment, but as
soon as he recovered, he called to the guard in the lower
chamber to bring up a torch. The order was promptly
obeyed; but, meanwhile, the sound had ceased, and,
though they searched about, they could not discover the
occasion of it.

This, however, was not so wonderful, for the singular
construction of the chamber, with its numerous cross-
beams, its deep embrasures and recesses, its insecure and
uneven floor, its steep ladder-like staircases, was highly
favourable to concealment, it being utterly impossible,
owing to the intersection of the beams, for the searchers
to see far before them, or to move about quickly. In the

midst of the chamber was a large wooden compartment inclosing the cumbrous and uncouth machinery of the castle clock, and through this box ran the cord communicating with the belfry above. At that time, pieces of ordnance were mounted in all the embrasures, but there is now only one gun, placed in a porthole commanding Thames Street, and the long thoroughfare leading to Eton. The view from this porthole of the groves of Eton, and of the lovely plains on the northwest, watered by the river, is enchanting beyond description.

Viewed from a recess which has been partly closed, the appearance of this chamber is equally picturesque and singular; and it is scarcely possible to pass beneath its huge beams, or to gaze at the fantastic, yet striking combinations they form in connection with the deep embrasures, the steep staircases, and trap-doors, and not feel that the whole place belongs to romance, and that a multitude of strange and startling stories must be connected with it. The old architects were indeed great romancers, and built for the painter and the poet.

Bouchier and his companions crept about under the great meshwork of beams—peered into all the embrasures, and beneath the carriages of the culverins. There was a heap of planks and beams lying on the floor beneath the two staircases, but no one was near it.

The result of their investigations did not tend to decrease their alarm. Bouchier would fain have had the man keep watch in the chamber, but neither threats nor entreaties could induce him to remain there. He was therefore sent below, and the captain returned to the roof. He had scarcely emerged upon the leads when the hammering recommenced more violently than before. In vain Bouchier ordered his men to go down. No one would stir; and superstitious fear had by this time obtained such mastery over the captain, that he hesitated to descend alone. To add to his vexation, the arquebusier had taken the torch with him, so that he should have to proceed in darkness. At length, he mustered up courage to make the attempt ; but he paused between each step, peering through the gloom, and half fancying he could discern the figure of Herne near the spot where the pile of wood lay. Certain it was that the sound of diabolical laughter, mingled with the rattling of the chain and the sharp blows of the hammer, smote his ears. The laughter became yet louder as Bouchier advanced, the hammering ceased, and the clanking of the chain showed that its mysterious wearer was approaching the foot of the steps to meet him. But the captain had not nerve enough for the encounter. Invoking the protection of the saints, he beat a precipitate retreat, and closed the little door at the head of the steps after him.

The demon was apparently satisfied with the alarm he had occasioned, for the hammering was not renewed at that time.

VIII

Showing the Vacillations of the King between Wolsey and Anne Boleyn

BEFORE returning to the state apartments, Henry took a turn on the ramparts on the north side of the castle, between the Curfew Tower and the Winchester Tower, and lingered for a short time on the bastion commanding that part of the acclivity where the approach, called the hundred steps, is now contrived. Here he cautioned the sentinels to be doubly vigilant throughout the night, and having gazed for a moment at the placid stream flowing at the foot of the castle, and tinged with the last rays of the setting sun, he proceeded to the royal lodgings, and entered the banquet-chamber, where supper was already served.

Wolsey sat on his right hand, but he did not vouchsafe him a single word, addressing the whole of his discourse to the Duke of Suffolk, who was placed on his left. As soon as the repast was over, he retired to his closet. But the cardinal would not be so repulsed, and sent one of his gentlemen to crave a moment's audience of the king, which, with some reluctance, was accorded.

"Well, cardinal!" cried Henry, as Wolsey presented himself, and the usher withdrew. "You are playing a deep game with me, as you think; but take heed, for I see through it!"

"I pray you dismiss these suspicions from your mind, my liege," said Wolsey. "No servant was ever more faithful to his master than I have been to you."

"No servant ever took better care of himself," cried the king fiercely. "Not alone have you wronged me to enrich yourself, but you are ever intriguing with my enemies. I have nourished in my breast a viper; but I will cast you off—will crush you as I would the noxious reptile!"

And he stamped upon the floor, as if he could have stamped the cardinal beneath his foot.

"Beseech you, calm yourself, my liege," replied Wolsey, in the soft and deprecatory tone which he had seldom known to fail with the king; "I have never thought of my own aggrandisement, but as it was likely to advance your power. For the countless benefits I have received at your hands, my soul overflows with gratitude. You have raised me from the meanest condition to the highest. You have made me your confidant, your adviser, your treasurer, and with no improper boldness I say it, your friend. But I defy the enemies who have poisoned your ears against me, to prove that I ever abused the trust placed in me. The sole fault that can be imputed to me is that I have meddled more with temporal matters than with spiritual; and it is a crime for which I must answer before Heaven. But I have so acted because I felt that I might thereby best serve your highness. If I have aspired to the papal throne—which you well know I have—it has been that I might be yet a more powerful friend to your majesty, and render you, what you are entitled to be, the first prince in Christendom."

" Tut, tut ! " exclaimed the king, who was, neverthe-less, moved by the artful appeal.

" The gifts I have received from foreign princes," pursued Wolsey, seeing the effect he had produced, " the wealth I have amassed, have all been with a view of benefiting your majesty."

" Humph ! " exclaimed the king.

" To prove that I speak the truth, sire," continued the wily cardinal, " the palace at Hampton Court, which I have just completed——"

" And at a cost more lavish than I myself should have expended on it," interrupted the king angrily.

" If I had destined it for myself, I should not have spent a tithe of what I have done," rejoined Wolsey. " Your highness's unjust accusations force me to declare my intentions somewhat prematurely. Deign," he cried, throwing himself at the king's feet,—" deign to accept that palace and all within it. You were pleased, during your late residence there, to express your approval of it. And I trust it will find equal favour in your eyes, now that it is your own."

" By holy Mary, a royal gift ! " cried Henry—" rise, cardinal. You are not the grasping, selfish person you have been represented."

" Declare as much to my enemies, sire, and I shall be more than content," replied Wolsey. " You will find the palace better worth acceptance than at first sight might appear."

" How so ? " cried the king.

" Your highness will be pleased to take this key," said the cardinal ; " it is the key of the cellar."

" You have some choice wine there," cried Henry significantly; " given you by some religious house—or sent you by some foreign potentate—ha ! "

" It is wine that a king might prize," replied the cardinal. " Your majesty will find a hundred hogsheads in that cellar—and each hogshead filled with gold."

" You amaze me ! " cried the king, feigning astonish-ment. " And all this you freely give me ? "

"Freely and fully, sire," replied Wolsey. "Nay, I have saved it for you. Men think I have cared for myself, whereas I have cared only for your majesty. Oh ! my dear liege, by the devotion I have just approved to you, and which I would also approve, if needful, with my life, I beseech you to consider well before you raise Anne Boleyn to the throne. In giving you this council, I know I hazard the favour I have just regained. But even at *that* hazard, I must offer it. Your infatuation blinds you to the terrible consequences of the step. The union is odious to all your subjects—but, most of all, to those not tainted with the new heresies and opinions. It will never be forgiven by the Emperor Charles the Fifth, who will seek to avenge the indignity offered to his illustrious relative ; while Francis will gladly make it a pretext for breaking his truce with you. Add to this, the displeasure of the apostolic see, and it must be apparent that, powerful as you are, your position will be one of infinite peril."

"Thus far advanced I cannot honourably abandon the divorce," said Henry.

"Nor do I advise its abandonment, sire," replied Wolsey; "but do not let it be a means of injuring you with all men. Do not let a mal-alliance place your very throne in jeopardy; as, with your own subjects and all foreign powers against you, must necessarily be the case."

"You speak warmly, cardinal," said Henry.

"My zeal prompts me to do so," replied Wolsey. "Anne Boleyn is in no respect worthy of the honour your propose her."

"And whom do you think more worthy ? " demanded Henry.

"Those whom I have already recommended to your majesty, the Duchess d'Alençon, or the Princess Renée," replied Wolsey; "by a union with either of whom you would secure the cordial co-operation of Francis, and the interests of the See of Rome, which, in the event of a war with Spain, you may need."

"No, Wolsey," replied Henry, taking a hasty turn across the chamber; "no considerations of interest or security shall induce me to give up Anne. I love her too well for that. Let the lion Charles roar, the fox Francis snarl, and the hydra-headed Clement launch forth his flames, I will remain firm to my purpose. I will not play the hypocrite with you, whatever I may do with others. I cast off Catherine that I may wed Anne, because I cannot otherwise obtain her. And shall I now, when I have dared so much, and when the prize is in my grasp, abandon it? Never! Threats, expostulations, entreaties, are alike unavailing."

"I grieve to hear it, my liege," replied Wolsey, heaving a deep sigh; "it is an ill-omened union, and will bring woe to you, woe to your realm, and woe to the Catholic Church."

"And woe also to you, false cardinal," cried Anne Boleyn, throwing aside the arras, and stepping forward. "I have overheard what has passed; and from my heart of hearts I thank you, Henry, for the love you have displayed for me. But I here solemnly vow never to give my hand to you till Wolsey is dismissed from your councils."

"Anne!" exclaimed the king.

"My own enmity I could forego," pursued Anne vehemently, "but I cannot forgive him his duplicity and perfidy towards you. He has just proffered you his splendid Palace of Hampton, and his treasures—and wherefore?—I will tell you—because he feared they would be wrested from him. His jester had acquainted him with the discovery just made of the secret hoard, and he was therefore compelled to have recourse to this desperate move. But I was apprised of his intentions by Will Sommers, and have come in time to foil him."

"By my faith, I believe you are right, sweetheart," said the king.

"Go tell your allies, Francis and Clement, that the king's love for me outweighs his fear of them," cried

Anne, laughing spitefully. " As for you, I regard you as nothing."

" Vain woman, your pride will be abased," rejoined Wolsey bitterly.

" Vain man, you are already abased," replied Anne. " A few weeks ago I would have made terms with you. Now I am your mortal enemy, and will never rest till I have procured your downfall."

" The king will have an amiable consort, truly," sneered Wolsey.

" He will have one who can love him and hate his foes," replied Anne; " and not one who would side with them and thee, as would be the case with the Duchess d'Alençon or the Princess Renée. Henry, you know the sole terms on which you can procure my hand."

The king nodded a playful affirmative.

" Then dismiss him at once—disgrace him," said Anne.

" Nay, nay," replied Henry, " the divorce is not yet passed. You are angered now, and will view matters more coolly to-morrow."

" I shall never change my resolution," she replied.

" If my dismissal and disgrace can save my sovereign, I pray him to sacrifice me without hesitation," said Wolsey; " but while I have liberty of speech with him, and aught of power remaining, I will use it to his advantage. I pray your majesty suffer me to retire."

And receiving a sign of acquiescence from the king, he withdrew, amid the triumphant laughter of Anne.

IX

How Tristram Lyndwood was interrogated by the King

ANNE BOLEYN remained with her royal lover for a few minutes to pour forth her gratitude for the attachment he had displayed to her, and to confirm the advantage she had gained over Wolsey. As soon as she was gone, Henry summoned an usher, and giving him some instructions respecting Mabel Lyndwood, proceeded to the Curfew Tower.

Nothing was said to him of the strange noise that had been heard in the upper chamber, for the arquebusiers were fearful of exciting his displeasure by a confession of their alarm, and he descended at once to the dungeon.

" Well, fellow," he cried, sternly regarding the captive, who arose at his entrance, " you have now had ample time for reflection, and I trust you are in a better frame of mind than when I last spoke to you. I command you to declare all you know concerning Herne the hunter, and to give me such information respecting the proscribed felon, Morgan Fenwolf, as will enable me to accomplish his capture."

" I have already told your highness that my mouth is sealed by an oath of secrecy," replied Tristram humbly, but firmly.

" Obstinate dog ! thou shalt either speak, or I will hang thee from the top of this tower as I hanged Mark Fytton, the butcher," roared Henry.

" You will execute your sovereign pleasure, my liege," said the old man. " My life is in your hands. It is little matter whether it is closed now or a year hence. I have well-nigh run out my term."

" If thou carest not for thyself, thou mayst not be equally indifferent to another," cried the king. " What ho ! bring in his grand-daughter."

The old man started at the command, and trembled

violently. The next moment, Mabel was led into the dungeon by Shoreditch and Paddington. Behind her came Nicholas Clamp. On seeing her grandsire, she uttered a loud cry, and would have rushed towards him, but she was held back by her companions.

"Oh! grandfather," she cried; "what have you done?—why do I find you here?"

Tristram groaned, and averted his head.

"He is charged with felony and sorcery," said the king, sternly; "and you, maiden, come under the same suspicion."

"Believe it not, sire," cried the old man, flinging himself at Henry's feet ; " oh, believe it not. Whatever you may judge of me, believe her innocent. She was brought up most devoutly by a lay sister of the monastery of Chertsey; and she knows nothing, save by report, of what passes in the forest."

"Yet she has seen and conversed with Morgan Fenwolf," said the king.

"Not since he was outlawed," said Tristram.

"I saw him to-day, as I was brought to the castle," cried Mabel; "and"—but recollecting that she might implicate her grandfather, she suddenly stopped.

"What said he?—ha!" demanded the king.

"I will tell your majesty what passed," interposed Nicholas Clamp, stepping forward, " for I was with the damsel at the time. He came upon us suddenly from behind a great tree, and ordered her to accompany him to her grandsire."

"Ha!" exclaimed the king.

"But he had no authority for what he said, I am convinced," pursued Clamp. "Mabel disbelieved him, and refused to go, and I should have captured him if the fiend he serves had not lent him a helping hand."

"What says the prisoner himself to this?" observed the king. "Didst thou send Fenwolf on the errand?"

"I did," replied Tristram. "I sent him to prevent her from going to the castle."

Mabel sobbed audibly.

" Thou art condemned by thy own confession, caitiff ! " said the king, " and thou knowest upon what terms alone thou canst save thyself from the hangman, and thy grand-daughter from the stake ! "

" Oh, mercy, sire, mercy ! " shrieked Mabel.

" Your fate rests with your grandsire," said the king sternly. " If he chooses to be your executioner, he will remain silent."

" Oh ! speak, grandsire, speak ! " cried Mabel. " What matters the violation of an unholy vow ? "

" Give me till to-morrow for consideration, sire," said the old man.

" Thou shalt have till midnight," replied the king ; " and till then, Mabel shall remain with thee."

" I would rather be left alone," said Tristram.

" I doubt it not," replied the king; " but it shall not be."

And without bestowing a look at Mabel, whose supplications he feared might shake his purpose, he quitted the vault with his attendants, leaving her alone with her grandsire.

" I shall return at midnight," he said to the arquebusier stationed at the door; " and, meanwhile, let no one enter the dungeon—not even the Duke of Suffolk, unless," he added, holding forth his hand to display a ring, " he shall bring this signet."

X

Of the brief advantage gained by the Queen and the Cardinal

As the king, wholly unattended—for he had left the archers at the Curfew Tower—was passing at the back of St. George's Chapel, near the north transept, he paused for a moment to look at the embattled entrance to the New Commons—a structure erected in the eleventh year of his own reign, by James Denton, a canon, and afterwards Dean of Lichfield, for the accommodation of such chantry priests and choristers as had no place in the college. Over the doorway, surmounted by a niche, ran (and still runs) the inscription—" ÆDES PRO SACELLANORUM CHORISTARUM COVIVIIS EXTRUCTA, A.D. 1519." The building has since been converted into one of the canon's houses.

While he was contemplating this beautiful gateway, which was glimmering in the bright moonlight, a tall figure suddenly darted from behind one of the buttresses of the chapel, and seized his left arm with an iron grasp. The suddenness of the attack took him by surprise; but he instantly recovered himself, plucked away his arm, and drawing his sword, made a pass at his assailant, who, however, avoided the thrust, and darted with inconceivable swiftness through the archway leading to the choristers. Though Henry followed as quickly as he could, he lost sight of the fugitive, but just as he was about to enter the passage running between the tomb-house and the chapel, he perceived a person in the south ambulatory, evidently anxious to conceal himself, and rushing up to him, and dragging him to the light, he found it was no other than the cardinal's jester, Patch.

" What dost thou here, knave ? " cried Henry angrily.

" I am waiting for my master the cardinal," replied the jester, terrified out of his wits.

"Waiting for him here!" cried the king. "Where is he?"

"In that house," replied Patch, pointing to a beautiful bay-window, full of stained glass, overhanging the exquisite arches of the north ambulatory.

"Why that is Doctor Sampson's dwelling," cried Henry, "he who was chaplain to the queen, and is a strong opponent of the divorce. What doth he there?"

"I am sure I know not," replied Patch, whose terror increased each moment. "Perhaps I have mistaken the house. Indeed, I am sure it must be Doctor Voysey's, the next door."

"Thou liest, knave!" cried Henry fiercely; "thy manner convinces me there is some treasonable practice going forward. But I will soon find it out. Attempt to give the alarm, and I will cut thy throat."

With this, he proceeded to the back of the north ambulatory, and finding the door he sought unfastened, raised the latch, and walked softly in. But before he got half way down the passage, Doctor Sampson himself issued from an inner room with a lamp in his hand. He started on seeing the king, and exhibited great alarm.

"The Cardinal of York is here—I know it," said Henry, in a deep whisper. "Lead me to him."

"Oh! go not forward, my gracious liege," cried Sampson, placing himself in his path.

"Wherefore not?" rejoined the king. "Ha! what voice is that I hear in the upper chamber. Is she here, and with Wolsey? Out of my way, man," he added, pushing the canon aside, and rushing up the short wooden staircase.

When Wolsey returned from his interview with the king, which had been so unluckily interrupted by Anne Boleyn, he found his ante-chamber beset with a crowd of suitors, to whose solicitations he was compelled to listen, and having been detained in this manner for nearly half an hour he at length retired into an inner room.

"Vile sycophants!" he muttered, "they bow the knee before me, and pay me greater homage than they render the king—but though they have fed upon my bounty, and risen by my help, not one of them, if he was aware of my true position, but would desert me. Not one of them but would lend a helping hand to crush me. Not one but would rejoice in my downfall. But they have not deceived me. I knew them from the first —saw through their hollowness, and despised them. While power lasts to me, I will punish some of them. While power lasts!" he repeated. "Have I any power remaining? I have already given up Hampton and my treasures to the king; and the work of spoliation once commenced, the royal plunderer will not be content until he has robbed me of all; while his minion, Anne Boleyn, has vowed my destruction. Well, I will not yield tamely, nor fall unavenged."

As these thoughts passed through his mind, Patch, who had waited for a favourable moment to approach him, delivered him a small billet carefully sealed, and fastened with a silken thread. Wolsey took it, and broke it open; and as his eyes eagerly scanned its contents, the expression of his countenance totally changed. A flash of joy and triumph irradiated his fallen features; and thrusting the note into the folds of his robe, he inquired of the jester by whom it had been brought, and how long?

"It was brought by a messenger from Dr. Sampson," replied Patch, "and was committed to me with special injunctions to deliver it to your grace immediately on your return, and secretly."

The cardinal sat down, and for a few moments appeared lost in deep reflection; he then arose, and telling Patch he should return presently, quitted the chamber. But the jester, who was of an inquisitive turn, and did not like to be confined to half a secret, determined to follow him, and accordingly tracked him along the great corridor, down a winding staircase, through a private door near the Norman Gateway, across the middle ward, and finally saw him enter Doctor Sampson's dwelling, at the back of the north ambulatory. He was reconnoitring the windows of the house from the opposite side of the cloisters, in the hope of discovering something, when he was caught, as before mentioned, by the king.

Wolsey, meanwhile, was received by Doctor Sampson at the doorway of his dwelling, and ushered by him into a small chamber, on the upper floor, wainscoted with curiously-carved and lustrously black oak. A silver lamp was burning on the table, and in the recess of the window, which was screened by thick curtains, sat a majestic lady, who rose on the cardinal's entrance. It was Catharine of Arragon.

"I attend your pleasure, madam," said Wolsey, with a profound inclination.

"You have been long in answering my summons," said the queen; "but I could not expect greater promptitude. Time was when a summons from Catharine of Arragon would have been quickly and cheerfully attended to; when the proudest noble in the land would have borne her message to you, and when you would have passed through crowds to her audience chamber. Now, another holds her place, and she is obliged secretly to enter the castle where she once ruled, to despatch a valet to her enemy, to attend his pleasure, and to receive him in the dwelling of an humble canon. Times are changed with me, Wolsey—sadly changed."

"I have been in attendance on the king, madam, or I should have been with you sooner," replied Wolsey. "It grieves me sorely to see you here."

"I want not your pity," replied the queen proudly. "I did not send for you to gratify your malice by exposing my abject state. I did not send for you to insult me by false sympathy; but in the hope that your own interest would induce you to redress the wrongs you have done me."

"Alas! madam, I fear it is now too late to repair the error I have committed," said Wolsey, in a tone of affected penitence and sorrow.

"You admit then it was an error," cried Catharine. "Well, that is something. Oh! that you had paused

269

before you had began your evil work—before you had raised a storm which will destroy me and yourself. Your quarrel with my nephew the Emperor Charles has cost *me* dear, but it will cost *you* yet more dearly."

" I deserve all your reproaches, madam," said Wolsey, with feigned meekness; " and I will bear them without a murmur. But you have sent for me for some specific object, I presume."

" I sent for you to give me aid, as much for your own sake as mine," replied the queen, " for you are in equal danger. Prevent this divorce—foil Anne and you retain the king's favour. Our interests are so far leagued together that you must serve me to serve yourself. My object is to gain time to enable my friends to act. Your colleague is secretly favourable to me. Pronounce no sentence here, but let the cause be removed to Rome. My nephew the emperor will prevail upon the pope to decide in my favour. "

" I dare not thus brave the king's displeasure, madam," replied Wolsey.

" Dissembler ! " exclaimed Catharine. " I now perceive the insincerity of your professions. Thus much I have said to try you. And now to my real motive for sending for you. I have in my possession certain letters that will ruin Anne Boleyn with the king."

" Ha ! " exclaimed the cardinal joyfully; " if that be the case, all the rest will be easy. Let me see the letters, I pray you, madam."

Before Catharine could reply, the door was thrown violently open, and the king stood before them.

" Soh ! " roared Henry, casting a terrible look at Wolsey, " I have caught you at your treasonable practices at last !—And you, madam," he added, turning to Catharine, who meekly but steadily, returned his gaze, " what brings you here again ? Because I pardoned your indiscretion yesterday, think not I shall always be so lenient. You will leave the castle instantly. As to Wolsey, he shall render me a strict account of his conduct."

" I have nothing to declare, my liege," replied Wolsey, recovering himself. " I leave it to the queen to explain why I came hither."

" The explanation shall be given at once," said Catharine. " I sent for the cardinal to request him to lay before your majesty these two letters from Anne Boleyn to Sir Thomas Wyat, that you might judge whether one who could write thus would make you a fitting consort. You disbelieved my charge of levity yesterday. Read these, sire, and judge whether I spoke the truth."

Henry glanced at the letters and his brow grew dark.

" What say you to them, my liege ? " cried Catharine, with a glance of triumph. " In the one she vows eternal constancy to Sir Thomas Wyat; and in the other— written after her engagement to you—she tells him that though they can never meet as heretofore, she will always love him."

" Ten thousand furies ! " cried the king. " Where got you these letters, madam ? "

" They were given to me by a tall dark man, as I quitted the castle last night," said the queen. " He said they were taken from the person of Sir Thomas Wyat while he lay concealed in the forest in the cave of Herne the hunter.

" If I thought she wrote them," cried Henry, in an access of jealous fury, " I would cast her off for ever."

" Methinks your majesty should be able to judge whether they are true or false," said Catharine. " I know her writing well—too well, alas !—and am satisfied they are genuine."

" I am well assured that Wyat was concealed in the Lady Anne's chamber when your majesty demanded admittance, and could not obtain it,—when the Earl of Surrey sacrificed himself for her, and for his friend," said Wolsey.

" Perdition ! " exclaimed the king, striking his brow with his clenched hand. " Oh, Catharine," he continued, after a pause, during which she intently watched the workings of his countenance, " and it was for this light-hearted creature I was about to cast you off ! "

" I forgive you, sire—I forgive you ! " exclaimed the queen, clasping his hands, and bedewing them with grateful tears. " You have been deceived. Heaven keep you in the same mind ! "

" You have preserved me," said Henry; " but you must not tarry here. Come with me to the royal lodgings."

" No, Henry," replied Catharine, with a shudder, " not while *she* is there."

" Make no conditions, madam," whispered Wolsey. " Go."

" She shall be removed to-morrow," said Henry.

" In that case I am content to smother my feelings," said the queen.

" Come, then, Kate," said Henry, taking her hand. " Lord cardinal, you will attend us."

" Right gladly, my liege," replied Wolsey. " If this mood will only endure," he muttered, " all will go well. But his jealousy must not be allowed to cool. Would that Wyat were here ! "

Doctor Sampson could scarcely credit his senses, as he beheld the august pair come forth together, and a word from Wolsey explaining what had occurred, threw him into transports of delight. But the surprise of the good canon was nothing to that exhibited as Henry and Catharine entered the royal lodgings, and the king ordered his own apartments to be instantly prepared for her majesty's reception.

XI

How Tristram Lyndwood and Mabel were liberated

INTELLIGENCE of the queen's return was instantly conveyed to Anne Boleyn, and filled her with indescribable alarm. All her visions of power and splendour seemed to melt away at once. She sent for her father, Lord Rochford, who hurried to her in a state of the utmost anxiety, and closely questioned her whether the extraordinary change had not been occasioned by some imprudence of her own. But she positively denied the charge; alleging that she had parted with the king scarcely an hour before on terms of the most perfect amity, and with the full conviction that she had accomplished the cardinal's ruin.

"You should not have put forth your hand against him till you were sure of striking the blow," said Rochford. "There is no telling what secret influence he has over the king; and there may yet be a hard battle to fight. But not a moment must be lost in counteracting his operations. Luckily, Suffolk is here; and his enmity to the cardinal will make him a sure friend to us. Pray Heaven you have not given the king fresh occasion for jealousy! That is all I fear."

And quitting his daughter, he sought out Suffolk, who, alarmed at what appeared like a restoration of Wolsey to favour, promised heartily to co-operate with him in the struggle, and that no time might be lost, the duke proceeded at once to the royal closet, where he found the king pacing moodily to and fro.

"Your majesty seems disturbed," said the duke.

"Disturbed!—ay!" exclaimed the king. "I have enough to disturb me, I will never love again. I will forswear the whole sex. Harkee, Suffolk, you are my brother, my second self, and know all the secrets of my heart. After the passionate devotion I have displayed for Anne Boleyn—after all I have done for her—all I have risked for her—I have been deceived."

"Impossible, my liege!" exclaimed Suffolk.

"Why, so I thought," cried Henry, "and I turned a deaf ear to all insinuations thrown out against her, till proof was afforded which I could no longer doubt."

"And what was the amount of the proof, my liege?" asked Suffolk.

"These letters," said Henry, handing them to him, "found on the person of Sir Thomas Wyat."

"But these only prove, my liege, the existence of a former passion—nothing more," remarked Suffolk, after he had scanned them.

"But she vows eternal constancy to him!" cried Henry; "says she shall ever love him!—says so at the time she professes devoted love for me! How can I trust her after that? Suffolk, I feel she does not love me exclusively; and my passion is so deep and devouring that it demands entire return. I must have her heart as well as her person; and I feel I have only won her in my quality of king."

"I am persuaded your majesty is mistaken," said the duke.

"Would I could think so!" sighed Henry. "But no —no, I cannot be deceived. I will conquer this fatal passion. Oh, Suffolk! it is frightful to be the bond-slave of a woman—a fickle, inconstant woman. But between the depths of love and hate is but a step; and I can pass from one to the other."

"Do nothing rashly, my dear liege," said Suffolk; "nothing that may bring with it after-repentance. Do not be swayed by those who have inflamed your jealousy, and who could practise upon it. Think the matter calmly over, and then act. And till you have decided, see neither Catharine nor Anne; and, above all, do not admit Wolsey to your secret councils."

"You are his enemy, Suffolk," said the king sternly.

"I am your majesty's friend," replied the duke.

"Beseech you, yield to me on this occasion, and I am sure of your thanks hereafter."

"Well, I believe you are right, my good friend and brother," said Henry, "and I will curb my impulses of rage and jealousy. To-morrow, before I see either the queen or Anne, we will ride forth into the forest, and talk the matter further over."

"Your highness has come to a wise determination," said the duke.

"Oh, Suffolk!" sighed Henry, "would I had never seen this siren! She exercises a fearful control over me, and enslaves my very soul."

"I cannot say whether it is for good or ill that you have met, my dear liege," replied Suffolk, "but I fancy I can discern the way in which your ultimate decision will be taken. But it is now near midnight. I wish your majesty sound and untroubled repose."

"Stay!" cried Henry, "I am about to visit the Curfew Tower, and must take you with me. I will explain my errand as we go. I had some thought of sending you there in my stead. Ha!" he exclaimed, glancing at his finger. "By St. Paul! it is gone."

"What is gone, my liege?" asked Suffolk.

"My signet," replied Henry. "I missed it not till now. It has been wrested from me by the fiend, during my walk from the Curfew Tower. Let us not lose a moment, or the prisoners will be set free by him—if they have not been liberated already."

So saying, he took a couple of dags—a species of short gun—from a rest on the wall, and giving one to Suffolk, thrust the other into his girdle. Thus armed, they quitted the royal lodgings, and hurried in the direction of the Curfew Tower. Just as they reached the Horse-shoe Cloisters, the alarm-bell began to ring.

"Did I not tell you so?" cried Henry furiously; "they have escaped. Ha! it ceases!—what has happened?"

About a quarter of an hour after the king had quitted the Curfew Tower, a tall man, enveloped in a cloak, and wearing a high conical cap, presented himself to the arquobusier stationed at the entrance to the dungeon, and desired to be admitted to the prisoners.

" I have the king's signet," he said, holding forth the ring.

On seeing this, the arquebusier, who recognised the ring, unlocked the door, and admitted him. Mabel was kneeling on the ground beside her grandsire, with her hands raised as in prayer, but as the tall man entered the vault she started to her feet, and uttered a slight scream.

" What is the matter, child ? " cried Tristram.

" He is here !—he is come ! " cried Mabel, in a tone of the deepest terror.

" Who—the king ! " cried Tristram, looking up. "Ah ! I see ! Herne is come to deliver me."

" Do not go with him, grandsire," cried Mabel. " In the name of all the saints, I implore you, do not."

" Silence her ! " said Herne, in a harsh, imperious voice, " or I leave you."

The old man looked imploringly at his grand-daughter.

" You know the conditions of your liberation ? " said Herne.

" I do—I do," replied Tristram hastily, and with a shudder.

" Oh, grandfather," cried Mabel, falling at his feet, " do not, I conjure you, make any conditions with this dreaded being, or it will be at the expense of your salvation. Better I should perish at the stake—better you should suffer the most ignominious death, than this should be."

" Do you accept them ? " cried Herne, disregarding her supplications.

Tristram answered in the affirmative.

" Recall your words, grandfather—recall your words !" cried Mabel. " I will implore pardon for you on my knees from the king, and he will not refuse me."

" The pledge cannot be recalled, damsel," said Herne;

" and it is to save you from the king, as much as to accomplish his own preservation, that your grandsire consents. He would not have you a victim to Henry's lust." And as he spoke, he divided the forester's bonds with his knife. " You must go with him, Mabel," he added.

" I will not ! " she cried. " Something warns me that a great danger awaits me."

" You *must* go, girl," cried Tristram angrily. " I will not leave you to Henry's lawless passion."

Meanwhile, Herne had passed into one of the large embrasures, and opened, by means of a spring, an entrance to a secret staircase in the wall. He then beckoned Tristram towards him, and whispered some instructions in his ear.

" I understand," replied the old man.

" Proceed to the cave," cried Herne, " and remain there till I join you."

Tristram nodded assent.

" Come, Mabel ! " he cried, advancing towards her, and seizing her hand.

" Away ! " cried Herne, in a menacing tone.

Terrified by the formidable looks and gestures of the demon, the poor girl offered no resistance, and her grandfather drew her into the opening, which was immediately closed after her.

About an hour after this, and when it was near upon the stroke of midnight, the arquebusier who had admitted the tall stranger to the dungeon, and who had momentarily expected his coming forth, opened the door to see what was going forward. Great was his astonishment to find the cell empty ! After looking around in bewilderment he rushed to the chamber above to tell his comrades what had happened.

" This is clearly the work of the fiend," said Shoreditch ; " it is useless to strive against him."

" That tall black man was doubtless Herne himself," said Paddington. " I am glad he did us no injury. I hope the king will not provoke his malice further."

"Well, we must inform Captain Bouchier of the mischance," said Shoreditch. "I would not be in thy skin, Mat Bee, for a trifle. The king will be here presently, and then——"

"It is impossible to penetrate through the devices of the Evil One," interrupted Mat. "I could have sworn it was the royal signet, for I saw it on the king's finger as he delivered the order. I wish such another chance of capturing the fiend would occur to me."

As the words were uttered, the door of a recess was thrown suddenly open, and Herne, in his wild garb, with his antlered helm upon his brow, and the rusty chain depending from his left arm, stood before them. His appearance was so terrific and unearthly that they all shrank aghast, and Mat Bee fell with his face on the floor.

"I am here!" cried the demon. "Now, braggart, wilt dare to seize me?"

But not a hand was moved against him. The whole party seemed transfixed with terror.

"You dare not brave my power, and you are right," cried Herne; "a wave of my hand would bring this old tower about your ears—a word would summon a legion of fiends to torment you."

"But do not utter it, I pray you, good Herne—excellent Herne," cried Mat Bee. "And, above all things, do not wave your hand, for we have no desire to be buried alive—have we, comrades? I should never have said what I did if I had thought your fiendship within hearing."

"Your royal master will as vainly seek to contend with me as he did to bury me beneath the oak-tree," cried Herne. "If you want me further, seek me in the upper chamber."

And with these words, he darted up the ladder-like flight of steps and disappeared.

As soon as they recovered from the fright that had enchained them, Shoreditch and Paddington rushed forth into the area in front of the turret, and shouting

to those on the roof, told them that Herne was in the
upper room—a piece of information which was altogether superfluous, as the hammering had recommenced,
and continued till the clock struck twelve, when it
stopped. Just then, it occurred to Mat Bee to ring
the alarm-bell, and he seized the rope, and began
to pull it; but the bell had scarcely sounded when
the cord, severed from above, fell down upon his
head.

At this juncture, the king and the Duke of Suffolk
arrived. When told what had happened, though prepared for it, Henry burst into a terrible passion, and
bestowed a buffet on Mat Bee that well-nigh broke his
jaw, and sent him reeling to the farther side of the
chamber. He had not at first understood that Herne
was supposed to be in the upper room; but as soon as
he was made aware of the circumstance, he cried
out:

" Ah, dastards ! have you let him brave you thus ? But
I am glad of it. His capture is reserved for my own
hand."

" Do not expose yourself to this risk, my gracious
liege," said Suffolk.

" What ! are you, too, a sharer in their womanish
fears, Suffolk ? " cried Henry. " I thought you had
been made of stouter stuff. If there is danger, I shall
be the first to encounter it. Come," he added, snatching
a torch from an arquebusier. And drawing his dag, he
hurried up the steep steps, while Suffolk followed his
example, and three or four arquebusiers ventured after
them.

Meanwhile, Shoreditch and Paddington ran out, and
informed Bouchier that the king had arrived, and was
mounting in search of Herne, upon which the captain,
shaking off his fears, ordered his men to follow him,
and opening the little door at the top of the stairs,
began cautiously to descend, feeling his way with his
sword. He had got about half-way down when Henry
sprang upon the platform. The light of the torch fell

upon the ghostly figure of Herne, with his arms folded upon his breast, standing near the pile of wood lying between the two staircases. So appalling was the appearance of the demon, that Henry stood still to gaze at him, while Bouchier and his men remained irresolute on the stairs. In another moment, the Duke of Suffolk had gained the platform, and the arquebusiers were seen near the head of the stairs.

"At last thou art in my power, accursed being!" cried Henry. "Thou art hemmed in on all sides, and canst not escape!"

"Ho! ho! ho!" laughed Herne.

"This shall prove whether thou art human or not," cried Henry, taking deliberate aim at him with the dag.

"Ho! ho! ho!" roared Herne.

And as the report rang through the room, he sank through the floor, and disappeared from view.

"Gone!" exclaimed Henry, as the smoke cleared off —"gone! Holy Mary! then it must indeed be the fiend. I made the middle of his skull my aim, and if he had not been invulnerable, the bullet must have pierced his brain."

"I heard it rebound from his horned helmet, and drop to the floor," said Bouchier.

"What is that chest?" cried Henry, pointing to a strange coffin-shaped box, lying, as it seemed, on the exact spot where the demon had disappeared.

No one had seen it before, though all called to mind the mysterious hammering; and they had no doubt that the coffin was the work of the demon.

"Break it open!" cried Henry; "for ought we know, Herne may be concealed within it."

The order was reluctantly obeyed by the arquebusiers. But no force was required, for the lid was not nailed down; and when it was removed, a human body, in the last stages of decay, was discovered.

"Pah! close it up," cried Henry, turning away in disgust. "How came it there?"

"It must have been brought by the powers of darkness," said Bouchier; "no such coffin was here when I searched the chamber two hours ago. But see," he added, stooping down, and picking up a piece of paper which had fallen from the coffin, "here is a scroll."

"Give it me!" cried Henry; and holding it to the light, he read the words, "*The body of Mark Fytton, the butcher, the victim of a tyrant's cruelty.*"

Uttering a terrible imprecation, Henry flung the paper from him; and bidding the arquebusiers burn the body at the foot of the gallows without the town, he quitted the tower without further search.

XII

How Wolsey was disgraced by the King

ON the following day, a reconciliation took place between the king and Anne Boleyn. During a ride in the Great Park with his royal brother, Suffolk not only convinced him of the groundlessness of his jealousy, but contrived to incense him strongly against Wolsey. Thus the queen and the cardinal lost the momentary advantage they had gained, while Anne's power was raised yet higher. Yielding to her entreaties not to see Catharine again, nor to hold further conference with Wolsey until the sentence of the court should be pronounced, Henry left the castle that very day, and proceeded to his palace of Bridewell. The distress of the unhappy queen at this sudden revolution of affairs may be conceived. Distrusting Wolsey, and putting her sole reliance on Heaven, and the goodness of her cause, she withdrew to Blackfriars, where she remained till the court met. As to the cardinal himself, driven desperate by his situation, and exasperated by the treatment he had experienced, he resolved, at whatever risk, to thwart Henry's schemes, and revenge himself upon Anne Boleyn.

Thus matters continued till the court met as before in the parliament-chamber, at Blackfriars. On this occasion Henry was present, and took his place under a cloth of estate—the queen sitting at some distance below him. Opposite them were the legates with the Archbishop of Canterbury, and the whole of the bishops. The aspect of the assemblage was grave and anxious.

Many eyes were turned on Henry, who looked gloomy and menacing, but the chief object of interest was the queen, who, though pale as death, had never in her highest days of power worn a more majestic and dignified air than on this occasion.

The proceedings of the court then commenced, and the king being called by the crier, he immediately answered to the summons. Catharine was next called, and instead of replying, she marched towards the canopy beneath which the king was seated, prostrated herself, and poured forth a most pathetic and eloquent appeal to him; at the close of which she arose, and making a profound reverence, walked out of the court, leaning upon the arm of her general receiver, Griffith. Henry desired the crier to call her back, but she would not return; and seeing the effect produced by her address upon the auditory, he endeavoured to efface it by an eulogium on her character and virtues, accompanied by an expression of deep regret at the step he was compelled to take in separating himself from her. But his hypocrisy availed him little, and his speech was received with looks of ill-disguised incredulity. Some further discourse then took place between the Archbishop of Canterbury and the Bishop of Rochester; but as the queen had absented herself, the court was adjourned to the next day, when it met again, and as she did not then appear, though summoned, she was pronounced contumacious. After repeated adjournments, the last session was held, and judgment demanded on the part of the king, when Campeggio, as had been arranged between him and Wolsey, declined to pronounce it until he had referred the matter to the pope, and the court dissolved.

About two months after this event, during which time the legates' commission had been revoked, while Henry was revolving the expediency of accomplishing the divorce through the medium of his own ecclesiastical courts, and without reference to that of Rome—a despatch was received from the pope by the two cardinals, requiring them to cite the king to appear before him by attorney on a certain day. At the time of the arrival of this instrument, Campeggio chanced to be staying with Wolsey at his palace at Esher, and as the king was then holding his court at Windsor, they both set out for the castle on the following day, attended by a retinue of nearly a hundred horsemen, splendidly equipped.

It was now the middle of September, and the woods, instead of presenting one uniform mass of green, glowed with an infinite variety of lovely tints. And yet, despite the beauty of the scene, there was something melancholy in witnessing the decline of the year, as marked by those old woods, and by the paths that led through them, so thickly strewn with leaves. Wolsey was greatly affected.

" These noble trees were ere long be reft of their glories," he thought—" and so, most likely, will it be with me—and perhaps my winter may come on sooner than theirs ! "

The cardinal and his train had crossed Staines Bridge, and passing through Egham, had entered the Great Park, near Englefield Green. They were proceeding along the high ridge overlooking the woody region between it and the castle, when a joyous shout in the glades beneath reached them; and looking down, they saw the king, accompanied by Anne Boleyn, and attended by his falconers and a large company of horsemen, pursuing the sport of hawking. The royal party appeared so much interested in their sport that they did not notice the cardinal and his train, and were soon out of sight. But as Wolsey descended Snow Hill, and entered the long avenue, he heard the trampling of horses at a little distance; and shortly afterwards, Henry and Anne issued from out the trees. They were somewhat more than a bow-shot in advance of the cardinal; but instead of halting till he came up, the king had no sooner ascertained who it was, than, despatching a messenger to the castle, who was seen galloping swiftly down the avenue, he rode off with Anne Boleyn towards the opposite side of the park. Though deeply mortified by the slight, Wolsey concealed his vexation from his brother cardinal, and pursued his way to the castle, before which he presently arrived. The gate was thrown open at his approach, but he had scarcely entered the lower ward, when Sir Henry Norris, the king's groom of the stole, advanced to meet him, and, with a sorrowful expression of countenance, said that his royal master had so many guests at the castle, that he could not accommodate him and his train.

" I understand your drift, sir," replied Wolsey—" you would tell me I am not welcome. Well, then, his eminence Cardinal Campeggio and myself must take up our lodging at some hostel in the town, for it is necessary we should see the king."

" If your grace is content to dismiss your attendants," said Norris in a low tone, " you and Cardinal Campeggio can be lodged in Henry the Third's Tower. Thus much I will take upon me; but I dare not admit you to the royal lodgings."

Wolsey tried to look unconcerned, and calling to his gentleman usher, George Cavendish, gave him some instructions in a low voice, upon which the other immediately placed himself at the head of the retinue, and ordered them to quit the castle with him, leaving only the jester, Patch, to attend upon his master. Campeggio's attendants being, comparatively speaking, few in number, were allowed to remain, and his litter was conveyed to Henry the Third's Tower—a fortification standing, as already stated, in the south side of the lower ward, near the edge of the dry moat surrounding the

Round Tower. At the steps of this tower Wolsey dismounted, and was about to follow Campeggio into the doorway, when Will Sommers, who had heard of his arrival, stepped forward, and with a salutation of mock formality, said, " I am sure it will grieve the king, my master, not to be able to accommodate your grace's train; but since it is larger than his own, you will scarce blame him his want of hospitality."

" Nor the courtesy of his attendants," rejoined Wolsey sharply. " I am in no mood for thy jesting now. Stand aside, sirrah, or I will have the rod applied to thy back ! "

" Take care the king does not apply the rod to your own, lord cardinal," retorted Will Sommers. " If he scourges you according to your deserts, your skin will be redder than your robe." And his mocking laugh pursued Wolsey, like the hiss of a snake, into the tower.

Some two hours after this, Henry and his attendants returned from the chase. The king seemed in a blithe humour, and Wolsey saw him laugh heartily as Will Sommers pointed with his bauble towards Henry the Third's Tower. The cardinal received no invitation to the royal banquet; and the answer to his solicitation for an interview was, that he and Campeggio would be received in the presence-chamber on the following morning, but not before.

That night a great revel was held in the castle. Masquing, dancing, and feasting filled up the evening, and the joyous sounds and strains reached Wolsey in his seclusion, and forced him to contrast it with his recent position, when he would have been second only to the king in the entertainment. He laid his head upon his pillow, but not to rest, and while tossing feverishly about his couch, he saw the arras with which the walls were covered move, and a tall, dark figure step from behind it. The cardinal would have awakened his jester, who slept in a small truckle-bed at his feet, but the strange visitor motioned him to be still.

" You may conjecture who I am, cardinal," he said, " but in case you should doubt, I will tell you. I am

Herne the hunter ! And now to my errand. There is a damsel, whom you once saw in the forest near the great lake, and whom you promised to befriend. You can assist her now—to-morrow it may be out of your power."

" I have enough to do to aid myself, without meddling with what concerns me not," said Wolsey.

" This damsel *does* concern you," cried Herne. " Read this, and you will see in what way."

And he tossed a letter to Wolsey, who glanced at it by the light of the lamp.

" Ha ! is it so ? " he exclaimed. " Is she——"

" Hush ! " cried Herne, " or you will wake this sleeper. It is as you suppose. Will you not aid her now ? Will you not bestow some of your treasure upon her before it is wholly wrested from you by the king ? I will do aught you wish, secretly and swiftly."

" Go, then, to my palace at Esher," cried the cardinal. " Take this key to my treasurer—it is the key of my coffers. Bid him deliver to you the six caskets in the cabinet in the gilt chamber. Here is a token by which he will know that you came from me," he added, delivering him a small chain of gold, " for it has been so agreed between us. But you will be sure to give the treasure to Mabel ? "

" Fear nothing," replied Herne. And stretching forth his hand to receive the key and the chain, he glided behind the tapestry, and disappeared.

This strange incident gave some diversion to Wolsey's thoughts; but ere long they returned to their former channel. Sleep would not be summoned, and as soon as the first glimpse of day appeared, he arose, and wrapping his robe around him, left his room and ascended a winding staircase leading to the roof of the tower.

The morning promised to be fine, but it was then hazy, and the greater part of the forest was wrapped in mist. The castle, however, was seen to great advantage. Above Wolsey rose the vast fabric of the Round Tower, on the summit of which the broad standard was at that moment being unfurled; while the different battlements and towers arose majestically around. But Wolsey's gaze rested chiefly upon the exquisite mausoleum lying immediately beneath him, in which he had partly prepared for himself a magnificent monument. A sharp pang shook him as he contemplated it, and he cried aloud, " My very tomb will be wrested from me by this rapacious monarch; and after all my care, and all my cost, I know not where I shall rest my bones ! "

Saddened by the reflection, he descended to his chamber, and again threw himself on the couch.

But Wolsey was not the only person in the castle who had passed a sleepless night. Of the host of his enemies many had been kept awake by the anticipation of his downfall on the morrow; and among these was Anne Boleyn, who had received an assurance from the king that her enmity should at length be fully gratified.

At the appointed hour, the two cardinals proceeded to the royal lodgings. They were detained for some time in the antechamber, where Wolsey was exposed to the taunts and sneers of the courtiers, who had lately so servilely fawned upon him. At length, they were ushered into the presence-chamber, at the upper end of which, beneath a canopy emblazoned with the royal arms woven in gold, sat Henry, with Anne Boleyn on his right hand. At the foot of the throne stood Will Sommers, and near him the Dukes of Richmond and Suffolk. Norfolk, Rochford, and a number of other nobles, all open enemies of Wolsey, were likewise present. Henry watched the advance of the cardinals with a stern look, and after they had made an obeisance to him, he motioned them to rise.

" You have sought an interview with me, my lords," he said, with suppressed rage. " What would you ? "

" We have brought an instrument to you, my liege," said Wolsey, " which has just been received from his holiness the pope."

" Declare its nature," said Henry.

"It is a citation," replied Wolsey, "enjoining your highness to appear by attorney in the papal court, under a penalty of ten thousand ducats."

And he presented a parchment, stamped with the great seal of Rome, to the king, who glanced his eye fiercely over it, and then dashed it to the ground, with an explosion of fury terrible to hear and to witness.

"Ha! by St. George!" he cried; "am I as nothing, that the pope dares to insult me thus?"

"It is a mere judicial form, your majesty," interposed Campeggio; "and is chiefly sent by his holiness to let you know we have no further jurisdiction in the matter of the divorce."

"I will take care you have not, nor his holiness either," roared the king. "By my father's head! he shall find I will be no longer trifled with."

"But, my liege——" cried Campeggio.

"Peace!" cried the king. "I will hear no apologies nor excuses. The insult has been offered, and cannot be effaced. As for you, Wolsey——"

"Sire!" exclaimed the cardinal, shrinking before the whirlwind of passion, which seemed to menace his utter extermination.

"As for you, I say," pursued Henry, extending his hand towards him, while his eyes flashed fire, "who by your outrageous pride have so long overshadowed our honour—who by your insatiate avarice and appetite for wealth have oppressed our subjects—who by your manifold acts of bribery and extortion have impoverished our realm, and by your cruelty and partiality have subverted the due course of justice, and turned it to your ends—the time is come when you shall receive due punishment for your offences."

"You wrong me, my dear liege," cried Wolsey abjectly. "These are the accusations of my enemies. Grant me a patient hearing, and I will explain all."

"I would not sharpen the king's resentment against you, lord cardinal," said Anne Boleyn, "for it is keen enough; but I cannot permit you to say that these charges are merely hostile. Those who would support the king's honour and dignity must desire to see you removed from his councils."

" I am ready to take thy place, lord cardinal," said Will Sommers; " and will exchange my bauble for thy chancellor's mace, and my fool's cap for thy cardinal's hat."

" Peace ! " thundered the king. " Stand not between me and the object of my wrath. Your accusers are not one but many, Wolsey; nay, the whole of my people cry out for justice against you. And they shall have it. But you shall hear the charges they bring. Firstly, contrary to our prerogative, and for your own advancement and profit, you have obtained authority legatine from the pope; by which authority you have not only spoiled and taken away their substance from many religious houses, but have usurped much of our own jurisdiction. You have also made a treaty with the King of France for the pope without our consent, and concluded another friendly treaty with the Duke of Ferrara, under our great seal, and in our name, without our warrant. And furthermore, you have presumed to couple yourself with our royal self in your letters and instructions, as if you were on an equality with us."

" Ha ! ha ! ' The king and I would have you do thus ! ' ' The king and I give you our hearty thanks ! ' Ran it not so, cardinal ? " cried Will Sommers. " You will soon win the cap and bells."

" In exercise of your legatine authority," pursued the king, " you have given away benefices contrary to our crown and dignity, for the which you are in danger of forfeiture of your lands and goods."

" A premunire, cardinal," cried Will Sommers. " A premunire !—ha ! ha ! "

" Then it has been your practice to receive all the ambassadors to our court first at your own palace," continued Henry—" to hear their charges and intentions, and to instruct them as you might see fit. You have also so practised that all our letters sent from beyond sea have first come to your own hands, by which you have acquainted yourself with their contents, and compelled us and our council to follow your devices. You have also written to all our ambassadors abroad in your own name concerning our affairs, without our authority ; and received letters in return from them by which you have sought to compass your own purposes. By your ambition and pride you have undone many of our poor subjects; have suppressed religious houses, and received their possessions; have seized upon the goods of wealthy spiritual men deceased; constrained all ordinaries yearly to compound with you; have gotten riches for yourself and servants by subversion of the laws, and by abuse of your authority in causing divers pardons of the pope to be suspended until you, by promise of a yearly pension, chose to revive them; and also by crafty and untrue tales have sought to create dissension among our nobles."

" That we can all avouch for," cried Suffolk. " It was never merry in England while there were cardinals among us."

" Of all men in England your grace should be the last to say so," rejoined Wolsey; " for if I had not been cardinal, you would not have had a head upon your shoulders to utter the taunt."

" No more of this ! " cried the king. " You have misdemeaned yourself in our court by keeping up as great state in our absence as if we had been there in person; and presumptuously have dared to join and imprint your badge—the cardinal's hat, under our arms, graven on our coins struck at York. And lastly— whenever in open parliament allusion hath been made to heresies and erroneous sects, you have failed to correct and notice them, to the danger of the whole body of good and Christian people of this our realm."

" This last charge ought to win me favour in the eyes of one who professes the opinions of Luther," said Wolsey to Anne. " But I deny it, as I do all the rest."

" I will listen to no defence, Wolsey," replied the

king. "I will make you a terrible example to others how they offend us and our laws hereafter."

"Do not condemn me unheard!" cried the cardinal, prostrating himself.

"I have heard too much, and I will hear no more!" cried the king fiercely. "I dismiss you from my presence for ever. If you are innocent, as you aver, justice will be done you. If you are guilty, as I believe you to be, look not for leniency from me, for I will show you none!"

And, seating himself, he turned to Anne, and said, in a low tone, "Are you content, sweetheart?"

"I am," she replied. "I shall not now break my vow. False cardinal!" she added aloud, "your reign is at an end."

"Your own may not be much longer, madam," rejoined Wolsey bitterly. "The shadow of the axe," he added, pointing to the reflection of a partisan on the floor, "is at your feet. Ere long it may rise to the head."

And accompanied by Campeggio, he slowly quitted the presence-chamber.

Book the Fifth

MABEL LYNDWOOD

I

How the Earl of Surrey and the fair Geraldine met in King James's bower in the moat; and how they were surprised by the Duke of Richmond

IN order to preserve unbroken the chain of events with which the last book of this chronicle concluded, it was deemed expedient to disturb the unity of time, so far as it related to some of the less important characters; and it will now be necessary, therefore, to return to the middle of June, when the Earl of Surrey's term of captivity was drawing to a close.

As the best means of conquering the anxiety produced by the vision exhibited to him by Herne, increased as it was by the loss of the relic he had sustained at the same time, the earl had devoted himself to incessant study, and for a whole month he remained within his chamber. The consequence of his unremitting application was, that though he succeeded in his design, and completely regained his tranquillity, his strength gave way under the effort, and he was confined for some days to his couch by a low fever.

As soon as he was sufficiently recovered to venture forth, he mounted to the summit of the Round Tower, in the hope that a walk round its breezy battlements might conduce to his restoration of health. The day was bright and beautiful, and a gentle wind was stirring; and as Surrey felt the breath of heaven upon his cheek, and gazed upon the glorious prospect before him, he wondered that his imprisonment had not driven him mad. Everything around him, indeed, was calculated to make the sense of captivity painful. The broad and beautiful meads, stretching out beneath him, seemed to invite a ramble over them; the silver river courted a plunge into its waves; the woods an hour's retirement into their shady recesses. The bells of Eton College rang out merrily, but their sound saddened rather than elated him. The road between Eton and Windsor, then marked by straggling cottages with gardens between them, with here and there a dwelling of a better kind, was thronged with herds of cattle and their drivers, for a fair was held that day in the town of Windsor, to which they were hastening. Then there were country maidens and youthful hinds in their holiday apparel, trooping towards the bridge. Booths were erected, near which, in the Brocas meads, the rustic sports of wrestling, running, and casting the bar, were going forward; while numbers of boats shot to and fro upon the river, and strains of music proceeded from a large gilt barge moored to its banks. Nearer, and in the broad green plain lying beneath the north terrace, were a company of archers shooting at the butts. But these sights, instead of affording pleasure to Surrey, only sharpened the anguish of his feelings by the contrast they offered to his present position.

To distract his thoughts, he quitted the near view, and let his eye run along the edge of the horizon, until it rested upon a small speck, which he knew to be the lofty spire of St. Paul's Cathedral. If, as he supposed, the fair Geraldine was in attendance upon Anne Boleyn, at the palace at Bridewell, she must be under the very shadow of this very spire; and the supposition, whether correct or not, produced such quick and stifling emotions, that the tears rushed to his eyes.

Ashamed of his weakness, he turned to the other side of the tower, and bent his gaze upon the woody heights of the Great Park. These recalled Herne the hunter; and burning with resentment at the tricks practised upon him by the demon, he determined that the first use he would make of his liberty should be to seek out, and, if possible, effect the capture of the mysterious being. Some of the strange encounters between Herne and the king had been related to him by the officer on guard at the Norman Tower; but these only served as stimulants to the adventure. After a couple of hours thus passed on the keep, he descended, refreshed and invigorated. The next day he was there again, and the day after that; when, feeling that his restoration was well-nigh complete, he requested permission to pass the following evening in the dry moat of the donjon. And this was readily accorded him.

Covered with green sod, and shaded by many tall trees, growing out of the side of the artificial mound on which the keep was built, the fosse offered all the advantages of a garden to the prisoners who were allowed to take exercise within it. Here, as has been mentioned, King James the First of Scotland first beheld from the battlements above, the lovely Jane Beaufort take her solitary walk, and by his looks and gestures contrived to make her sensible of the passion with which she inspired him; and here at last, in an arbour which, for the sake of the old and delightful legend connected with it, was kept up at the time of this chronicle, and then bore the name of the royal poet, they had secretly met, and interchanged their vows of affection.

Familiar with the story, familiar also with the poetic strains to which the monarch's passion gave birth, Surrey could not help comparing his own fate with that of the illustrious captive who had visited the spot before him. Full of such thoughts, he pensively tracked the narrow path winding between the grassy banks of the fosse—now casting up his eyes to the keep—now looking towards the arbour, and wishing that he had been favoured with such visitings as lightened the captivity of the Scottish king. At last, he sought the bower—a charming little nest of green leaves and roses, sheltering a bench which seemed only contrived for lovers— and taking out his tablets, began to trace within them some stanzas of that exquisite poem which has linked his name for ever with the Round Tower. Thus occupied, the time stole on insensibly, and he was not aware that he had overstayed the limits allowed him, till he was roused by the voice of the officer, who came to summon him back to his prison.

"You will be removed to your old lodging in the Round Tower to-morrow night, my lord," said the officer.

"For what reason?" demanded the earl, as he followed his conductor up the steep side of the mound. But receiving no reply, he did not renew the inquiry.

Entering a door in the covered way at the head of the flight of steps communicating with the Norman Tower, they descended them in silence. Just as they reached the foot of this long staircase, the earl chanced to cast back his eyes, and to his inexpressible astonishment, perceived on the landing at the head of the steps, and just before the piece of ordnance commanding the ascent, the figure of Herne the hunter.

Before he could utter an exclamation, the figure retreated through the adjoining archway. Telling the officer what he had seen, Surrey would fain have gone in quest of the fiendish spy; but the other would not permit him; and affecting to treat the matter as a mere creation of fancy, he hurried the earl to his chamber in the Curfew Tower.

The next day, Surrey was removed betimes to the Round Tower, and the cause of the transfer was soon explained by the discharge of ordnance, the braying of trumpets, and the rolling of drums, announcing the arrival of the king. From the mystery observed towards him, Surrey was led to the conclusion that the fair Geraldine accompanied the royal party; but he in vain sought to satisfy himself of the truth of the surmise by examining, through the deep embrasure of his window, the cavalcade that soon afterwards entered the upper quadrangle. Amid the throng of beautiful dames surrounding Anne Boleyn he could not be certain that he detected the fair Geraldine; but he readily distinguished the Duke of Richmond among the nobles, and the sight awakened a pang of bitter jealousy in his breast.

The day wore away slowly, for he could not fix his attention upon his books, neither was he allowed to go forth upon the battlements of the tower. In the evening, however, the officer informed him he might take exercise within the dry moat if he was so inclined, and he gladly availed himself of the permission.

After pacing to and fro along the walk for a short time, he entered the arbour, and was about to throw himself upon the bench, when he observed a slip of paper lying upon it. He took it up, and found a few lines traced upon it in hurried characters. They ran thus :—

" The fair Geraldine arrived this morning in the castle. If the Earl of Surrey desires to meet her, he will find her within this arbour at midnight."

This billet was read and re-read by the young earl with feelings of indescribable transport; but a little reflection damped his ardour, and made him fear it might be a device to ensnare him. There was no certainty that the note proceeded in any way from the fair Geraldine, nor could he even be sure that she was in the castle. Still, despite these misgivings, the attraction was too powerful to be resisted, and he turned over the means of getting out of his chamber, but the scheme seemed wholly impracticable. The window was at a considerable height above the ramparts of the keep, and even if he could reach them, and escape the notice of the sentinels, he should have to make a second descent into the fosse. And supposing all this accomplished, how was he to return ? The impossibility of answering this latter mental interrogation compelled him to give up all idea of the attempt.

On returning to his prison chamber, he stationed himself at the embrasure overlooking the ramparts, and listened to the regular tread of the sentinel below, half resolved, be the consequences what they might, to descend. As the appointed time approached, his anxiety became almost intolerable, and quitting the window, he began to pace hurriedly to and fro within the chamber, which, as has been previously observed, partook of the circular form of the keep, and was supported in certain places by great wooden pillars and cross beams. But instead of dissipating his agitation, his rapid movements seemed rather to increase it, and at last, wrought to a pitch of uncontrollable excitement, he cried aloud, " If the fiend were to present himself now, and offer to lead me to her, I would follow him."

Scarcely were the words uttered than a hollow laugh broke from the farther end of the chamber, and a deep voice exclaimed, " I am ready to take you to her."

" I need not ask who addresses me," said Surrey, after a pause, and straining his eyes to distinguish the figure of the speaker in the gloom.

" I will tell you who I am," rejoined the other. " I am he who visited you once before—who showed you a vision of the fair Geraldine—and carried off your vaunted relic—ho ! ho ! "

" Avoid thee, false fiend ! " rejoined Surrey, " thou temptest me now in vain."

" You have summoned me," returned Herne, " and I will not be dismissed. I am ready to convey you to your mistress, who awaits you in King James's bower, and marvels at your tardiness."

" And with what design dost thou offer me this service ? " demanded Surrey.

" It will be time enough to put that question when I make any condition," replied Herne. " Enough, I am willing to aid you. Will you go ? "

" Lead on ! " replied Surrey, marching towards him.

Suddenly, Herne drew a lantern from beneath the cloak in which he was wrapped, and threw its light on a trap-door lying open at his feet.

" Descend ! "

Surrey hesitated a moment, and then plunged down the steps. In another instant, the demon followed. Some hidden machinery was then set in motion, and the trap-door returned to its place. At length, Surrey arrived at a narrow passage, which appeared to correspond in form with the bulwarks of the keep. Here Herne passed him, and taking the lead, hurried along the gallery and descended another flight of steps, which brought them to a large vault, apparently built in the foundation of the Tower. Before the earl had time to gaze round this chamber, the demon masked the lantern, and taking his hand, drew him through a narrow passage, terminated by a small iron door, which flew open at a touch, and they emerged among the bushes clothing the side of the mound.

" You can now proceed without my aid," said Herne; " but take care not to expose yourself to the sentinels."

Keeping under the shade of the trees, for the moon was shining brightly, Surrey hastened towards the arbour, and as he entered it, to his inexpressible delight found that he had not been deceived, but that the fair Geraldine was indeed there.

" How did you contrive this meeting ? " she cried, after their first greetings had passed. " And how did you learn I was in the castle, for the strictest instructions were given that the tidings should not reach you ? "

The only response made by Surrey was to press her lily hand devotedly to his lips.

" I should not have ventured hither," pursued the fair Geraldine, " unless you had sent me the relic as a token. I knew you would never part with it, and I therefore felt sure there was no deception."

" But how did you get here ? " inquired Surrey.

" Your messenger provided a rope-ladder, by which I descended in the moat," she replied.

Surrey was stupefied.

" You seem astonished at my resolution," she continued; " and, indeed, I am surprised at it myself; but I could not overcome my desire to see you, especially as this meeting may be our last. The king, through the Lady Anne Boleyn, has positively enjoined me to think no more of you, and has given your father, the Duke of Norfolk, to understand that your marriage without the royal assent will be attended by the loss of all the favour he now enjoys."

" And think you I will submit to such tyranny ? " cried Surrey.

301

"Alas!" replied the fair Geraldine, in a mournful tone, "I feel we shall never be united. This conviction, which has lately forced itself upon my mind, has not made me love you less, though it has in some degree altered my feelings towards you."

"But I may be able to move the king," cried Surrey. "I have some claim beside that of kindred on the Lady Anne Boleyn—and she will obtain his consent."

"Do not trust to her," replied the fair Geraldine. "You may have rendered her an important service, but be not too sure of a return. No, Surrey, I here release you from the troth you plighted to me in the cloisters."

"I will not be released from it!" cried the earl hastily; "neither will I release you. I hold the pledge as sacred and as binding as if we had been affianced together before Heaven."

"For your own sake, do not say so, my dear lord," rejoined the fair Geraldine; "beseech you, do not. That your heart is bound to me now, I well believe—and that you could become inconstant I will not permit myself to suppose. But your youth forbids a union between us for many years; and if during that time you should behold some fairer face than mine, or should meet some heart you may conceive more loving—though that can hardly be—I would not have a hasty vow restrain you. Be free then—free at least for three years—and if at the end of that time your affections are still unchanged, I am willing you should bind yourself to me for ever."

"I cannot act with equal generosity to you," rejoined Surrey, in a tone of deep disappointment. "I would sooner part with life than relinquish the pledge I have received from you. But I am content that my constancy should be put to the test you propose. During the long term of my probation, I will shrink from no trial of faith. Throughout Europe I will proclaim your beauty in the lists, and will maintain its supremacy against all comers. But, oh! sweet Geraldine, since we have met in this spot, hallowed by the loves of James of Scotland

and Jane Beaufort, let us here renew our vows of eternal constancy, and agree to meet again at the time you have appointed, with hearts as warm and loving as those we bring together now."

And as he spoke he drew her towards him and imprinted a passionate kiss on her lips.

" Let that ratify the pledge," he said.

" Ho ! ho ! ho ! " laughed a deep voice without.

" What was that ? " demanded the fair Geraldine, in a tone of alarm.

" You have the relic, have you not ? " inquired the earl, in a low tone.

" No," she replied; " your messenger merely showed it to me. But why do you ask ? " Ah ! I understand. The fiendish laughter that just now sounded in my ears proceeded from——"

" Herne the hunter," replied Surrey, in a whisper. " But fear nothing. I will defend you with my life. Ah ! accursed chance ! I have no weapon."

" None would avail against him," murmured the fair Geraldine. " Lead me forth; I shall die if I stay here."

Supporting her in his arms, Surrey complied, but they had scarcely gained the entrance of the arbour, when a tall figure stood before them. It was the Duke of Richmond. A gleam of moonlight penetrating through the leaves fell upon the group, and rendered them distinctly visible to each other.

" Soh ! " exclaimed the duke, after regarding the pair in silence for a moment, " I have not been misinformed. You have contrived a meeting here."

" Richmond," said Surrey sternly, " we once were dear and loving friends, and we are still honourable foes. I know that I am safe with you. I know you will breathe no word about this meeting, either to the fair Geraldine's prejudice or mine."

" You judge me rightly, my lord," replied the duke, in a tone of equal sternness. " I have no thought of betraying you; though, by a word to my royal father, I could prevent all chance of future rivalry on your part.

I shall, however, demand a strict account from you on your liberation."

" Your grace acts as beseems a loyal gentleman," replied Surrey. " Hereafter I will not fail to account to you for my conduct in any way you please."

" Oh ! let me interpose between you, my lords," cried the fair Geraldine, " to prevent the disastrous consequences of this quarrel. I have already told your grace I cannot love you—and that my heart is devoted to the Earl of Surrey. Let me appeal to your noble nature— to your generosity—not to persist in a hopeless suit."

" You have conquered, madam," said the duke, after a pause. " I have been to blame in this matter. But I will make amends for my error. Surrey, I relinquish her to you."

" My friend ! " exclaimed the earl, casting himself into the duke's arms.

" I will now endeavour to heal the wounds I have unwittingly occasioned," said the fair Geraldine. " I am surprised your grace should be insensible to attractions so far superior to mine as those of the Lady Mary Howard."

" The Lady Mary is very beautiful, I confess," said the duke; " and if you had not been in the way, I should assuredly have been her captive."

" I ought not to betray the secret, perhaps," hesitated the fair Geraldine, " but gratitude prompts me to do so. The lady is not so blind to your grace's merits as I have been."

" Indeed ! " exclaimed the duke. " If it be so, Surrey, we may yet be brothers as well as friends."

" And that it is so I can avouch, Richmond," rejoined the earl. " for I am in my sister's secret as well as the fair Geraldine. But now that this explanation has taken place, I must entreat your grace to conduct the fair Geraldine back to her lodgings, while I regain, the best way I can, my chamber in the Round Tower."

" I marvel how you escaped from it," said Richmond; " but I suppose it was by the connivance of the officer."

" He who set me free—who brought the fair Geraldine hither—and who, I suspect, acquainted you with our meeting, was no other than Herne the hunter," replied Surrey.

" You amaze me ! " exclaimed the duke; " it was indeed a tall dark man, muffled in a cloak, who informed me that you were to meet at midnight in King James's bower in the moat, and I therefore came to surprise you."

" Your informant was Herne," replied Surrey.

" Right ! " exclaimed the demon, stepping from behind a tree, where he had hitherto remained concealed; " it was I—I, Herne the hunter. And I contrived the meeting in anticipation of a far different result from that which has ensued. But I now tell you, my Lord Surrey, that it is idle to indulge a passion for the fair Geraldine. You will never wed her."

" False fiend, thou liest ! " cried Surrey.

" Time will show," replied Herne. " I repeat you will wed another—and more, I tell you, you are blinder than Richmond has shown himself—for the most illustrious damsel in the kingdom has regarded you with eyes of affection, and yet you have not perceived it."

" The Princess Mary ? " demanded Richmond.

" Ay, the Princess Mary," repeated Herne. " How say you now, my lord ?—will you let ambition usurp the place of love ? "

" No," replied Surrey. " But I will hold no further converse with thee. Thou wouldst tempt to perdition. Hence, fiend ! "

" Unless you trust yourself to my guidance you will never reach your chamber," rejoined Herne, with a mocking laugh. " The iron door in the mound cannot be opened on this side, and you well know what the consequence of a discovery will be. Come, or I leave you to your fate." And he moved down the path on the right.

" Go with him, Surrey," cried Richmond.

Pressing the fair Geraldine to his breast, the earl committed her to the charge of his friend, and tearing himself

away, followed the steps of the demon. He had not proceeded far when he heard his name pronounced by a
voice issuing from the tree above him. Looking up, he
beheld Herne in one of the topmost branches, and at a
sign, instantly climbed up to him. The thick foliage
screened them from observation, and Surrey concluded
his guide was awaiting the disappearance of the sentinel,
who was at that moment approaching the tree. But such
apparently was not the other's intentions; for the man
had scarcely passed than Herne sprang upon the arm-
parts, and the poor fellow turning at the sound, was
almost scared out of his senses at the sight of the dreaded
fiend. Dropping his halbert, he fell upon his face with a
stifled cry. Herne then motioned Surrey to descend, and
they marched together quickly to a low door opening
into the keep. Passing through it, and ascending a flight
of steps they stood upon the landing at the top of the
staircase communicating with the Norman Tower, and
adjoining the entrance to Surrey's chamber.

Apparently familiar with the spot, Herne took down
a large key from a nail in the wall against which it hung,
and unlocked the door.

" Enter ! " he said to Surrey, " and do not forget the
debt you owe to Herne the hunter."

And as the earl stepped into the chamber, the door was
locked behind him.

I I

How Sir Thomas Wyat found Mabel in the Sandstone
Cave; and what happened to him there

A WEEK after the foregoing occurrence, the Earl of Surrey
was set free. But his joy at regaining his liberty was
damped by learning that the fair Geraldine had departed
for Ireland. She had left the tenderest messages for him
with his sister, the Lady Mary Howard, accompanied
with assurances of unalterable attachment.

But other changes had taken place, which were calculated to afford him some consolation. Ever since the
night on which he had been told that the Lady Mary was
not indifferent to him, Richmond had devoted himself
entirely to her; and matters had already proceeded so
far, that he had asked her in marriage of the Duke of
Norfolk, who, after ascertaining the king's pleasure on
the subject, had gladly given his consent, and the youthful
pair were affianced to each other. Surrey and Richmond
now became closer friends than ever; and if, amid the
thousand distractions of Henry's gay and festive court,
the young earl did not forget the fair Geraldine, he did
not, at least, find the time hang heavily on his hands.

About a week after Wolsey's dismissal, while the court
was still sojourning at Windsor, Surrey proposed to
Richmond, to ride one morning with him in the Great
Park. The duke willingly assented, and mounting their
steeds they galloped towards Snow Hill, wholly unattended. While mounting this charming ascent at a
more leisurely pace, the earl said to his companion, " I
will now tell you why I proposed this ride to you,
Richmond. I have long determined to follow up the
adventure of Herne the hunter, and I wish to confer with
you about it, and ascertain whether you are disposed to
join me."

" I know not what to say, Surrey," replied the duke gravely, and speaking in a low tone; " the king, my father, failed in his endeavours to expel the demon, who still lords it in the forest."

" The greater glory to us if we succeed," said Surrey.

" I will take counsel with the Lady Mary on the subject before I give an answer," rejoined Richmond.

" Then there is little doubt what your grace's decision will be," laughed Surrey. " To speak truth, it was the fear of your consulting her that made me bring you here. What say you to a ride in the forest to-morrow night ? "

" I have little fancy for it," replied Richmond, " and if you will be ruled by me, you will not attempt the enterprise yourself."

" My resolution is taken," said the earl; " but now, since we have reached the brow of the hill, let us push forward to the lake "

A rapid ride of some twenty minutes brought them to the edge of the lake, and they proceeded along the verdant path leading to the forester's hut. On arriving at the dwelling, it appeared wholly deserted, but they nevertheless dismounted, and tying their horses to the trees at the back of the cottage, entered it. While they were examining the lower room, the plash of oars reached their ears, and rushing to the window, they descried the skiff rapidly approaching the shore. A man was seated within it, whose attire, through sombre, seemed to proclaim him of some rank, but as his back was towards them, they could not discern his features. In another instant the skiff touched the strand, and the rower leaping ashore, proved to be Sir Thomas Wyat. On making this discovery they both ran out to him, and the warmest greetings passed between them. When these were over, Surrey expressed his surprise to Wyat at seeing him there, declaring he was wholly unaware of his return from the court of France.

" I came back about a month ago," said Wyat. " His majesty supposes me at Allington; nor shall I return to court without a summons."

" I am not sorry to hear it," said Surrey; " but what are you doing here ? "

" My errand is a strange and adventurous one," replied Wyat. " You may have heard that before I departed for France I passed some days in the forest in company with Herne the hunter. What then happened to me I may not disclose; but I have vowed never to rest till I have freed this forest from the weird being who troubles it."

" Say you so ! " cried Surrey; " then you are most fortunately encountered, Sir Thomas, for I myself, as Richmond will tell you, am equally bent upon the fiend's expulsion. We will be companions in the adventure."

" We will speak of that anon," replied Wyat. " I was sorry to find this cottage uninhabited, and the fair damsel who dwelt within it, when I beheld it last, gone. What has become of her ? "

" It is a strange story," said Richmond. And he proceeded to relate all that was known to have befallen Mabel.

Wyat listened with profound attention to the recital, and at its close, said, " I think I can find a clue to this mystery, but to obtain it I must go alone. Meet me here at midnight to-morrow, and I doubt not we shall be able to accomplish our design."

" May I not ask for some explanation of your scheme?" said Surrey.

" Not yet," rejoined Wyat. " But I will freely confess to you that there is much danger in the enterprise— danger that I would not willingly any one should share with me, especially you, Surrey, to whom I owe so much. If you do not find me here, therefore, to-morrow night, conclude that I have perished, or am captive."

" Well, be it as you will, Wyat," said Surrey; " but I would gladly accompany you, and share your danger."

" I know it, and I thank you," returned Wyat, warmly grasping the other's hand; " but much—nay, all—may remain to be done to-morrow night. You had better bring some force with you, for we may need it."

"I will bring half a dozen stout archers," replied Surrey—"and if you come not, depend upon it, I will either release you or avenge you."

"I did not intend to prosecute this adventure further," said Richmond; "but since you are both resolved to embark in it, I will not desert you."

Soon after this, the friends separated—Surrey and Richmond taking horse and returning to the castle, discoursing on the unlooked-for meeting with Wyat, while the latter again entered the skiff, and rowed down the lake. As soon as the hut was clear, two persons descended the steps of a ladder leading to a sort of loft in the roof, and sprang upon the floor of the hut.

"Ho! ho! ho!" laughed the foremost, whose antlered helm and wild garb proclaimed him to be Herne; "they little dreamed who were the hearers of their conference. So they think to take me, Fenwolf—ha!"

"They know not whom they have to deal with," rejoined the latter.

"They *should* do so by this time," said Herne; "but I will tell thee why Sir Thomas Wyat has undertaken this enterprise. It is not to capture me, though that may be one object that moves him. But he wishes to see Mabel Lyndwood. The momentary glimpse he caught of her bright eyes was sufficient to inflame him."

"Ah!" exclaimed Fenwolf; "think you so?"

"I am assured of it," replied Herne. "He knows the secret of the cave, and will find her there."

"But he will never return to tell what he has seen," said Fenwolf moodily.

"I know not that," replied Herne. "I have my own views respecting him. I want to renew my band."

"He will never join you," rejoined Fenwolf.

"What if I offer him Mabel as a bait?" said Herne.

"You will not do so, dread master?" rejoined Fenwolf, trembling and turning pale. "She belongs to me."

"To thee, fool!" cried Herne, with a derisive laugh. "Thinkest thou I would resign such a treasure to

310

thee? No, no. But rest easy, I will not give her to Wyat."

"You mean her for yourself, then?" said Fenwolf.

"Darest thou to question me!" cried Herne, striking him with the hand armed with the iron gyves. "This to teach thee respect!"

"And this to prove whether thou art mortal or not!" rejoined Fenwolf, plucking his hunting-knife from his belt, and striking it with all his force against the other's breast.

But though surely and forcibly dealt, the blow glanced off as if the demon were cased in steel, and the intended assassin fell back in amazement, while an unearthly laugh rang in his ears. Never had Fenwolf seen Herne wear so formidable a look as he at that moment assumed. His giant frame dilated; his eyes flashed fire; and the expression of his countenance was so fearful that Fenwolf shielded his eyes with his hands.

"Ah! miserable dog!" thundered Herne; "dost thou think I am to be hurt by mortal hands, or mortal weapons? Thy former experience should have taught thee differently. But since thou hast provoked it, take thy fate!"

Uttering these words, he seized Fenwolf by the throat, clutching him with a terrific gripe, and in a few seconds the miserable wretch would have paid the penalty of his rashness, if a person had not at the moment appeared at the doorway. Flinging his prey hastily backwards, Herne turned at the interruption, and perceived old Tristram Lyndwood, who looked appalled at what he beheld.

"Ah! it is thou, Tristram," cried Herne; "thou art just in time to witness the punishment of this rebellious hound."

"Spare him, dread master!—oh, spare him!" cried Tristram imploringly.

"Well," said Herne, gazing at the half-strangled caitiff, "he may live. He will not offend again. But why has thou ventured from thy hiding-place, Tristram?"

"I came to inform you that I have just observed a

person row across the lake in the skiff," replied the old man. " He appears to be taking the direction of the secret entrance to the cave."

" It is Sir Thomas Wyat," replied Herne; " I am aware of his proceedings. Stay with Fenwolf till he is able to move, and then proceed with him to the cave. But mark me, no violence must be done to Wyat if you find him there. Any neglect of my orders in this respect will be followed by severe punishment. I shall be at the cave ere long; but, meanwhile, I have other business to transact."

And quitting the hut, he plunged into the wood.

Meanwhile Sir Thomas Wyat having crossed the lake, landed, and fastened the skiff to a tree, struck into the wood, and presently reached the open space in which lay the secret entrance to the cave. He was not long in finding the stone, though it was so artfully concealed by the brushwood that it would have escaped any uninstructed eye, and removing it, the narrow entrance to the cave was revealed.

Committing himself to the protection of Heaven, Wyat entered, and having taken the precaution of drawing the stone after him, which was easily accomplished by a handle fixed to the inner side of it, he commenced the descent. At first, he had to creep along, but the passage gradually got higher, until at length, on reaching the level ground, he was able to stand upright. There was no light to guide him, but by feeling against the sides of the passage, he found that he was in the long gallery he had formerly threaded. Uncertain which way to turn, he determined to trust to chance for taking the right direction, and drawing his sword proceeded slowly to the right.

For some time, he encountered no obstacle, neither could he detect the slightest sound, but he perceived that the atmosphere grew damp, and that the sides of the passage were covered with moisture. Thus warned, he proceeded with greater caution, and presently found, after emerging into a more open space, and striking off on the left, that he had arrived at the edge of the pool of water which he knew lay at the end of the large cavern.

While considering how he should next proceed, a faint gleam of light became visible at the upper end of the vault. Changing his position, for the pillars prevented him from seeing the source of the glimmer, he discovered that it issued from a lamp borne by a female hand, who he had no doubt was Mabel. On making this discovery, he sprang forward, and called to her, but instantly repented his rashness, for as he uttered the cry the light was extinguished.

Wyat was now completely at a loss how to proceed. He was satisfied that Mabel was in the vault; but in what way to guide himself to her retreat, he could not tell; and it was evident she herself would not assist him. Persuaded, however, if he could but make himself known, he should no longer be shunned, he entered one of the lateral passages, and ever and anon, as he proceeded, repeated Mabel's name in a low, soft tone. The stratagem was successful. Presently he heard a light footstep approaching him, and a gentle voice inquired—

" Who calls me ? "

" A friend," replied Wyat.

" Your name ? " she demanded.

" You will not know me if I declare myself, Mabel," he replied; " but I am called Sir Thomas Wyat."

" The name *is* well known to me," she replied, in trembling tones; " and I have seen you once—at my grandfather's cottage. But why have you come here ?— Do you know where you are ? "

" I know that I am in the cave of Herne the hunter," replied Wyat; " and one of my motives for seeking it was to set you free. But there is nothing to prevent your flight now."

" Alas ! there is," she replied. " I am chained here by bonds I cannot break. Herne has declared that any attempt at escape on my part shall be followed by the death of my grandsire. And he does not threaten idly, as no doubt you know. Besides, the most terrible vengeance would fall on my own head. No—I cannot—dare not fly. But let us not talk in the dark. Come with me to procure a light. Give me your hand, and I will lead you to my cell."

Taking the small, trembling hand offered him, Wyat followed his conductress down the passage. A few steps brought them to a door, which she pushed aside and disclosed a small chamber, hewn out of the rock, in a recess of which a lamp was burning. Lighting the other lamp which she had recently extinguished she placed it on a rude table.

"Have you been long a prisoner here?" asked Wyat, fixing his regards upon her countenance, which, though it had lost somewhat of its bloom, had gained much in interest and beauty.

"For three months, I suppose," she replied; "but I am not able to calculate the lapse of time. It has seemed very—very long. Oh, that I could behold the sun again, and breathe the fresh, pure air!"

"Come with me, and you shall do so," rejoined Wyat.

"I have told you I cannot fly," she answered. "I cannot sacrifice my grandsire."

"But if he is leagued with this demon he deserves the worst fate that can befall him," said Wyat. "You should think only of your own safety. What can be the motive of your detention?"

"I tremble to think of it," she replied; "but I fear that Herne has conceived a passion for me."

"Then indeed you must fly," cried Wyat; "such unhallowed love will lead to perdition of soul and body."

"Oh, that there was any hope for me!" she ejaculated.

"There *is* hope," replied Wyat. "I will protect you—will care for you—will love you."

"Love me!" exclaimed Mabel, a deep blush overspreading her pale features. "You love another."

"Absence has enabled me to overcome the vehemence of my passion," replied Wyat, "and I feel that my heart is susceptible of new emotions. But you, maiden," he added coldly, " you were captivated by the admiration of the king."

" My love, like yours, is past," she answered, with a faint smile; " but if I were out of Herne's power I feel that I could love again, and far more deeply than I loved before—for that, in fact, was rather the result of vanity than of real regard."

" Mabel," said Wyat, taking her hand, and gazing into her eyes, " if I set you free, will you love me ? "

" I love you already," she replied; " but if that could be, my whole life should be devoted to you.—Ha ! " she exclaimed, with a sudden change of tone, " footsteps are approaching; it is Fenwolf. Hide yourself within that recess."

Though doubting the prudence of the course, Wyat yielded to her terrified and imploring looks, and concealed himself in the manner she had indicated. He was scarcely ensconced in the recess, when the door opened, and Morgan Fenwolf stepped in, followed by her grandfather. Fenwolf gazed suspiciously round the little chamber, and then glanced significantly at old Tristram, but he made no remark.

" What brings you here ? " demanded Mabel tremlingly.

" You are wanted in the cave," said Fenwolf.

" I will follow you anon," she replied.

" You must come at once," rejoined Fenwolf, authoritatively. " Herne will become impatient."

Upon this, Mabel rose, and, without daring to cast a look towards the spot where Wyat was concealed, quitted the cell with them. No sooner were they all out, than Fenwolf, hastily shutting the door, turned the key in the lock, and taking it out, exclaimed, " So we have secured you, Sir Thomas Wyat. No fear of your revealing the secret of the cave now, or flying with Mabel— ha ! ha ! "

III

In what manner Herne declared his passion for Mabel

UTTERLY disregarding her cries and entreaties, Fenwolf dragged Mabel into the great cavern, and forced her to take a seat on a bench near the spot where a heap of ashes showed that the fire was ordinarily lighted. All this while, her grandfather had averted his face from her, as if fearing to meet her regards, and he now busied himself in striking a light and setting fire to a pile of fagots and small logs of wood.

" I thought you told me Herne was here," said Mabel, in a tone of bitter reproach, to Fenwolf, who seated himself beside her on the bench.

" He will be here ere long," he replied sullenly.

" Oh, do not detain Sir Thomas Wyat ! " cried Mabel piteously; " do not deliver him to your dread master ! Do what you will with me—but let him go."

" I will tell you what I will do," replied Fenwolf, in a low tone; " I will set Sir Thomas at liberty, and run all risks of Herne's displeasure, if you will promise to be mine."

Mabel replied by a look of unutterable disgust.

" Then he will await Herne's coming where he is," rejoined Fenwolf.

Saying which he arose, and pushing a table near the bench, took the remains of a huge venison pasty and a loaf from a hutch standing on one side of the cavern.

By this time, old Tristram having succeeded in lighting the fire, placed himself at the farther end of the table, and fell to work upon the viands with Fenwolf. Mabel was pressed to partake of the repast, but she declined the offer. A large stone bottle was next produced and emptied of its contents by the pair, who seemed well contented with their regale.

Meanwhile, Mabel was revolving the possibility of

flight, and had more than once determined to make an attempt, but fear restrained her. Her grandsire, as has been stated, sedulously avoided her gaze, and turned a deaf ear to her complaints and entreaties. But once, when Fenwolf's back was turned, she caught him gazing at her with peculiar significance, and then comprehended the meaning of his strange conduct. He evidently only awaited an opportunity to assist her.

Satisfied at this, she became more tranquil, and about an hour having elapsed, during which nothing was said by the party, the low winding of a horn was heard, and Fenwolf started to his feet, exclaiming—

" It is Herne ! "

The next moment, the demon-huntsman rode from one of the lateral passages into the cave. He was mounted on a wild-looking black horse, with flowing mane and tail, eyes glowing like carbuncles, and in all respects resembling the sable steed he had lost in the forest.

Springing to the ground, he exchanged a few words with Fenwolf, in a low tone, and delivering his steed to him, with orders to take it to the stable, signed to Tristram to go with him, and approached Mabel.

" So you have seen Sir Thomas Wyat, I find," he said, in a stern tone.

Mabel made no answer, and did not even raise her eyes towards him.

" And he has told you he loves you, and has urged you to fly with him—ha ? " pursued Herne.

Mabel still did not dare to look up, but a deep blush overspread her cheek.

" He was mad to venture hither," continued Herne; " but having done so, he must take the consequences."

" You will not destroy him ? " cried Mabel imploringly.

" He will perish by a hand as terrible as mine," laughed Herne—" by that of famine. He will never quit the dungeon alive, unless——"

" Unless what ? " gasped Mabel.

" Unless he is leagued with me," replied Herne. " And now let him pass, for I would speak of myself. I have already told you that I love you, and am resolved to make you mine. You shudder, but wherefore ? It is a glorious destiny to be the bride of the wild hunter—the fiend who rules the forest, and who in his broad domain is more powerful than the king. The old forester, Robin Hood, had his maid Marian; and what was he compared to me ? He had neither my skill, nor my power. Be mine, and you shall accompany me on my midnight rides; shall watch the fleet stag dart over the moonlight glade, or down the lengthened vista. You shall feel all the unutterable excitement of the chase. You shall thread with me the tangled grove; swim the river and the lake; and enjoy a thousand pleasures hitherto unknown to you. Be mine, and I will make you mistress of all my secrets, and compel the band whom I will gather round me to pay you homage. Be mine, and you shall have power of life and death over them, as if you were absolute queen. And from me, whom all fear, and all obey, you shall have love and worship."

And he would have taken her hand, but she recoiled from him with horror.

" Though I now inspire you with terror and aversion," pursued Herne, " the time will come when you will love me as passionately as I was beloved by one of whom you are the image."

" And she is dead ? " asked Mabel, with curiosity.

" Dead ! " exclaimed Herne. " Thrice fifty years have flown since she dwelt upon earth. The acorn which was then shed in the forest has grown into a lusty oak, while trees at that time in their pride have fallen and decayed away. Dead !—yes, she has passed from all memory save mine, where she will ever dwell. Generations of men have gone down to the grave since her time—a succession of kings have lodged within the castle—but I am still a denizen of the forest. For crimes I then committed, I am doomed to wander within it; and I shall haunt it, unless released, till the crack of doom."

" Liberate me ! " cried Mabel; " liberate your other prisoner, and we will pray for your release."

"No more of this!" cried Herne fiercely. "If you would not call down instant and terrible punishment on your head—punishment that I cannot avert, and must inflict, you will mention nothing sacred in my hearing— and never allude to prayer. I am beyond the reach of salvation."

"Oh, say not so!" cried Mabel, in a tone of commiseration.

"I will tell you how my doom was accomplished," rejoined Herne wildly. "To gain her of whom I have just spoken, and who was already vowed to Heaven, I invoked the powers of darkness. I proffered my soul to the Evil One if he would secure her to me; and the condition demanded by him was that I should become what I am—the fiend of the forest, with power to terrify and to tempt, and with other more fearful and fatal powers besides."

"Oh!" exclaimed Mabel.

"I grasped at the offer," pursued Herne. "She I loved became mine. But she was speedily snatched from me by death, and since than I have known no human passion except hatred and revenge. I have dwelt in this forest, sometimes alone, sometimes at the head of a numerous band, but always exerting a baneful influence over mankind. At last, I saw the image of her I loved again appear before me, and the old passion was revived within my breast. Chance has thrown you in my way, and mine you shall be, Mabel!"

"I will die rather," she replied, with a shudder.

"You cannot escape me," rejoined Herne, with a triumphant laugh; "you cannot avoid your fate. But I want not to deal harshly with you. I love you, and would win you rather by persuasion than by force. Consent to be mine, then, and I give Wyat his life and liberty."

"I cannot—I cannot!" she replied.

"Not only do I offer you Wyat's life as the price of your compliance," persevered Herne; "but you shall have whatever else you may seek—jewels, ornaments, costly attire, treasure—for of such I possess a goodly store."

" And of what use would they be to me here ? " said Mabel.

" I will not always confine you to this cave," replied Herne. " You shall go where you please—and live as you please—but you must come to me whenever I summon you."

" And what of my grandsire ? " she demanded.

" Tristram Lyndwood is no relative of yours," replied Herne. " I will now clear up the mystery that hangs over your birth. You are the offspring of one who for years has exercised greater sway than the king within this realm, but who is now disgraced and ruined, and nigh his end. His priestly vows forbid him to own you, even if he desired to do so."

" Have I seen him ? " demanded Mabel.

" You have," replied Herne—" and he has seen you —and little did he know when he sought you out, that he was essaying to maintain his own power, and overturn that of another by the dishonour of his daughter—though if he had done so," he added, with a scoffing laugh, " it might not have restrained him."

" I know whom you mean," said Mabel. " And is it possible he can be my father ? "

" It is as I have told you," replied Herne. " You now know my resolve. To-morrow at midnight our nuptials shall take place."

" Nuptials ! " echoed Mabel.

" Ay, at that altar," he cried, pointing to the Druid pile of stones—" there you shall vow yourself to me and I to you before terrible witnesses. I shall have no fear that you will break your oath. Reflect upon what I have said."

With this he placed the bugle to his lips, blew a low call upon it, and Fenwolf and Tristram immediately answering the summons, he whispered some instructions to the former, and disappeared down one of the side passages.

Fenwolf's deportment was now more sullen than before. In vain did Mabel inquire from him what Herne was about to do with Sir Thomas Wyat. He returned no answer, and at last, wearied by her importunity, desired her to hold her peace. Just then, Tristram quitted the cavern for a moment, when he instantly changed his manner, and said to her quickly—

"I overheard what passed between you and Herne. Consent to be mine, and I will deliver you from him."

"That were to exchange one evil for another," she replied. "If you would serve me, deliver Sir Thomas Wyat."

"I will only deliver him on the terms I have mentioned," replied Fenwolf.

At this moment, Tristram returned, and the conversation ceased.

Fresh logs were then thrown on the fire by Fenwolf, and, at his request, Tristram proceeded to a hole in the rock, which served as a sort of larder, and brought from it some pieces of venison, which were broiled upon the embers.

At the close of the repast, of which she sparingly partook, Mabel was conducted by Morgan Fenwolf into a small chamber opening out of the great cavern, which was furnished, like the cell she had lately occupied, with a small straw pallet. Leaving her a lamp, Fenwolf locked the door and placed the key in his girdle.

IV

How Sir Thomas Wyat was visited by Herne in the cell

MADE aware by the clangour of the lock, and Fenwolf's exulting laughter, of the snare in which he had been caught, Sir Thomas Wyat instantly sprang from his hiding-place, and rushed to the door; but being framed of the stoutest oak, and strengthened with plates of iron, it defied all his efforts, nerved as they were by rage and despair, to burst it open. Mabel's shrieks as she was dragged away reached his ears, and increased his anguish; and he called out loudly to her companions to return, but his vociferations were only treated with derision.

Finding it useless to struggle further, Wyat threw himself upon the bench, and endeavoured to discover some means of deliverance from his present hazardous position. He glanced round the cell to see whether there was any other outlet than the doorway, but he could discern none, except a narrow grated loophole opening upon the passage, and contrived, doubtless, for the admission of air to the chamber. No dungeon could be more secure.

Raising the lamp, he examined every crevice, but all seemed solid stone. The recess in which he had taken shelter proved to be a mere hollow in the wall. In one corner lay a small straw pallet, which, no doubt, had formed the couch of Mabel, and this, together with the stone bench and rude table of the same material, constituted the sole furniture of the place.

Having taken this careful survey of the cell, Wyat again sat down upon the bench with the conviction that escape was out of the question; and he therefore endeavoured to prepare himself for the worst, for it was more than probable he would be allowed to perish of starvation. To a fiery nature like his, the dreadful uncertainty in which he was placed was more difficult

of endurance than bodily torture. And he was destined
to endure it long. Many hours flew by, during which
nothing occurred to relieve the terrible monotony of his
situation. At length, in spite of his anxiety, slumber
stole upon him unawares; but it was filled with frightful
visions.

How long he slept he knew not, but when he awoke
he found that the cell must have been visited in the
interval, for there was a manchet of bread, part of a cold
neck of venison, and a flask of wine on the table. It was
evident, therefore, that his captors did not mean to
starve him, and, yielding to the promptings of appetite,
he attacked the provisions, determined to keep strict
watch when his jailer should next visit him.

The repast finished, he again examined the cell, but
with no better success than before; and he felt almost
certain, from the position in which the bench was placed,
that the visitor had not found entrance through the
door.

After another long and dreary interval, finding that
sleep was stealing over him fast, he placed the bench
near the door, and leaned his back against the latter,
certain that in this position he should be awakened if
any one attempted to gain admittance in that way. His
slumber was again disturbed by fearful dreams; and he
was at length aroused by a touch upon the shoulder,
while a deep voice shouted his own name in his ears.

Starting to his feet, and scarcely able to separate the
reality from the hideous phantasms that had troubled
him, he found that the door was still fastened, and the
bench unremoved, while before him stood Herne the
hunter.

" Welcome again to my cave, Sir Thomas Wyat ! "
cried the demon, with a mocking laugh; " I told you,
on the night of the attempt upon the king, that though
you escaped *him*, you would not escape *me*. And so it
has come to pass. You are now wholly in my power,
body and soul—ha ! ha ! "

" I defy you, false fiend," replied Wyat. " I was mad

enough to proffer you my soul on certain conditions; but they have never been fulfilled."

"They may yet be so," rejoined Herne.

"No," replied Wyat, "I have purged my heart from the fierce and unhallowed passion that swayed it. I desire no assistance from you."

"If you have changed your mind that is nought to me," rejoined the demon derisively—"I shall hold you to your compact."

"Again I say I renounce you, infernal spirit !" cried Wyat—"you may destroy my body—but you can work no mischief to my soul."

"You alarm yourself without reason, good Sir Thomas," replied Herne, in a slightly sneering tone. "I am not the malignant being you suppose me; neither am I bent upon fighting the battles of the enemy of mankind against Heaven. I may be leagued with the powers of darkness, but I have no wish to aid them; and I therefore leave you to take care of your own soul in your own way. What I desire from you is your service while living. Now listen to the conditions I have to propose. You must bind yourself by a terrible oath, the slightest infraction of which shall involve the perdition of the soul you are so solicitous to preserve, not to disclose aught you may see, or that may be imparted to you here. You must also swear implicit obedience to me in all things—to execute any secret commissions, of whatever nature, I may give you—to bring associates to my band—and to join me in any enterprise I may propose. This oath taken, you are free. Refuse it, and I leave you to perish."

"I do refuse it," replied Wyat boldly. "I would die a thousand deaths rather than so bind myself. Neither do I fear being left to perish here. You shall not quit this cell without me."

"You are a stout soldier, Sir Thomas Wyat," rejoined the demon, with a scornful laugh; "but you are scarcely a match for Herne the hunter, as you will find, if you are rash enough to make the experiment. Beware !"

he exclaimed in a voice of thunder, observing the knight lay his hand upon his sword, " I am invulnerable, and you will, therefore, vainly strike at me. Do not compel me to use the dread means, which I could instantly employ, to subject you to my will. I mean you well, and would rather serve than injure you. But I will not let you go, unless you league yourself with me. Swear, therefore, obedience to me, and depart hence to your friends, Surrey and Richmond, and tell them you have failed to find me."

" You know, then, of our meeting ? " exclaimed Wyat.

" Perfectly well," laughed Herne. " It is now eventide, and at midnight the meeting will take place in the forester's hut. If *you* attend it not, *I* will. They will be my prisoners as well as you. To preserve yourself and save them, you must join me."

" Before I return an answer," said Wyat, " I must know what has become of Mabel Lyndwood."

" Mabel Lyndwood is nought to you, Sir Thomas," rejoined Herne coldly.

" She is so much to me that I will run a risk for her which I would not run for myself," replied Wyat. " If I promise obedience to you, will you liberate her—will you let her depart with me ? "

" No," replied Herne peremptorily. " Banish all thoughts of her from your breast. You will never behold her again. I will give you time for reflection on my proposal. An hour before midnight I shall return, and if I find you in the same mind, I abandon you to your fate."

And with these words, he stepped back towards the lower end of the cell. Wyat instantly sprang after him, but before he could reach him a flash of fire caused him to recoil, and to his horror and amazement he beheld the rock open, and yield a passage to the retreating figure.

When the sulphureous smoke, with which the little cell was filled, had in some degree cleared off, Wyat examined the sides of the rock, but could not find the slightest trace of a secret outlet, and therefore concluded that the disappearance of the demon had been effected by magic.

V

How Mabel escaped from the cave with Sir Thomas Wyat

THE next day Mabel was set at liberty by her jailer, and the hours flew by without the opportunity of escape, for which she sighed, occurring to her. As night drew on, she became more anxious, and at last expressed a wish to retire to her cell. When about to fasten the door, Fenwolf found that the lock had got strained, and the bolts would not move, and he was therefore obliged to content himself with placing a bench against it, on which he took a seat.

About an hour after Mabel's retirement, old Tristram offered to relieve guard with Fenwolf, but this the other positively declined, and leaning against the door, disposed himself to slumber. Tristram then threw himself on the floor, and in a short time all seemed buried in repose.

By and by, however, when Fenwolf's heavy breathing gave token of the soundness of his sleep, Tristram raised himself upon his elbow, and gazed round. The lamp placed upon the table imperfectly illumined the cavern, for the fire which had been lighted to cook the evening meal had gone out completely. Getting up cautiously, and drawing his hunting-knife, the old man crept towards Fenwolf, apparently with the intent of stabbing him, but he suddenly changed his resolution and dropped his arm.

At that moment, as if preternaturally warned, Fenwolf opened his eyes, and seeing the old forester standing by, sprang upon him and seized him by the throat.

" Ah ! traitor ! " he exclaimed, " what are you about to do ? "

326

" I am no traitor," replied the old man. " I heard a noise in the passage leading to Wyat's cell, and was about to rouse you, when you awakened of your own accord, probably disturbed by the noise."

" It may be," replied Fenwolf, satisfied with the excuse, and relinquishing his grasp; " I fancied I heard something in my dreams. But come with me to Wyat's cell. I will not leave you here."

And snatching up the lamp, he hurried with Tristram into the passage. They were scarcely gone, when the door of the cell was opened by Mabel, who had overheard what had passed; and so hurriedly did she issue forth that she overturned the bench, which fell to the ground with a considerable clatter. She had only just time to replace it, and to conceal herself in an adjoining passage, when Fenwolf rushed back into the cavern.

" It was a false alarm," he cried. " I saw Sir Thomas Wyat in his cell through the loophole, and I have brought the key away with me. But I am sure I heard a noise here."

" It must have been mere fancy," said Tristram. " All is as we left it."

" It seems so, certes," replied Fenwolf doubtfully. " But I will make sure."

While he placed his ear to the door, Mabel gave a signal to Tristram that she was safe. Persuaded that he heard some sound in the chamber, Fenwolf nodded to Tristram that all was right, and resumed his seat.

In less than ten minutes he was again asleep. Mabel then emerged from her concealment, and cautiously approached Tristram, who feigned, also, to slumber. As she approached him, he rose noiselessly to his feet.

" The plan has succeeded," he said, in a low tone. " It was I who spoiled the lock. But come with me. I will lead you out of the cavern."

" Not without Sir Thomas Wyat," she replied; " I will not leave him here."

" You will only expose yourself to risk, and fail to deliver him," rejoined Tristram. " Fenwolf has the key of his cell.—Nay, if you are determined upon it, I will not hinder you. But you must find your own way out, for I shall not assist Sir Thomas Wyat."

Motioning him to silence, Mabel crept slowly, and on the points of her feet, towards Fenwolf.

The key was in his girdle. Leaning over him, she suddenly and dexterously plucked it forth.

At the very moment she possessed herself of it, Fenwolf stirred, and she dived down, and concealed herself beneath the table. Fenwolf, who had been only slightly disturbed, looked up, and seeing Tristram in his former position, which he had resumed when Mabel commenced her task, again disposed himself to slumber.

Waiting till she was assured of the soundness of his repose, Mabel crept from under the table, signed to Tristram to remain where he was, and glided with swift and noiseless footsteps down the passage leading to the cell. In a moment, she was at the door, the key was in the lock, and she stood before Sir Thomas Wyat.

A few words sufficed to explain to the astonished knight how she came there, and comprehending that not a moment was to be lost, he followed her forth.

In the passage they held a brief consultation together, in a low tone, as to the best means of escape, for they deemed it useless to apply to Tristram. The outlet with which Sir Thomas Wyat was acquainted lay on the other side of the cavern; nor did he know how to discover the particular passage leading to it. As to Mabel, she could offer no information, but she knew that the stable lay in an adjoining passage.

Recollecting, from former experience, how well the steeds were trained, Sir Thomas Wyat eagerly caught at the suggestion, and Mabel led him farther down the passage, and striking off through an opening on the left, brought him, after a few turns, to a large chamber, in which two or three black horses were kept.

Loosening one of them, Wyat placed a bridle on his neck, sprang upon his back, and took up Mabel beside him. He then struck his heels against the sides of the animal, who needed no further incitement to dash along the passage, and in a few seconds brought them into the cavern.

The trampling of the horse wakened Fenwolf, who started to his feet, and ran after them, shouting furiously. But he was too late. Goaded by Wyat's dagger, the steed dashed furiously on, and, plunging with its double burden into the pool at the bottom of the cavern, disappeared.

VI

Of the Desperate Resolution Formed by Tristram and Fenwolf; and how the Train was Laid

TRANSPORTED with rage at the escape of the fugitives, Fenwolf turned to old Tristram, and, drawing his knife, threatened to make an end of him. But the old man, who was armed with a short hunting-sword, stood upon his defence, and they remained brandishing their weapons at each other for some minutes, but without striking a blow.

"Well, I leave you to Herne's vengeance," said Fenwolf, returning his knife to his belt. "You will pay dearly for allowing them to escape."

"I will take my chance," replied Tristram moodily; "my mind is made up to the worst. I will no longer serve this fiend."

"What! dare you break your oath?" cried Fenwolf. "Remember the terrible consequences."

"I care not for them," replied Tristram. "Harkee, Fenwolf, I know you will not betray me, for you hate him as much as I do, and have as great a desire for revenge. I will rid the forest of this fell being."

"Would you could make good your words, old man!" cried Fenwolf. "I would give my life for vengeance upon him."

"I take the office," said Tristram—"you *shall* have vengeance."

" But how ? " cried the other. " I have proved that he is invulnerable, and the prints of his hands are written in black characters upon my throat. If we could capture him, and deliver him to the king, we might purchase our own pardon."

" No, that can never be," said Tristram. " My plan is to destroy him."

" Well, let me hear it," said Fenwolf.

" Come with me, then," rejoined Tristram.

And taking up the lamp, he led the way down a narrow lateral passage. When about half-way down it, he stopped before a low door, cased with iron, which he opened, and showed that the recess was filled with large canvas bags.

" Why, this is the powder-magazine," said Fenwolf; " I can now guess how you mean to destroy Herne. I like the scheme well enough; but it cannot be executed without certain destruction to ourselves."

" I will take all risk upon myself," said Tristram; " I only require your aid in the preparations. What I propose to do is this. There is powder enough in the magazine, not only to blow up the cave, but to set fire to all the wood surrounding it. It must be scattered among the dry brushwood in a great circle round the cave, and connected by a train with this magazine. When Herne comes back, I will fire the train."

" There is much hazard in the scheme, and I fear it will fail," replied Fenwolf, after a pause; " nevertheless, I will assist you."

" Then, let us go to work at once," said Tristram, " for we have no time to lose. Herne will be here before mid-night, and I should like to have all ready for him."

Accordingly, they each shouldered a couple of the bags, and returning to the cavern, threaded a narrow passage, and emerged from the secret entrance in the grove.

While Fenwolf descended for a fresh supply of powder, Tristram commenced operations. Though autumn was now far advanced, there had been remarkably fine weather of late; the ground was thickly strewn with yellow leaves; the fern was brown and dry; and the brushwood crackled and broke as a passage was forced through it. The very trees were parched by the long-continued drought. Thus favoured in his design, Tristram scattered the contents of one of the bags in a thick line among the fern and brushwood, depositing here and there, among the roots of a tree, several pounds of powder, and covering the heaps over with dried sticks and leaves.

While he was thus employed, Fenwolf appeared with two more bags of powder, and descended again for a fresh supply. When he returned, laden as before, the old forester had already described a large portion of the circle he intended to take.

Judging that there was now powder sufficient, Tristram explained to his companion how to proceed; and the other commenced laying a train on the left of the secret entrance, carefully observing the instructions given him.

In less than an hour, they met together at a particular tree, and the formidable circle was complete.

" So far well ! " said Tristram, emptying the contents of his bag beneath the tree, and covering it with leaves and sticks, as before; " and now to connect this with the cavern."

With this, he opened another bag, and drew a wide train towards the centre of the space. At length, he paused at the foot of a large hollow tree.

" I have ascertained," he said, " that this tree stands immediately over the magazine; and by following this rabbit's burrow I have contrived to make a small entrance into it. A hollow reed introduced through the hole, and filled with powder, will be sure to reach the store below."

" An excellent idea ! " replied Fenwolf. " I will fetch one instantly."

And starting off to the side of the lake, he presently returned with several long reeds, one of which was selected by Tristram, and thrust into the burrow. It proved of the precise length required; and as soon as it touched the bottom it was carefully filled with powder

331

from a horn. Having connected this tube with the side train, and scattered powder for several yards around, so as to secure its instantaneous ignition, Tristram pronounced that the train was complete.

"We have now laid a trap from which Herne will scarcely escape," he observed, with a moody laugh, to Fenwolf.

They then prepared to return to the cave; but had not proceeded many yards when Herne, mounted on his sable steed, burst through the trees.

"Ah! what make you here?" he cried, instantly checking his career. "I bade you keep strict watch over Mabel. Where is she?"

"She has escaped with Sir Thomas Wyat," replied Fenwolf; "and we have been in search of them——"

"Escaped!" exclaimed Herne, springing from his steed, and rushing up to him; "dogs! you have played me false. But your lives shall pay the penalty of your perfidy."

"We had no hand in it whatever," replied Fenwolf doggedly. "She contrived to get out of a chamber in which I placed her, and to liberate Sir Thomas Wyat. They then procured a steed from the stable, and plunged through the pool into the lake."

"Hell's malison upon them, and upon you both!" cried Herne. "But you shall pay dearly for your heedlessness—if, indeed, it has not been something worse. How long have they been gone?"

"It may be two hours," replied Fenwolf.

"Go to the cave," cried Herne, "and await my return there; and if I recover not the prize woe betide you both!"

And with these words he vaulted upon his steed and disappeared.

"And woe betide you too, false fiend!" cried Fenwolf. "When you come back you shall meet with a welcome you little expect. Would we had fired the train, Tristram, even though we had perished with him!"

"It will be time enough to fire it on his return," replied the old forester; "it is but postponing our vengeance for a short time. And now to fix our positions. I will take my station in yon brake."

" And I in that hollow tree," said Fenwolf. " Whoever first beholds him shall fire the train."

" Agreed ! " replied Tristram. " Let us now descend to the cave, and see that all is right in the magazine, and then we will return and hold ourselves in readiness for action."

VII

How the Train was Fired ; and what Followed the Explosion

ABOUT ten o'clock in the night under consideration, Surrey and Richmond, accompanied by the Duke of Shoreditch and half a dozen other archers, set out from the castle, and took their way along the Great Park, in the direction of the lake.

They had not ridden far when they were overtaken by two horsemen who, as far as they could be discerned in that doubtful light, appeared stalwart personages, and well mounted, though plainly attired. The new-comers very unceremoniously joined them.

" There are ill reports of the park, my masters," said the foremost of these persons to Surrey, " and we would willingly ride with you across it."

" But our way may not be yours, friend," replied Surrey, who did not altogether relish this proposal. " We are not going farther than the lake."

" Our road lies in that direction," replied the other, " and, if you please, we will bear you company as far as we go. Come, tell me frankly," he added, after a pause, " are you not in search of Herne the hunter ? "

" Why do you ask, friend ? " rejoined the earl, somewhat angrily.

" Because if so," replied the other, " I shall be right

glad to join you, and so will my friend, Tony Cryspyn, who is close behind me. I have an old grudge to settle with this Herne, who has more than once attacked me, and I shall be glad to pay it."

" If you will take my advice, Hugh Dacre, you will ride on, and leave the achievement of the adventure to these young galliards," interposed Cryspyn.

" Nay, by the mass ! that shall never be," rejoined Dacre, " if they have no objection to our joining them. If they have, they have only to say so, and we will go on."

" I will be plain with you, my masters," said Surrey. " We are determined this night, as you have rightly conjectured, to seek out Herne the hunter ; and we hope to obtain such clue to him as will ensure his capture. If, therefore, you are anxious to join us, we shall be glad of your aid. But you must be content to follow, and not lead, and to act as you may be directed ; or you will only be in the way, and we would rather dispense with your company."

" We are content with the terms—are we not, Tony ? " said Dacre.

His companion answered somewhat ⸲sullenly in the affirmative.

" And now that the matter is arranged, may I ask when you propose to go ? " he continued.

" We are on our way to a hut on the lake, where we expect a companion to join us," replied Surrey.

" What ! Tristram Lyndwood's cottage ? " demanded Dacre.

" Ay," replied the earl, " and we hope to recover his fair granddaughter from the power of the demon."

" Ha ! say you so ? " cried Dacre ; " that were a feat indeed ! "

The two strangers then rode apart for a few moments, and conversed together in a low tone, during which Richmond expressed his doubts of them to Surrey, adding that he was determined to get rid of them.

The new-comers, however, were not easily shaken off. As soon as they perceived the duke's design, they stuck more pertinaciously to him and the earl than before, and made it evident they would not be dismissed.

By this time they had passed Spring Hill, and were within a mile of the valley in which lay the marsh, when a cry for help was heard in the thicket on the left, and the troop immediately halted. The cry was repeated, and Surrey, bidding the others follow him, dashed off in the direction of the sound.

Presently they perceived two figures beneath the trees, whom they found, on a nearer approach, were Sir Thomas Wyat, with Mabel in a state of insensibility in his arms.

Dismounting by the side of his friend, Surrey hastily demanded how he came there, and what had happened.

"It is too long a story to relate now," said Wyat; "but the sum of it is that I have escaped, by the aid of this damsel, from the clutches of the demon. Our escape was effected on horseback, and we had to plunge into the lake. The immersion deprived my fair preserver of sensibility, so that as soon as I landed, and gained a covert where I fancied myself secure, I dismounted, and tried to restore her. While I was thus occupied, the steed I had brought with me broke his bridle and darted off into the woods. After a while Mabel opened her eyes, but she was so weak that she could not move, and I was fain to make her a couch in the fern, in the hope that she would speedily revive. But the fright and suffering had been too much for her, and a succession of fainting fits followed, during which I thought she would expire. This is all. Now let us prepare a litter for her, and convey her where proper assistance can be rendered."

Meanwhile the others had come up, and Hugh Dacre, flinging himself from his horse, and pushing Surrey somewhat rudely aside, advanced towards Mabel, and taking her hand, said, in a voice of some emotion, " Alas ! poor girl ! I did not expect to meet thee again in this state."

"You knew her, then ? " said Surrey.

Dacre muttered an affirmative.

"Who is this man ? " asked Wyat of the earl.

"I know him not," answered Surrey. "He joined us on the road hither."

"I am well known to Sir Thomas Wyat," replied Dacre, in a significant tone, "as he will avouch when I recall certain matters to his mind. But do not let us lose time here. This damsel claims our first attention. She must be conveyed to a place of safety, and where she can be well tended. We can then return to search for Herne."

Upon this, a litter of branches was speedily made, and Mabel being laid upon it, the simple conveyance was sustained by four of the archers. The little cavalcade then quitted the thicket, and began to retrace its course towards the castle. Wyat had been accommodated with a horse by one of the archers, and rode in a melancholy manner by the side of the litter.

They had got back nearly as far as the brow of Spring Hill, when a horseman, in a wild garb, and mounted on a coal-black steed, dashed suddenly and at a furious pace out of trees on the right. He made towards the litter, overturning Sir Thomas Wyat, and, before any opposition could be offered him, seized the inanimate form of Mabel, and placing her before him on his steed, dashed off as swiftly as he came, and with a burst of loud, exulting laughter.

"It is Herne! it is Herne!" burst from every lip. And they all started in pursuit, urging the horses to their utmost speed. Sir Thomas Wyat had instantly remounted his steed, and he came up with the others.

Herne's triumphant and demoniacal laugh was heard as he scoured with the swiftness of the wind down the long glade. But the fiercest determination animated his pursuers, who, being all admirably mounted, managed to keep him fully in view.

Away! away! he speeded in the direction of the lake; and after him they thundered, straining every sinew in the desperate chase. It was a wild and extraordinary sight, and partook of the fantastical character of a dream.

At length, Herne reached the acclivity at the foot of

which lay the waters of the lake glimmering in the starlight, and by the time he had descended to its foot his pursuers had gained its brow.

The exertions made by Sir Thomas Wyat had brought him a little in advance of the others. Furiously goading his horse, he dashed down the hillside at a terrific pace.

All at once, as he kept his eye on the flying figure of the demon, he was startled by a sudden burst of flame in the valley. A wide circle of light was rapidly described, a rumbling sound was heard like that preceding an earthquake, and a tremendous explosion followed, hurling trees and fragments of rock into the air.

Astounded at the extraordinary occurrence, and not knowing what might ensue, the pursuers reined in their steeds. But the terror of the scene was not yet over. The whole of the brushwood had caught fire, and blazed up with the fury and swiftness of lighted flax. The flames caught the parched branches of the trees, and in a few seconds the whole grove was on fire.

The sight was awfully grand, for the wind, which was blowing strongly, swept the flames forward, so that they devoured all before them.

When the first flash was seen, the demon had checked his steed, and backed him, so that he had escaped without injury, and he stood at the edge of the flaming circle watching the progress of the devastating element; but at last, finding that his pursuers had taken heart, and were approaching him, he bestirred himself, and rode round the blazing zone.

Having by this time recovered from their surprise, Wyat and Surrey dashed after him, and got so near him that they made sure of his capture. But at the very moment they expected to reach him, he turned his horse's head, and forced him to leap over the blazing boundary.

In vain the pursuers attempted to follow. Their horses refused to encounter the flames; while Wyat's steed, urged on by its frantic master, reared bolt upright, and dislodged him.

But the demon held on his way, apparently unscathed, in the midst of the flames, casting a look of grim defiance at his pursuers. As he passed a tree, from which volumes of fire were bursting, the most appalling shrieks reached his ear, and he beheld Morgan Fenwolf emerging from a hole in the trunk. But without bestowing more than a glance upon his unfortunate follower, he dashed forward, and becoming involved in the wreaths of flame and smoke, was lost to sight.

Attracted by Fenwolf's cries, the beholders perceived him crawl out of the hole, and clamber into the upper part of the tree, where he roared to them most piteously for aid. But even if they had been disposed to render it it was impossible to do so now; and after terrible and protracted suffering, the poor wretch, half stifled with smoke, and unable longer to maintain his hold of the branch to which he had crept, fell into the flames beneath, and perished.

Attributing its outbreak to supernatural agency, the party gazed on in wonder at the fire, and rode round it as closely as their steeds would allow them. But though they tarried till the flames had abated, and little was left of the noble grove but a collection of charred and smoking stumps, nothing was seen of the fiend or of the hapless girl he had carried off. It served to confirm the notion of the supernatural origin of the fire, in that it was confined within the mystic circle, and did not extend farther into the woods.

At the time that the flames first burst forth, and revealed the countenances of the lookers-on, it was discovered that the self-styled Dacre and Cryspyn were no other than the king and the Duke of Suffolk.

"If this mysterious being is mortal, he must have perished now," observed Henry; "and if he is not, it is useless to seek for him further."

Day had begun to break as the party quitted the scene of devastation. The king and Suffolk, with the archers, returned to the castle; but Wyat, Surrey, and Richmond rode towards the lake, and proceeded along its banks in the direction of the forester's hut.

Their progress was suddenly arrested by the sound of lamentation, and they perceived, in a little bay, overhung by trees, which screened it from the path, an old man kneeling beside the body of a female, which he had partly dragged out of the lake. It was Tristram Lyndwood, and the body was that of Mabel. Her tresses were dishevelled, and dripping with wet, as were her garments; and her features white as marble. The old man was weeping bitterly.

With Wyat, to dismount and grasp the cold hand of the hapless maiden was the work of a moment.

" She is dead ! " he cried in a despairing voice, removing the dank tresses from her brow, and imprinting a reverent kiss upon it. " Dead !—lost to me for ever ! "

" I found her entangled among those water-weeds," said Tristram, in tones broken by emotion, " and had just dragged her to shore when you came up. As you hope to prosper, now and hereafter, give her a decent burial. For me all is over."

And, with a lamentable cry, he plunged into the lake, struck out to a short distance, and then sank to rise no more.

JANE SEYMOUR

I

Of Henry's attachment to Jane Seymour

ON the anniversary of St. George, 1536, and exactly seven years from the opening of this chronicle, Henry assembled the knights-companions within Windsor Castle to hold the grand feast of the most noble Order of the Garter.

Many important events had occurred in the wide interval thus suffered to elapse. Wolsey had long since sunk under his reverses—for he never regained the royal favour after his dismissal—and had expired at Leicester Abbey, on 26th November, 1530.

But the sufferings of Catharine of Arragon were prolonged up to the commencement of the year under consideration. After the divorce, and the elevation of Anne Boleyn to the throne in her stead, she withdrew to Kimbolton Castle, where she dwelt in the greatest retirement, under the style of the princess dowager. Finding her end approaching, she sent a humble message to the king, imploring him to allow her one more interview with her daughter, that she might bestow her blessing upon her; but the request was refused.

A touching letter, however, which she wrote to the king on her death-bed, moved him to tears; and having ejaculated a few expressions of his sense of her many noble qualities, he retired to his closet to indulge his grief in secret. Solemn obsequies were ordered to be performed at Windsor and Greenwich on the day of her interment, and the king and the whole of his retinue put on mourning for her.

With this arrangement Anne Boleyn cared not to comply. Though she had attained the summit of her ambition; though the divorce had been pronounced, and she was crowned queen; though she had given birth to

343

a daughter—the Princess Elizabeth, afterwards the illustrious queen of that name—two years before; and though she could have no reasonable apprehensions from her, the injured Catharine, during her lifetime, had always been an object of dread to her. She heard of her death with undisguised satisfaction, clapped her hands, exclaiming to her attendants, " Now I am indeed queen!" and put the crowning point to her unfeeling conduct by decorating herself and her dames in the gayest apparel on the day of the funeral.

Alas ! she little knew that at that very moment the work of retribution commenced, and that the wrongs of the injured queen, whose memory she thus outraged, were soon to be terribly and bloodily avenged.

Other changes had likewise taken place, which may be here recorded. The Earl of Surrey had made the tour of France, Italy, and the Empire, and had fully kept his word, by proclaiming the supremacy of the fair Geraldine's beauty at all tilts and tournaments, at which he constantly bore away the prize. But the greatest reward, and that which he hoped would crown his fidelity—the hand of his mistress—was not reserved for him.

At the expiration of three years, he returned home, polished by travel, and accounted one of the bravest and most accomplished cavaliers of the day. His reputation had preceded him, and he was received with marks of the highest distinction and favour by Henry, as well as by Anne Boleyn. But the king was still averse to the match, and forbade the fair Geraldine to return to court.

Finding so much opposition on all sides, the earl was at last brought to assent to the wish of the fair Geraldine, that their engagement should be broken off. In her letters, she assured him that her love had undergone no abatement—and never would do so—but that she felt they must give up all idea of a union.

These letters, probably the result of some manœuvring on his own part, set on foot by the royal mandate, were warmly seconded by the Duke of Norfolk, and after many and long solicitations, he succeeded in wringing from his son a reluctant acquiescence to the arrangement.

The disappointment produced its natural consequences on the ardent temperament of the young earl, and completely chilled and blighted his feelings. He became moody and discontented; took little share in the amusements and pastimes going forward; and from being the blithest cavalier at court became the saddest. The change in his demeanour did not escape the notice of Anne Boleyn, who easily divined the cause, and she essayed by raillery and other arts to wean him from his grief. But all was for some time of no avail. The earl continued inconsolable. At last, however, by the instrumentality of the queen and his father, he was contracted to the Lady Francis Vere, daughter of the Earl of Oxford, and was married to her in 1535.

Long before this, the Duke of Richmond had been wedded to the Lady Mary Howard.

For some time previous to the present era of this chronicle Anne Boleyn had observed a growing coolness towards her on the part of the king, and latterly it had become evident that his passion for her was fast subsiding, if indeed it had not altogether expired.

Though Anne had never truly loved her royal consort, and though at that very time she was secretly encouraging the regards of another, she felt troubled by this change, and watched all the king's movements with jealous anxiety to ascertain if any one had supplanted her in his affections.

At length her vigilance was rewarded by discovering a rival in one of the loveliest of her dames, Jane Seymour. This fair creature, the daughter of Sir John Seymour, of Wolff Hall, in Wiltshire, and who was afterwards, it is almost needless to say, raised to as high a dignity as Anne Boleyn herself, was now in the very pride of her beauty. Tall, exquisitely proportioned, with a complexion of the utmost brilliancy and delicacy, large liquid blue eyes, bright chestnut tresses, and lovely features, she possessed charms that could not fail to captivate the amorous monarch. It seems marvellous that Anne Boleyn should have such an attendant; but perhaps she felt confident in her own attractions.

Skilled in intrigue herself, Anne, now that her eyes were opened, perceived all the allurements thrown out by Jane to ensnare the king, and she intercepted many a furtive glance between them. Still she did not dare to interfere. The fireceness of Henry's temper kept her in awe, and she well knew that the slightest opposition would only make him the more determined to run counter to her will. Trusting, therefore, to get rid of Jane Seymour by some stratagem, she resolved not to attempt to dismiss her except as a last resource.

A slight incident occurred which occasioned a departure from the prudent course she had laid down to herself.

Accompanied by her dames, she was traversing the great gallery of the palace at Greenwich, when she caught the reflection of Jane Seymour, who was following her, in a mirror, regarding a jewelled miniature. She instantly turned round at the sight, and Jane, in great confusion, thrust the picture into her bosom.

" Ah ! what have you there ? " cried Anne.

" A picture of my father, Sir John Seymour," replied Jane, blushing deeply.

" Let me look at it ! " cried Anne, snatching the picture from her. " Ah ! call you this your father ? To my thinking it is much more like my royal husband. Answer me frankly minion—answer me, as you value your life ! Did the king give you this ? "

" I must decline answering the question," replied Jane, who by this time had recovered her composure.

" Ah ! am I to be thus insolently treated by one of my own dames ! " cried Anne.

" I intend no disrespect to your majesty," replied Jane, " and I will, since you insist upon it, freely confess that I received the portrait from the king. I did not conceive there could be any harm in doing so, because I saw your majesty present your own portrait, the other day, to Sir Henry Norris."

Anne Boleyn turned as pale as death, and Jane Seymour perceived that she had her in her power.

" I gave the portrait to Sir Henry as a recompense for an important service he rendered me," said Anne, after a slight pause.

" No doubt," replied Jane; " and I marvel not that he should press it so fervently to his lips, seeing he must value the gift highly. The king likewise bestowed his portrait upon me for rendering him a service."

" And what was that ? " asked Anne.

" Nay, there your majesty must hold me excused," replied the other. " It were to betray his highness's confidence to declare it. I must refer you to him for an explanation."

" Well, you are in the right to keep the secret," said Anne, forcing a laugh. " I dare say there is no harm in the portrait—indeed, I am sure there is not, if it was given with the same intent that mine was bestowed upon Norris. And so we will say no more upon the matter— except that I must beg you to be discreet with the king. If others should comment upon your conduct, I may be compelled to dismiss you."

" Your majesty shall be obeyed," said Jane, with a look that intimated that the request had but slight weight with her.

" Catharine will be avenged by means of this woman," muttered Anne, as she turned away. " I already feel some of the torments with which she threatened me. And she suspects Norris. I must impress more caution on him. Ah ! when a man loves deeply, as he loves me, due restraint is seldom maintained."

But though alarmed, Anne was by no means aware of the critical position in which she stood. She could not persuade herself that she had entirely lost her influence with the king, and she thought that when his momentary passion had subsided, it would return to its old channels.

She was mistaken. Jane Seymour was absolute mistress

of his heart; and Anne was now as great a bar to him as she had before been an attraction. Had her conduct been irreproachable, it might have been difficult to remove her; but, unfortunately, she had placed herself at his mercy by yielding to the impulses of vanity, and secretly encouraging the passion of Sir Henry Norris, groom of the stole.

This favoured personage was somewhat above the middle size, squarely and strongly built. His features were regularly and finely formed, and he had a ruddy complexion, brown, curling hair, good teeth, and fine eyes of a clear blue. He possessed great personal strength, was expert in all manly exercises, and shone especially at the jousts and the manège. He was of an ardent temperament, and Anne Boleyn had inspired him with so desperate a passion that he set at naught the fearful risk he ran to obtain her favour.

In all this seemed traceable the hand of fate—in Henry's passion for Jane Seymour, and Anne's insane regard for Norris—as if in this way, and by the same means in which she herself had been wronged, the injured Catharine of Arragon was to be avenged.

How far Henry's suspicions of his consort's regard for Norris had been roused did not at the time appear. Whatever he felt in secret, he took care that no outward manifestation should betray him. On the contrary, he loaded Norris, who had always been a favourite with him, with new marks of regard, and encouraged rather than interdicted his approach to the queen.

Things were in this state when the court proceeded to Windsor, as before related, on St. George's Day.

II

How Anne Boleyn received proof of Henry's passion for Jane Seymour

ON the day after the solemnisation of the grand feast of the Order of the Garter, a masqued fête of great splendour and magnificence was held within the castle. The whole of the state apartments were thrown open to the distinguished guests, and universal gaiety prevailed. No restraint was offered to the festivity by the king, for though he was known to be present, he did not choose to declare himself.

The queen sat apart, on a fauteuil in the deep embrasure of a window; and as various companies of fantastic characters advanced towards her she more than once fancied she detected amongst them the king, but the voices convinced her of her mistake. As the evening was wearing, a mask in a blue domino drew near her, and whispered, in a devoted and familiar tone, " My queen!"

" Is it you, Norris ? " demanded Anne, under her breath.

" It is," he replied. " Oh, madam ! I have been gazing at you the whole evening, but have not dared to approach you till now."

" I am sorry you have addressed me at all, Norris," she rejoined. " Your regard for me has been noticed by others, and may reach the king's ears. You must promise never to address me in the language of passion again."

" If I may not utter my love, I shall go mad," replied Norris. " After raising me to the verge of Paradise, do not thrust me to the depths of Tartarus."

" I have neither raised you, nor do I cast you down," rejoined Anne. " That I am sensible of your devotion, and grateful for it, I admit, but nothing more. My love and allegiance are due to the king."

" True," replied Norris bitterly; " they are so, but he

349

is wholly insensible to your merits. At this very moment, he is pouring his love-vows in the ear of Jane Seymour."

"Ah! is he so?" cried Anne. "Let me have proof of his perfidy, and I may incline a more favourable ear to you."

"I will instantly obtain you the proof, madam," replied Norris, bowing and departing.

Scarcely had he quitted the queen, and mixed with the throng of dancers, than he felt a pressure upon his arm, and turning at the touch, beheld a tall monk, the lower part of whose face was muffled up, leaving only a pair of fierce black eyes, and a large aquiline nose visible.

"I know what you want, Sir Henry Norris," said the tall monk, in a low deep voice; "you wish to give the queen proof of her royal lord's inconstancy. It is easily done. Come with me."

"Who are you?" demanded Norris doubtfully.

"What matters it who I am?" rejoined the other; "I am one of the masquers, and chance to know what is passing around me. I do not inquire into your motive, and therefore you have no right to inquire into mine."

"It is not for my own satisfaction that I desire this proof," said Norris, "because I would rather shield the king's indiscretions than betray them. But the queen has conceived suspicions which she is determined to verify."

"Think not to impose upon me," replied the monk, with a sneer. "Bring the queen this way, and she shall be fully satisfied."

"I can run no risk in trusting you," said Norris, "and therefore I accept your offer."

"Say no more," cried the monk disdainfully, "I will await you here."

And Norris returned to the queen.

"Have you discovered anything?" she cried.

"Come with me, madam," said Norris, bowing, and taking her hand.

Proceeding thus, they glided through the throng of dancers, who respectfully cleared a passage for them as they walked along, until they approached the spot where the tall monk was standing. As they drew near him, he moved on, and Norris and the queen followed in silence. Passing from the great hall in which the crowd of dancers was assembled, they descended a short flight of steps, at the foot of which the monk paused, and pointed with his right hand to a chamber, partly screened by the folds of a curtain.

At this intimation, the queen and her companion stepped quickly on, and as she advanced, Anne Boleyn perceived Jane Seymour and the king seated on a couch within the apartment. Henry was habited like a pilgrim, but he had thrown down his hat, ornamented with the scallop-shell, his vizard, and his staff, and had just forced his fair companion to unmask.

At the sight, Anne was transfixed with jealous rage, and was for the moment almost unconscious of the presence of Norris, or of the monk, who remained behind the curtain, pointing to what was taking place.

" Your majesty is determined to expose my blushes," said Jane Seymour, slightly struggling with her royal lover.

" Nay, I only want to be satisfied that it is really yourself, sweetheart," cried Henry passionately. " It was in mercy to me, I suppose, that you insisted upon shrouding those beauteous features from my view."

" Hear you that, madam,? " whispered Norris to Anne. The queen answered by a convulsive clasp of the hand.

" Your majesty but jests with me," said Jane Seymour.

" Jests ! " cried Henry passionately. " By my faith, I never understood the power of beauty till now. No charms ever moved my heart like yours; nor shall I know a moment's peace till you become mine."

" I am grieved to hear it, my liege," replied Jane Seymour, " for I never can be yours, unless as your queen."

Again Norris hazarded a whisper to Anne Boleyn, which was answered by another nervous grasp of the hand.

" That is as much as to say," pursued Jane, seeing the

gloomy reverie into which her royal lover was thrown,
" I can give your majesty no hopes at all."

" You have been schooled by Anne Boleyn, sweetheart," said Henry.

" How so, my liege ? " demanded Jane Seymour.

" Those were the very words she used to me when I
wooed her, and which induced me to divorce Catharine
of Arragon," replied Henry. " Now they may bring
about her own removal."

" Just Heaven ? " murmured Anne.

" I dare not listen to your majesty," said Jane Seymour,
in a tremulous tone; " and yet, if I dared speak——"

" Speak on fearlessly, sweetheart," said Henry.

" Then I am well assured," said Jane, " that the queen
no longer loves you; nay, that she loves another."

" It is false, minion ! " cried Anne Boleyn, rushing
forward, while Norris hastily retreated—" it is false ! It
is you who would deceive the king for your own purposes.
But I have fortunately been brought hither to prevent
the injury you would do me. Oh ! Henry, have I deserved
this of you ? "

" You have chanced to overhear part of a scene in a
masquerade, madam—that is all," said the king.

" I have chanced to arrive most opportunely for
myself," said Anne. " As for this slanderous and
deceitful minion, I shall dismiss her from my service. If
your majesty is determined to prove faithless to me, it
shall not be with one of my own dames."

" Catharine of Arragon should have made that
speech," retorted Jane Seymour bitterly; " she had reason to complain that she was supplanted by one much
beneath her. And she never played the king falsely."

" Nor have I ! " cried Anne fiercely; " if I had my will
I should strike thee dead, for the insinuation. Henry—
my lord—my love—if you have any regard for me,
instantly dimiss Jane Seymour."

" It may not be, madam," replied Henry, in a freezing
tone. " She has done nothing to deserve dismissal. If
any one is to blame in the matter, it is myself."

"And will you allow her to make these accusations against me without punishment?" cried Anne.

"Peace, madam!" cried the king sternly; "and thank my good nature that I go no further into the matter. If you are weary of the masque, I pray you retire to your own apartments. For myself, I shall lead Jane Seymour to the bransle."

"And if your majesty should need a partner," said Jane, walking up to Anne, and speaking in a low tone, "you will doubtless find Sir Henry Norris disengaged."

The queen looked as if stricken by a thunderbolt. She heard the triumphant laugh of her rival; she saw her led forth, all smiles and beauty and triumph, by the king to the dance; and she covered her face in agony. While she was in this state, a deep voice breathed in her ears, "The vengeance of Catharine of Arragon begins to work!"

Looking up, she beheld the tall figure of the monk retreating from the chamber.

III

What passed between Norris and the tall Monk

TOTTERING to the seat which Henry and Jane had just quitted, Anne sank into it. After a little time, having in some degree recovered her composure, she was about to return to the great hall, when Norris appeared.

"I did not deceive you, madam," he said, "when I told you the king was insensible to your charms. He only lives for Jane Seymour."

"Would I could dismiss her!" cried Anne furiously.

"If you were to do so, she would soon be replaced by another," rejoined Norris. "The king delights only in change. With him, the last face is ever the most beautiful."

"You speak fearful treason, sir!" replied Anne; "but I believe it to be the truth."

" Oh, then, madam ! " pursued Norris, " since the king is so regardless of you, why trouble yourself about him ?—there are those who would sacrifice a thousand lives, if they possessed them, for your love."

" I fear it is the same with all men," rejoined Anne. " A woman's heart is a bauble which, when obtained, is speedily tossed aside."

" Your majesty judges our sex too harshly," said Norris. " If I had the same fortune as the king, I should never change."

" The king himself once thought so—once swore so," replied Anne petulantly. " It is the common parlance of lovers. But I may not listen to such discourse longer."

" Oh, madam," cried Norris, " you misjudge me greatly. My heart is not made of the same stuff as that of the royal Henry. I can love deeply—devotedly—lastingly."

" Know you not that by these rash speeches you place your head in jeopardy ? " said Anne.

" I would rather lose it than not be permitted to love you," he replied.

" But your rashness endangers me," said the queen. " Your passion has already been noticed by Jane Seymour, and the slightest further indiscretion will be fatal."

" Nay, if that be so," cried Norris, " and your majesty should be placed in peril on my account, I will banish myself from the court, and from your presence, whatever the effort may cost me ! "

" No," replied Anne, " I will not tax you so hardly. I do not think," she added tenderly, " deserted as I am by the king, that I could spare you."

" You confess, then, that I have inspired you with some regard ? " he cried rapturously.

" Do not indulge in these transports, Norris," said Anne mournfully. " Your passion will only lead to your destruction—perchance to mine ! Let the certainty that I *do* love, content you, and seek not to tempt your fate further."

" Oh ! madam, you make me the happiest of men by the avowal," he cried. " I envy not now the king, for I feel raised above him by your love."

" You must join the revel, Norris," said Anne—" your absence from it will be observed."

And extending her hand to him, he knelt down, and pressed it passionately to his lips.

" Ah ! we are observed," she cried suddenly, and almost with a shriek. " Rise, sir ! "

Norris instantly sprang to his feet, and to his inexpressible dismay, saw the figure of the tall monk gliding away. Throwing a meaning look at the almost sinking queen, he followed the mysterious observer into the great hall, determining to get rid of him in some way, before he should have time to make any revelations.

Avoiding the brilliant throng, the monk entered the adjoining corridor, and descending the great staircase, passed into the upper quadrangle. From thence, he proceeded towards the cloisters near St. George's Chapel, where he was overtaken by Norris, who had followed him closely.

" What would you with me, Sir Henry Norris ? " cried the monk, halting.

" You may guess," said Norris sternly, and drawing his sword. " There are secrets which are dangerous to the possessor. Unless you swear never to betray what you have seen and heard, you die."

The tall monk laughed derisively.

" You know that your life is in my power," he said, " and therefore you threaten mine. Well, e'en take it, if you can.'"

As he spoke, he drew a sword from beneath his robe, and stood upon his defence. After a few passes, Norris's weapon was beaten from his grasp.

" You are now completely at my mercy," said the monk, " and I have nothing to do but to call the guard, and declare all I have heard to the king."

" I would rather you plunged your sword into my heart," said Norris.

"There is one way—and only one, by which my secrecy may be purchased," said the monk.

"Name it," replied Norris. "Were it to be purchased by my soul's perdition, I would embrace it."

"You have hit the point exactly," rejoined the monk dryly. "Can you not guess with whom you have to deal?"

"Partly," replied Norris; "I never found such force in mortal arm as you have displayed."

"Probably not," laughed the other—"most of those who have ventured against me have found their match. But come with me into the park, and you shall learn the condition of my secrecy."

"I cannot quit the castle," replied Norris; "but I will take you to my lodgings, where we shall be wholly unobserved."

And crossing the lower ward, they proceeded to the tower of the south side of it, now appropriated to the governor of the alms knights.

About an hour after this, Norris returned to the revel. His whole demeanour was changed, and his looks ghastly. He sought out the queen, who had returned to the seat in the embrasure.

"What has happened?" said Anne, in a low tone, as he approached her. "Have you killed him?"

"No," he replied; "but I have purchased our safety at a terrible price."

"You alarm me, Norris—what mean you?" she cried.

"I mean this," he answered, regarding her with passionate earnestness—"that you *must* love me now, for I have perilled my salvation for you. That tall monk was Herne the hunter."

IV

*Of the Secret Interview between Norris and Anne Boleyn;
and of the Dissimulation practised by the King*

HENRY'S attentions to Jane Seymour at the masqued fête
were so marked, that the whole court was made aware of
his passion. But it was not anticipated that any serious
and extraordinary consequence would result from the
intoxication—far less that the queen herself would be
removed to make way for her successful rival. It was
afterwards, however, remembered that at this time Henry
held frequent, long, and grave conferences with the Dukes
of Suffolk and Norfolk, and appeared to be engrossed in
the meditation of some project.

After the scene at the revel, Anne did not make another
exhibition of jealousy; but it was not that she was reconciled to her situation, or in any way free from uneasiness.
On the contrary, the unhappy Catharine of Arragon did
not suffer more in secret; but she knew, from experience,
that with her royal consort all reproaches would be
unavailing.

One morning, when she was alone within her chamber,
her father, who was now Earl of Wiltshire, obtained
admittance to her.

"You have a troubled look, my dear lord," she said, as
she motioned him to a seat.

"And with good reason," he replied. "Oh, Anne,
words cannot express my anxiety at the present state
of things."

"It will speedily pass by, my lord," she replied; "the
king will soon be tired of his new idol."

"Not before he has overthrown the old one, I fear,"
rejoined the earl. "Jane Seymour's charms have usurped
entire sovereignty over him. With all her air of in-
genuousness and simplicity, the minion is artful and

357

dangerous. She has a high mark, I am persuaded—no less than the throne."

" But Henry cannot wed her—he cannot divorce me," said Anne.

" So thought Catharine of Arragon," replied her father; " and yet she was divorced. Anne, I am convinced a plot is hatching against you."

" You do not fear for my life, father ! " she cried, trembling.

" I trust there are no grounds for charges against you by which it might be brought in jeopardy," replied the earl gravely.

" None, father—none ! " she exclaimed.

" I am glad of it," rejoined the earl; " for I have heard that the king said to one who suggested another divorce to him, ' No, if the queen comes within the scope of the divorce, she also comes within the pale of the scaffold.' "

" A pledge was extorted from him to that effect," said Anne, in a hollow voice.

" That an attempt will be made against you, I firmly believe," replied the earl; " but if you are wholly innocent you have nothing to fear."

" Oh, father ! I know not that," cried Anne. " Innocence avails little with the stony-hearted Henry."

" It will prove your best safeguard," said the earl. " And now farewell, daughter ! Heaven guard you ! Keep the strictest watch upon yourself."

So saying, he quitted the apartment, and as soon as she was left alone, the unhappy Anne burst into an agony of tears.

From this state of affliction she was roused by hearing her own name pronounced in low accents, and looking up, she beheld Sir Henry Norris.

" Oh, Norris ! " she said, in a tone of reproach, " you have come hither to destroy me."

" No one knows of my coming," he said; " at least, no one will betray me. I was brought hither by one who will take care we are not observed."

" By Herne ? " demanded Anne.

Norris answered in the affirmative.

" Would you had never leagued yourself with him ! " she cried ; " I fear the rash act will bring destruction upon us both."

" It is too late to retract now," he replied ; " besides, there was no help for it. I sacrificed myself to preserve you."

" But will the sacrifice preserve me ? " she cried. " I fear not. I have just been told that the king is preparing some terrible measure against me—that he meditates removing me, to make way for Jane Seymour."

" You have heard the truth, madam," replied Norris ; " he will try to bring you to the block."

" And with him, to try is to achieve," said Anne. " Oh ! Norris, it is a fearful thing to contemplate such a death ! "

" But why contemplate it, madam ? " said Norris ; " why, if you are satisfied that the king has such designs against you—why, if you feel that he will succeed, tarry for the fatal blow ? Fly with me—fly with one who loves you, and will devote his whole life to you—who regards you, not as the queen, but as Anne Boleyn. Relinquish this false and hollow grandeur, and fly with me to happiness and peace."

" And relinquish my throne to Jane Seymour ? " rejoined Anne. " Never ! I feel that all you assert is true—that my present position is hazardous—that Jane Seymour is in the ascendant, while I am on the decline, if not wholly sunk—that you love me entirely, and would devote your life to me—still, all these motives for dread, I cannot prevail upon myself voluntarily to give up my title, and to abandon my post to a rival."

" You do not love me, then, as I love you, Anne," said Norris. " If I were king, I would abandon my throne for you."

" You think so now, Norris, because you are *not* king," she replied. " But I *am* queen, and will remain so, till I am forced to abandon my dignity."

" I understand, madam," rejoined Norris gloomily.
" But, oh ! bethink you to what risks you expose yourself. You know the king's terrible determination—his
vindictiveness, his ferocity."

" Full well," she replied—" full well; but I will rather
die a queen than live disgraced and ruined. In wedding
Henry the Eighth, I laid my account to certain risks, and
those I must brave."

Before Norris could urge anything further, the door
was suddenly opened, and a tall, dark figure entered the
chamber, and said hastily—

" The king is at hand."

" One word more, and it is my last," said Norris to
Anne. " Will you fly with me to-night ?—all shall be
ready."

" I cannot," replied Anne.

" Away ! " cried Herne, dragging Norris forcibly
behind the tapestry.

Scarcely had they disappeared when Henry entered the
chamber. He was in a gayer mood than had been usual
with him of late.

" I am come to tell you, madam," he said, " that I am
about to hold jousts in the castle on the first of May, at
which your good brother and mine, the Lord Rochford,
will be the challenger, while I myself shall be the defend-
ant. You will adjudge the prize."

" Why not make Jane Seymour queen of the jousts ? "
said Anne, unable to resist the remark.

" She will be present at them," said Henry, " but I
have my own reasons," he added significantly, " for not
wishing her to appear as queen on this occasion."

" Whatever may be your reasons, the wish is sufficient
for me," said Anne. " Nay, will you not tarry a moment
with me ? It is long since we have had any converse in
private together."

" I am busy at this moment," replied Henry bluffly;
" but what is it you would say to me ? "

" I would only reproach you for some lack of tenderness, and much neglect," said Anne. " Oh ! Henry ! do

you remember how you swore by your life—your crown
—your faith—all that you held sacred or dear—that you
would love me ever ? "

" And so would I, if I could," replied the king; " but
unfortunately the heart is not entirely under control.
Have you, yourself, for instance, experienced no change
in your affections ? "

" No," replied Anne; " I have certainly suffered
severely from your too evident regard for Jane Seymour;
but though deeply mortified and distressed, I have never
for a moment been shaken in my love for your majesty."

" A loyal and loving reply," said Henry. " I thought
I had perceived some slight diminution in your regard."

" You did yourself grievous injustice by the supposition," replied Anne.

" I would fain believe so," said the king; " but there
are some persons who would persuade me that you have
not only lost your affection for me, but have even cast
eyes of regard on another."

" Those who told you so lied ! " cried Anne passionately. " Never woman was freer from such imputation
than myself."

" Never woman was more consummate hypocrite,"
muttered Henry.

" You do not credit me, I see ? " cried Anne.

" If I did not, I should know how to act," replied the
king. " You remember my pledge."

" Full well," replied Anne; " and if love and duty
would not restrain me, fear would."

" So I felt," rejoined the king; " but there are some
of your sex upon whom nothing will operate as a warning
—so faithless and inconstant are they by nature. It has
been hinted to me that you are one of these. But I
cannot think it. I can never believe that a woman for
whom I have placed my very throne in jeopardy—for
whom I have divorced my queen—whose family I have
elevated and ennobled—and whom I have placed upon
the throne—would play me false. It is monstrous !—
incredible ! "

" It is—it is ! " replied Anne.

" And now farewell," said Henry. " I have stayed longer than I intended; and I should not have mentioned these accusations, which I regard as wholly groundless, unless you had reproached me."

And he quitted the chamber, leaving Anne in a strange state of perplexity and terror.

V

What Happened at the Jousts

THE first of May arrived; and though destined to set in darkness and despair, it arose in sunshine and smiles.

All were astir at an early hour within the castle, and preparations were made for the approaching show. Lists were erected in the upper quadrangle, and the whole of the vast area was strewn with sand. In front of the royal lodgings was raised a gallery, the centre of which, being set apart for the queen and her dames, was covered with cloth-of-gold and crimson velvet, on which the royal arms were gorgeously emblazoned. The two wings were likewise richly decorated, and adorned with scutcheons and pennons, while from the battlements of the eastern side of the court were hung a couple of long flags.

As soon as these preparations were completed, a throng of pages, esquires, armourers, archers, and henchmen entered it from the Norman Gateway, and took up positions within the barriers, the space without the pales being kept by a double line of halberdiers. Next came the trumpeters, mounted on richly-caparisoned horses, and having their clarions decorated with silken bandrols, fringed with gold. Stationing themselves at the principal entrance of the lists, they were speedily joined by the heralds, pursuivants, and other officers of the tilt-yard.

Presently afterwards, the Duke of Suffolk, who was appointed judge of the lists, appeared, and rode round the arena to see that all was in order. Apparently well satisfied with the survey, he dismounted, and proceeded to the gallery.

Meanwhile, the crowd within the court was increased by a great influx of the different members of the household, amongst whom were Shoreditch, Paddington, and Hector Cutbeard.

" Marry, this promises to be a splendid sight ! " said the clerk of the kitchen; " the king will, no doubt, do his devoir gallantly for the sake of the bright eyes that will look upon him."

" You mean the queen's, of course ? " said Shoreditch.

" I mean hers who may be queen," replied Cutbeard— " Mistress Jane Seymour."

" *May* be queen ! " exclaimed Shoreditch. " You surely do not think the king will divorce his present consort ? "

" Stranger things have happened," replied Cutbeard significantly. " If I am not greatly out of my reckoning," he added, " these are the last jousts Queen Anne will behold."

" The saints forfend ! " cried Shoreditch; " what reason have you for thinking so ? "

" That I may not declare," replied Cutbeard; " but before the jousts are over, you will see whether I have been rightly informed or not."

" Hush ! " exclaimed Shoreditch. " There is a tall monk eyeing us strangely; and I am not certain that he has not overheard what you have said."

" He is welcome to the intelligence," replied Cutbeard; " the end will prove its truth."

Though this was uttered in a confident tone, he, nevertheless, glanced with some misgiving at the monk, who stood behind Paddington. The object of the investigation was a very tall man, with a cowl drawn over his brow. He had a ragged black beard, fierce dark eyes, and a complexion like bronze. Seeing Cutbeard's glance anxiously fixed upon him, he advanced towards him, and said, in a low tone—

363

"You have nothing to fear from me; but talk not so loud, if you value your head."

So saying, he proceeded to another part of the lists.

"Who is that tall monk?" asked Paddington.

"Devil knows!" answered Cutbeard. "I never saw him before; but he has a villainous, cut-throat look."

Soon afterwards, a flourish of trumpets was heard, and amid their joyous bruit, the queen, sumptuously arrayed in cloth-of-gold and ermine, and having a small crown upon her brow, entered the gallery, and took her seat within it. Never had she looked more beautiful than on this fatal morning; and in the eyes of all the beholders she completely eclipsed her rival, Jane Seymour. The latter, who stood on her right hand, and was exquisitely attired, had a thoughtful and anxious air, as if some grave matter weighed upon her mind.

While the queen's attendants were taking their places, Lord Rochford, accompanied by Sir Henry Norris, and the Earls of Surrey and Essex, entered the lists. The four knights were completely armed, and mounted on powerful steeds barded with rich cloth-of-gold, embroidered with silver letters. Each had a great crimson plume in his helmet. They rode singly round the arena, and bowed as they passed the royal gallery, Norris bending almost to his saddle-bow while performing his salutation to the queen.

The field being thus taken by the challengers, who retired to the upper end of the court, a trumpet was thrice sounded by a herald, and an answer was immediately made by another herald, stationed opposite Henry the Seventh's buildings. When the clamour ceased, the king, fully armed, and followed by the Marquess of Dorset, Sir Thomas Wyat, and the Lord Clifford, rode into the lists.

Henry was equipped in a superb suit of armour, inlaid with gold, and having a breastplate of the globose form then in vogue. His helmet was decorated with a large snow-white plume. The trappings of his steed were of crimson velvet embroidered with the royal arms, and edged with great letters of massive gold bullion, full of pearls and precious stones. He was attended by a hundred gentlemen, armourers, and other officers, arrayed in white velvet.

Having ridden round the court like the others, and addressed his salutation exclusively to Jane Seymour, Henry took his station with his companions near the base of the Round Tower, the summit of which was covered with spectators, as were the towers and battlements around.

A trumpet was now sounded, and the king and the Lord Rochford having each taken a lance from his esquire, awaited the signal to start from the Duke of Suffolk, who was seated in the left wing of the royal gallery. It was not long delayed. As the clarion sounded clearly and loudly for the third time, he called out that the champions might go.

No sooner were the words uttered, than the thundering tramp of the steeds resounded, and the opponents met midway. Both their lances were shivered; but as the king did not, in the slightest degree, change his position, he was held to have the best of it. Courses were then run by the others, with varied success, the Marquess of Dorset being unhorsed by Sir Henry Norris, whose prowess was rewarded by the plaudits of the assemblage, and what was infinitely more dear to him, by the smiles of the queen.

" You have ridden well, Norris," cried Henry, advancing towards him. " Place yourself opposite me, and let us splinter a lance together."

As Norris reined back his steed, in compliance with the injunction, the tall monk stepped from out the line, and drawing near him, said, " If you wish to prove victorious, aim at the upper part of the king's helmet." And with these words he withdrew.

By the time Norris had placed his lance in the rest, the trumpet sounded. The next moment the word was given, and the champion started. Henry rode with great impetuosity, and struck Norris in the gorget with such good will that both he and his steed were shaken.

But Norris was more fortunate. Following the advice of the monk, he made the upper part of the king's helmet his mark, and the blow was so well dealt, that, though it did not dislodge the royal horseman, it drove back his steed on its haunches.

The success was so unequivocal, that Norris was at once declared the victor by the judge. No applause, however, followed the decision, from a fear of giving offence to the king.

Norris dismounted, and committing his steed to the care of an esquire, and his lance to a page, took off his helmet, and advanced towards the royal gallery, near which the Earl of Surrey and Sir Thomas Wyat were standing talking with the other dames. As Norris drew near, Anne leaned over the edge of the gallery, smiled at him tenderly, and, whether by design or accident, let fall her embroidered handkerchief.

Norris stooped to pick it up, regarding her, as he did so, with a glance of the most passionate devotion. A terrible gaze, however, was fixed on the unfortunate pair at that moment. It was that of the king. While Henry was careering in front of the gallery to display himself before Jane Seymour, a tall monk approached him, and said, " Look at Sir Henry Norris ! "

Thus addressed, Henry raised his beaver, that he might see more distinctly, and beheld Norris take up the embroidered handkerchief, which he recognised as one that he had given, in the early days of his affection, to the queen.

The sight stung him almost to madness, and he had great difficulty in repressing his choler. But if this slight action, heightened to importance, as it was, by the looks of the parties, roused his ire, it was nothing to what followed. Instead of restoring it to the queen, Norris, unconscious of the danger in which he stood, pressed the handkerchief fervently to his lips.

" I am hitherto the victor of the jousts," he said; " may I keep this as the prize ? "

Anne smiled assent.

" It is the proudest I ever obtained," pursued Norris. And he placed it within his helmet.

" Does your majesty see that ? " cried the tall monk, who still remained standing near the king.

" Death of my life ! " exclaimed Henry, " it is the very handkerchief I gave her before our union ! I can contain myself no longer, and must perforce precipitate matters. What ! ho ! " he cried, riding up to that part of the gallery where the Duke of Suffolk was seated—" let the jousts be stopped ! "

" Wherefore, my dear liege ? " said Suffolk. " The Earl of Surrey and Sir Thomas Wyat are about to run a course."

" Let them be stopped, I say," roared Henry, in a tone that admitted of no dispute. And wheeling round his charger, he dashed into the middle of the barriers, shouting in loud, authoritative accents, " The jousts are at an end ! Disperse ! "

The utmost consternation was occasioned by the announcement. The Duke of Suffolk instantly quitted his seat, and pressed through the crowd to the king, who whispered a few hasty words in his ear. Henry then called to the Earl of Surrey, the Marquess of Dorset, the Lord Clifford, Wyat, and some others, and bidding them attend him, prepared to quit the court. As he passed the royal gallery, Anne called to him, in an agonised voice—

" Oh, Henry ! what is the matter !—what have I done ? "

But without paying the slightest attention to her, he dashed through the Norman Gate, galloped down the lower quadrangle, and quitted the castle.

The confusion that ensued may be imagined. All saw that something extraordinary and terrible had taken place, though few knew precisely what it was. Dismay sat in every countenance, and the general anxiety was heightened by the agitation of the queen, who, uttering a piercing scream, fell back, and was borne off in a state of insensibility by her attendants.

Unable to control himself at the sight, Norris burst through the guard, and rushing up the great staircase, soon gained the apartment to which the queen had been conveyed. Owing to the timely aid afforded her, she was speedily restored; and the first person her eyes fell upon was her lover. At the sight of him, a glance of affection illumined her features, but it was instantly changed into an expression of alarm.

At this juncture, the Duke of Suffolk, who, with Bouchier and a party of halberdiers had entered the room, stepped up to the queen, and said—

"Will it please you, madam, to retire to an inner department. I grieve to say, you are under arrest."

"Arrest!" exclaimed Anne: "for what crime, your grace?"

"You are charged with incontinency towards the king's highness," replied Suffolk sternly.

"But I am innocent?" cried Anne—"as Heaven shall judge me, I am innocent!"

"I trust you will be able to prove yourself so, madam," said Suffolk. "Sir Henry Norris, your person is likewise attached."

"Then I am lost indeed!" exclaimed Anne distractedly.

"Do not let these false and malignant accusations alarm you, madam," said Norris. "You have nothing to fear. I will die protesting your innocence."

"Sir Henry Norris," said the duke coldly, "your own imprudence has brought about this sad result."

"I feel it," replied Norris; "and I deserve the worst punishment that can be inflicted upon me for it. But I declare to you—as I will declare upon the rack, if I am placed upon it—that the queen is wholly innocent. Let her not suffer for my fault."

"You hear what Sir Henry says," cried Anne; "and I call upon you to recollect the testimony he has borne."

"I shall not fail to do so, madam," replied Suffolk. "Your majesty will have strict justice."

" Justice ! " echoed Anne, with a laugh of bitter incredulity. " Justice from Henry the Eighth ? "

" Beseech you, madam, do not destroy yourself," said Norris, prostrating himself before her. " Recollect by whom you are surrounded. My folly and madness have brought you into this strait, and I sincerely implore your pardon for it."

" You are not to blame, Norris," said Anne—" it is fate, not you, that has destroyed me. The hand that has dealt this blow is that of a queen within the tomb."

" Captain Bouchier," said the Duke of Suffolk, addressing that officer who stood near him, " you will convey Sir Henry Norris to the strong-room in the lower gateway, whence he will be removed to the Tower."

" Farewell, for ever, Norris ! " cried Anne. " We shall meet no more on earth. In what has fallen on me, I recognise the hand of retribution. But the same measure which has been meted to me shall be dealt to others. I denounce Jane Seymour before Heaven ! She shall not long retain the crown she is about to snatch from me ! "

" That imprecation had better have been spared, madam," said the duke.

" Be advised, my gracious mistress ! " cried Norris; " and do not let your grief and distraction place you in the power of your enemies. All may yet go well."

" I denounce her ! " persisted Anne, wholly disregarding the caution; " and I also denounce the king. No union of his shall be happy, and other blood than mine shall flow ! "

At a sign from the duke, she was here borne, half suffocated with emotion, to an inner apartment, while Norris was conveyed by Bouchier and a company of halberdiers to the lower gateway, and placed within the prison-chamber.

VI

What passed between Anne Boleyn and the Duke of Suffolk; and how Herne the Hunter appeared to her in the Oratory

FOR some hours, Anne Boleyn's attendants were alarmed for her reason, and there seemed good grounds for the apprehension—so wildly and incoherently did she talk, and so violently comport herself—she who was usually so gentle—now weeping as if her soul would pass away in tears—now breaking into fearful hysterical laughter. It was a piteous sight, and deeply moved all who witnessed it. But towards evening she became calmer, and desired to be left by herself. Her wish being complied with, she fell upon her knees, and besought Heaven's forgiveness for her manifold offences.

" May my earthly sufferings," she cried, " avail me hereafter, and may my blood wash out my guilt ! I feel the enormity of my offence, and acknowledge the justice of my punishment. Pardon me, oh ! injured Catharine— pardon me, I implore thee ! Thou seest in me the most abject, pitiable woman, in the whole realm ! Overthrown, neglected, despised—about to die a shameful death— what worse can befall me ! Thine anguish was great, but it was never sharpened by remorse like mine. Oh ! that I could live my life over again ! I would resist all the dazzling temptations I have yielded to; above all, I would not injure thee. Oh, that I had resisted Henry's love—his false vows—his fatal lures ! But it is useless to repine. I have acted wrongfully, and must pay the penalty of my crime. May my tears, my penitence, my blood operate as an atonement, and procure me pardon from the Merciful Judge before whom I shall shortly appear ! "

In such prayers and lamentations she passed more than an hour, when her attendants entered to inform her that the Duke of Suffolk and the Lords Audley and Cromwell

were without, and desired to see her. She immediately
went forth to them.

" We are come to acquaint you, madam," said Suffolk,
" that you will be removed, at an early hour to-morrow
morning, to the Tower, there to abide during the king's
pleasure."

" If the king will have it so, my lords," she replied,
" I must needs go; but I protest my innocence, and will
protest it to the last. I have ever been a faithful and
loyal consort to his highness, and though I may not have
demeaned myself to him so humbly and gratefully as I
ought to have done—seeing how much I owe him—yet
I have lacked nothing in affection and duty. I have had
jealous fancies and suspicions of him, especially of late,
and have troubled him with them, but I pray his forgiveness for my folly, which proceeded from too much regard,
and if I am acquitted of my present charge, I will offend
him so no more."

" We will report what you say to the king," rejoined
Suffolk gravely. " But we are bound to add, that his
highness does not act on mere suspicion, the proofs of
your guilt being strong against you."

" There can be no such proofs," cried Anne quickly.
" Who are my accusers, and what do they state ? "

" You are charged with conspiring against the king's
life, and dishonouring his bed," replied Suffolk sternly.
" Your accusers will appear in due season."

" They are base creatures suborned for the purpose ! "
cried Anne. " No loyal person would so forswear
himself."

" Time will show you who they are, madam," said
Suffolk. " But having now answered all your questions,
I pray you permit us to retire."

" Shall I not see the king before I am taken to the
Tower ? " said Anne, upon whom the terror of her
situation rushed with new force.

" His highness has quitted the castle," replied Suffolk,
" and there is no likelihood of his return to-night."

" You tell me so to deceive me," cried Anne. " Let

371

me see him—let me throw myself at his feet. I can convince him of my innocence—can move him to compassion. Let me see him, I implore yon—l charge you ! "

" I swear to you, madam, that the king has departed for Hampton Court," replied Suffolk.

" Then take me to him there, under strong guard, or as secretly as you please ! " she cried passionately. " I will return with you instantly if I am unsuccessful."

" Were I to comply with your request, it would be fruitless, madam," replied Suffolk; " the king would not see you."

" Oh, Suffolk ! " cried Anne, prostrating herself before him, " I have shown you many kindnesses in my season of power, and have always stood your friend with the king. Do me this favour now. I will never forget it. Introduce me to the king. I am sure I can move his heart, if I can only see him."

" It would cost me my head, madam," said the duke, in an inexorable tone. " Rise, I pray you."

" You are more cruel than the king," said Anne, obeying. " And now, my lords," she continued with more composure and dignity, " since you refuse my last request, and plainly prove to me the sort of justice I may expect, I will not detain you longer. I shall be ready to attend you to the Tower to-morrow."

" The barge will proceed an hour before dawn," said Suffolk.

" Must I then go by water ? " asked Anne.

" Such are the king's commands," replied Suffolk.

" It is no matter," she rejoined. " I shall be ready when you will, for I shall not retire to rest during the night."

Upon this, Suffolk and the others withdrew, and Anne again retired to the oratory.

She remained alone, brooding, in a state of indescribable anguish, upon the probable fate awaiting her, when all at once, raising her eyes, she beheld a tall, dark figure near the arras.

Even in the gloom she recognised Herne the hunter, and with difficulty repressed a scream.

" Be silent ! " cried Herne, with an emphatic gesture. " I am come to deliver you."

Anne could not repress a joyful cry.

" Not so loud," rejoined Herne, " or you will alarm your attendants. I will set you free on certain conditions."

" Ah ! conditions ! " exclaimed Anne, recoiling—" if they are such as will effect my eternal welfare, I cannot accept them."

" You will repent it when it is too late," replied Herne. " Once removed to the Tower, I can no longer aid you. My power extends only to the forest and the castle."

" Will you take me to the king at Hampton Court ? " said Anne.

" It would be useless," replied Herne. " I will only do what I have stated. If you fly with me, you can never appear again as Anne Boleyn. Sir Henry Norris shall be set free at the same time, and you shall both dwell with me in the forest. Come ! "

" I cannot go," said Anne, holding back ; " it were to fly to a worse danger. I may save my soul now, but if I embrace your offer I am lost for ever."

Herne laughed derisively.

" You need have no fear on that score," he said.

" I will not trust you," replied Anne. " I have yielded to temptation already, and am now paying the penalty of it."

" You are clinging to the crown," said Herne, " because you know that by this step you will irrecoverably lose it. And you fancy that some change may yet operate to your advantage with the king. It is a vain delusive hope. If you leave this castle for the Tower, you will perish ignominiously on the block."

" What will be, must be ! " replied Anne. " I will not save myself in the way you purpose."

" Norris will say, and with reason, that you love him not," cried Herne.

" Then he will wrong me," replied Anne ; " for I *do*

love him. But of what account were a few years of fevered happiness compared with endless torture ! "

" I will befriend you in spite of yourself," vociferated Herne, seizing her arm; " you *shall* go with me ! "

" I will not," said Anne, falling on her knees. " Oh, Father of Mercy ! " she cried energetically, " deliver me from this fiend ! "

" Take your fate, then ! " rejoined Herne, dashing her furiously backwards.

And when her attendants, alarmed by the sound, rushed into the chamber, they found her stretched on the floor in a state of insensibility.

VII

How Herne appeared to Henry in the Home Park

On that same night, at a late hour, a horseman, mounted on a powerful steed, entered the eastern side of the Home Park, and stationed himself beneath the trees. He had not been there long, when the castle clock tolled forth the hour of midnight, and ere the deep strokes died away, a second horseman was seen galloping across the moonlit glade towards him.

" Has all been done as I directed, Suffolk ? " he demanded, as the new-comer approached him.

" It has, my liege," replied the duke. " The queen is imprisoned within her chamber, and will be removed, at early dawn, to the Tower."

" You had better start in an hour from this time," said the king. " It is a long passage by water, and I am anxious to avoid all chance of attempt at rescue."

" Your wishes shall be obeyed," replied the duke. " Poor soul ! her grief was most agonising, and I had much ado to maintain my composure. She implored, in the most passionate manner, to be allowed to see your highness before her removal. I told her it was impossible ; and that even if you were at the castle, you would not listen to her supplications.

" You did right," rejoined Henry ; " I will never see her more—not that I fear being moved by her prayers, but that, knowing how deceitful and faithless she is, I loathe to look upon her. What is expressed upon the matter by the household ? Speak frankly ! "

" Frankly, then," replied the duke, " your highness's proceedings are regarded as harsh and unjustifiable. The general opinion is, that you only desire to remove Anne to make way for Mistress Jane Seymour."

" Ha ! they talk thus, do they ? " cried the king. " I

will silence their saucy prating ere long. Tell all who venture to speak to you on the subject that I have long suspected the queen of a secret liking for Norris, but that I determined to conceal my suspicions till I found I had good warrant for them. That occurred, as you know, some weeks ago. However, I awaited a pretext for proceeding against them, and it was furnished by their own imprudence to-day. Convinced that something would occur, I had made my preparations; nor was I deceived. You may add, also, that not until my marriage is invalidated, Anne's offspring illegitimatised, and herself beheaded, shall I consider the foul blot upon my name removed."

"Has your majesty any further commands?" said Suffolk. "I saw Norris in his prison before I rode forth to you."

"Let him be taken to the Tower, under a strong escort, at once," said Henry. "Lord Rochford, I suppose, has already been removed there?"

"He has," replied the duke. "Shall I attend your majesty to your followers?"

"It is needless," replied the king. "They are waiting for me, close at hand, at the foot of Datchet Bridge. Farewell, my good brother; look well to your prisoners. I shall feel more easy when Anne is safely lodged within the Tower."

So saying, he wheeled round, and striking spurs into his steed, dashed through the trees, while the duke rode back to the castle.

Henry had not proceeded far, when a horseman, mounted on a sable steed, emerged from the thicket, and galloped up to him. The wild attire and antlered helm of this personage proclaimed the forest fiend.

"Ah! thou here, demon!" cried the king, his lion nature overmastered by superstitious fear for a moment. "What wouldst thou?"

"You are on the eve of committing a great crime," replied Herne; "and I told you that at such times I would always appear to you."

"To administer justice is not to commit crime," rejoined the king. "Anne Boleyn deserves her fate."

"Think not to impose on me as you have imposed on Suffolk!" cried Herne, with a derisive laugh. "I know your motives better; I know you have no proof of her guilt, and that in your heart of hearts you believe her innocent. But you destroy her because you would wed Jane Seymour! We shall meet again ere long—ho! ho! ho!"

And giving the rein to his steed, he disappeared among the trees.

VIII

The Signal Gun

ANNE BOLEYN'S arraignment took place in the great hall of the White Tower, on the 16th of May, before the Duke of Norfolk, who was created lord high steward for the occasion, and twenty-six peers. The duke had his seat under a canopy of state, and beneath him sat the Earl of Surrey as deputy earl-marshal.

Notwithstanding an eloquent and impassioned defence, Anne was found guilty; and having been required to lay aside her crown and the other insignia of royalty, was condemned to be burned or beheaded at the king's pleasure.

On the following day, she was summoned to the archiepiscopal palace at Lambeth, whither she was privately conveyed; and her marriage with the king was declared by Cranmer to be null and void, and to have always been so. Death by the axe was the doom awarded to her by the king, and the day appointed for the execution was Friday, the 19th of May, at the hour of noon.

Leaving the conduct of the fatal ceremony to the Duke of Suffolk, who had orders to have a signal gun fired from the summit of the White Tower, which was to be

377

answered from various points, when all was over, Henry repaired to Windsor Castle on the evening of Thursday. Before this, he had formally offered his hand to Jane Seymour; and while the unfortunate queen was languishing within the Tower, he was basking in the smiles of his new mistress, and counting the hours till he could make her his own. On the Tuesday before the execution, Jane Seymour retired to her father's mansion, Wolff Hall, in Wiltshire, where preparations were made for the marriage, which it was arranged should take place there in private on the Saturday.

On arriving at the castle, Henry gave out that he should hunt on the following morning in the Great Park, and retired to his closet. But he did not long remain there, and putting on the garb of a yeoman of the guard, descended by the narrow flight of steps (already mentioned as occupying the same situation as the existing Hundred Steps), to the town, and proceeded to the Garter, where he found several guests assembled, discussing the affairs of the day, and Bryan Bowntance's strong ale at the same time. Amongst the number were the Duke of Shoreditch, Paddington, Hector Cutbeard, and Kit Coo. At the moment of the king's entrance, they were talking of the approaching execution.

" Oh ! the vanity of worldly greatness ! " exclaimed Bryan, lifting up his hands. " Only seven years ago last St. George's day, this lovely queen first entered the castle with the king, amid pomp, and splendour, and power, and with a long life, apparently, of happiness before her. And now she is condemned to die ! "

" But if she has played the king false, she deserves her doom ! " replied Shoreditch. " I would behead my own wife if she served me the same trick—that is, if I could."

" You do right to say ' if you could,' " rejoined Paddington. " The beheading a wife is a royal privilege, and cannot be enjoyed by a subject."

" Marry, I wonder how the king could prefer Mistress Jane Seymour, for my part ! " said Hector Cutbeard.

" To my thinking, she is not to be compared with Queen Anne."

" She has a lovely blue eye, and a figure as straight as an arrow," returned Shoreditch. " How say you, master?" he added, turning to the king. " What think you of Mistress Jane Seymour ? "

" That she is passably fair, friend," replied Henry.

" But now as compared with the late—that is, the present queen; for, poor soul ! she has yet some hours to live ! " rejoined Shoreditch. " How, as compared with her ? "

" Why, I think Jane Seymour the more lovely, undoubtedly," replied Henry. " But I may be prejudiced."

" Not in the least, friend," said Cutbeard. " You but partake of your royal master's humour. Jane Seymour is beautiful, no doubt; and so was Anne Boleyn. Marry, we shall see many fair queens on the throne. The royal Henry has good taste and good management. He sets his subjects a rare example, and shows them how to get rid of troublesome wives. We shall all divorce or hang our spouses when we get tired of them. I almost wish I was married myself, that I might try the experiment—ha ! ha ! "

" Well, here's to the king's health ! " cried Shoreditch; " and wishing him as many wives as he may desire. What say you, friend ? " he added, turning to Henry. " Will you not drink that toast ? "

" That will I," replied Henry; " but I fancy the king will be content for the present with Mistress Jane Seymour."

" For the present, no doubt," said Hector Cutbeard; " but the time will come—and ere long—when Jane will be as irksome to him as Anne is now."

" Ah ! God's death, knave ! darest thou say so ? " cried Henry furiously.

" Why, I have said nothing treasonable, I hope," rejoined Cutbeard, turning pale. " I only wish the king to be happy in his own way; and as he seems to delight in change of wives, I pray that he may have it to his heart's content."

" A fair explanation," replied Henry, laughing.

" Let me give a health, my masters ! " cried a tall archer, whom no one had hitherto noticed, rising in one corner of the room. " It is—The headsman of Calais, and may he do his work featly to-morrow ! "

" Ha ! ha ! ha ! a good toast," cried Hector Cut-beard.

" Seize him who has proposed it ! " cried the king, rising; " it is Herne the hunter ! "

" I laugh at your threats here as elsewhere, Harry," cried Herne. " We shall meet to-morrow."

And flinging the horn-cup in the face of the man nearest him, he sprang through an open window at the back, and disappeared.

Both Cutbeard and Shoreditch were much alarmed lest the freedom of their expressions should be taken in umbrage by the king; but he calmed their fears by bestowing a good-humoured buffet on the cheek of the latter of them, and quitting the hostel, returned to the castle by the same way he had left it.

On the following morning, about ten o'clock, he rode into the Great Park, attended by a numerous train. His demeanour was moody and stern, and a general gloom pervaded the company. Keeping on the western side of the park, the party crossed Cranbourne Chase; but though they encountered several fine herds of deer, the king gave no orders to uncouple the hounds.

At last they arrived at that part of the park where Sandpit Gate is now situated, and pursuing a path bordered by noble trees, a fine buck was suddenly un-harboured, upon which Henry gave orders to the hunts-men and others to follow him, adding that he himself should proceed to Snow Hill, where they would find him an hour hence.

All understood why the king wished to be alone, and for what purpose he was about to repair to the eminence in question, and therefore, without a word, the whole company started off in the chase.

Meanwhile, the king rode slowly through the woods, often passing to listen to the distant sounds of the hunters, and notice the shadows on the greensward as they grew shorter, and proclaimed the approach of noon. At length he arrived at Snow Hill, and stationed himself beneath the trees on its summit.

From this spot a magnificent view of the castle, towering over its pomp of woods, now covered with foliage of the most vivid green, was commanded. The morning was bright and beautiful; the sky cloudless; and a gentle rain had fallen overnight, which had tempered the air, and freshened the leaves and the greensward. The birds were singing blithely in the trees, and at the foot of the hill couched a herd of deer. All was genial and delightful, breathing of tenderness and peace, and calculated to soften the most obdurate heart.

The scene was not without its effect upon Henry; but a fierce tumult raged within his breast. He fixed his eyes on the Round Tower, which was distinctly visible, and from which he expected the signal, and then tried to peer into the far horizon. But he could discern nothing. A cloud passed over the sun, and cast a momentary gloom over the smiling landscape. At the same time, Henry's fancy was so powerfully excited, that he fancied he could behold the terrible tragedy enacting at the Tower.

" She is now issuing forth into the green in the front of St. Peter's Chapel," said Henry to himself. " I can see her as distinctly as if I were there. Ah! how beautiful she looks—and how she moves all hearts to pity. Suffolk, Richmond, Cromwell, and the lord mayor are there to meet her. She takes leave of her weeping attendants—she mounts the steps of the scaffold firmly—she looks around, and addresses the spectators. How silent they are, and how clearly and musically her voice sounds. She blesses me! I hear it—I feel it here! Now she disrobes herself, and prepares for the fatal axe. It is wielded by the skilful executioner of Calais, and he is now feeling its edge. Now she takes leave of her dames, and bestows a parting gift on each. Again she kneels and prays. She rises. The fatal moment is at hand. Even now she retains her courage—she approaches the block, and places her head upon it. The axe is raised—ha ! "

The exclamation was occasioned by a flash of fire from the battlements of the Round Tower, followed by a volume of smoke, and, in another second, the deep boom of a gun was heard.

At the very moment that the flash was seen, a wild figure, mounted on a coal-black steed, galloped from out of the wood, and dashed towards Henry, whose horse reared and plunged as he passed.

" There spoke the death-knell of Anne Boleyn ! " cried Herne, regarding Henry sternly, and pointing to the Round Tower. " The bloody deed is done, and thou art free to wed once more. Away to Wolff Hall, and bring thy new consort to Windsor Castle ! "